Company Insurance Handbook

Second edition

CW01498544

under the editorship of the
Association of Insurance and Risk Managers in
Industry and Commerce

A Gower Handbook

First edition published 1973 by Gower Press Limited

Second edition published by
Gower Publishing Company Limited, Gower House, Croft Road, Aldershot, Hants GU11 3HR, England.

British Library Cataloguing in Publication Data

Company insurance handbook.—2nd ed
  1. Insurance, Business—Great Britain—
Handbooks, manuals, etc
  I. Association of Insurance and Risk Managers
in industry and commerce
  368   HG8051

  ISBN 0-566-02299-0

Library of Congress Cataloguing in Publication Data
Main entry under title:

Company insurance handbook.

  Includes index.
  1. Insurance, Business—Handbooks, manuals, etc.
I. Association of Insurance Managers in Industry and
Commerce.
HG8059.C65 1984   368   83-20738

  ISBN 0-566-02299-0

Typeset in Great Britain by
Guildford Graphics Limited, Guildford, Surrey.
Printed in Great Britain at the
University Press, Cambridge.

Company Insurance Handbook

Second edition

Contents

*The author of this chapter wishes to remain anonymous.

Foreword

T. E. Sparkes, FCII, Chairman, The Association of Insurance and Risk Managers in Industry and Commerce (AIRMIC)

Since it was first published over ten years ago, *Company Insurance Handbook* has proved extremely valuable for managers of industrial and commercial companies who have responsibility for arranging insurance protection for their companies' assets and liabilities.

Risk management has assumed even greater importance in the last few years to ensure that risks are controlled on the most cost-effective basis in a period when the economic pressures on the business community exceed those which existed when the first edition appeared. The purchasing of insurance remains the cornerstone of a truly effective risk management policy and this new edition updates developments during the intervening period.

The Association of Insurance and Risk Managers in Industry and Commerce is pleased to sponsor this new edition which it is hoped will reach an even larger number of those involved with the handling and insurance of industrial risks. It is an attempt to share the Association's members' extensive accumulated experience, and contributors have been selected from AIRMIC's active membership; this has meant certain changes in authorship from the previous edition to ensure that all are currently qualified to write on their chosen subject. I would like to thank all authors for their contributions and to pay special thanks to P. H. Liechti and A. S. D. Cross, both past Chairmen of AIRMIC, for their diligence and patience in acting as editors.

I hope and believe readers, and their employers, will find this fully revised edition as useful as did those who acquired its predecessor, to judge by the evidence of that edition's considerable success. It should also prove extremely valuable to all students in the insurance industry, for in one volume the basic principles of most forms of non-life cover are given in a very practical form.

Editorial Note

Marine (hull) and aviation (hull) insurances and certain other very specialised types of insurance are not covered by this book as they were considered not to be of sufficient interest to the intended readership.

Life and Pensions Assurance are also excluded as they represent very specialised fields and could not be dealt with satisfactorily in a book of this nature.

Except where otherwise indicated the information provided in the various chapters is according to law and practice in England.

The Role of AIRMIC

T. E. Sparkes, FCII, Chairman of AIRMIC and Insurance Manager, Metal Box plc

The Association of Insurance Managers in Industry and Commerce was formed in December 1963 (the title being subsequently altered to the Association of Insurance and Risk Managers in Industry and Commerce) and by catering for the special interests of private and public industry, commerce and local authorities it grew rapidly and now forms the largest national representative body of insurance and risk managers in Europe. In addition, the Association has widened its scope of membership and now admits persons from industry, commerce, local or national government undertakings who have a responsibility for insurance and risk management matters.

The aims of AIRMIC are:
To provide a forum for the exchange of views, ideas and experience between those engaged in insurance and risk management in industry and commerce;
To further the profession of insurance and risk management in industry and commerce;
To ascertain and advise the members of changes in insurance law and practice and other matters relating to insurance and risk control generally;
To promote within the members' sphere of influence a better understanding of risk management and its techniques, including insurance management;
To represent, where appropriate, a body of opinion within fields of interest to insurance and risk managers and insurance consumers in industry and commerce;
To co-operate and liaise, where appropriate, with other organisations in furtherance of these and related objects;
To undertake any other activities in furtherance of these or related objects.

The Association is limited by guarantee and is administered by an elected Board of Directors of twelve members and honorary officers appointed by it. It has a full time secretary-general and an administrative secretary who operate from its office in London and there are various committees reporting to the Executive Committee who handle specific aspects of the Association's work including education and training, finance membership, programme and technical matters.

Throughout the UK there are regional groups and branches to cater for the needs of members located in the various areas, with a programme of meetings, conferences and seminars designed specifically to interest the large numbers of members. The annual dinner in London is recognised as one of the highlights of the insurance calendar.

In addition, there are working interest groups covering a wide range of specialist subjects including captives, risk management, contractors, liabilities, motor, property and a recently formed group for affiliate members. This last group represents a category of membership available to those who have a responsibility for insurance or risk management but who do not qualify for Full Membership because they are not their main responsibilities and it is aimed at Company Secretaries, Financial Directors, Administrative Directors and the like.

AIRMIC is the United Kingdom member of the Association Européene des Assurés de l'Industrie (AEAI) which was formed to represent the interests of similar national associations of members' countries in the European Economic Community and maintains close contact with other overseas bodies including the Risk and Insurance Management Society (RIMS) in the United States.

Membership of the Association, for those eligible, provides an additional practical reference source on a day-to-day basis and continuity of professional information relating to matters treated in this Handbook. Publications are produced on a range of topics which are issued either free to members or at a nominal charge and there is a membership list issued which is private and confidential listing members by name and the companies employing them for easy reference.

Anyone interested in joining the Association is welcome to apply for membership details to The Secretary-General, AIRMIC, Plantation House, 31/35 Fenchurch Street, London EC3M 7DX (telephone 01–621 0337) who will be pleased to supply further information of its activities.

Notes on Contributors

M. J. Angel (Fire and extended perils insurance), joined the Insurance Department of Flight Refuelling Ltd in 1956 and is now Senior Administrative Officer with responsibility for the group's insurance and risk management programme.

A. P. Benson (The insurance market) is Group Risk Manager of Arthur Guinness & Sons plc. He graduated as a BA(Hons) at Corpus Christi College, Oxford in 1958, and has worked for Guardian Royal Exchange Group in UK and West Africa, as Insurance Manager, and Managing Director of Glaxo Risk Management Ltd within the Glaxo Group until joining his present employers. He is a past chairman of AIRMIC and is a frequent contributor to insurance periodicals, seminars and the like.

Robert L. Carter (Insurance and risk management) is Norwich Union Professor of Insurance Studies in the Department of Industrial Economics, Accountancy and Insurance at Nottingham University. Before his academic career, Dr Carter was with the Norwich Union and was Assistant Insurance Manager with Dunlop Company plc. He is the author of *Economics and Insurance* (2nd ed. 1979, P.H. Press), *Reinsurance* (2nd ed. 1983, Kluwer), & *Theft in the Market* (Institute of Economic Affairs, 1976) and the editor of *Handbook of Insurance* and *Handbook of Risk Management* (Kluwer). He has contributed to many other books and journals and prepared tuition courses for the Chartered Insurance Institute. He is a Fellow of the Chartered Insurance Institute.

W. A. Chrzanowski (Business interruption insurance) joined Rowntree Mackintosh plc in 1962 in the Sales Division, two years later transferred to their Insurance Department. After nine years of training and UK work, he took over responsibility for the European Division risk and insurance programme. Five years ago, on H. H. Parker's retirement, succeeded him as Group Insurance Manager. He is an Associate of the Chartered Insurance Institute and is current Chairman of North East Branch of AIRMIC.

The late *Brian F. Conner* (Fidelity, bonds, guarantees and credit insurance) was Manager of Group Insurance and Risk Department of Barclays Bank Group. He worked in insurance for over 30 years and had been an Associate of the Chartered Insurance Institute.

D. A. Curd (Engineering insurance) is a Director of NEI Furness (Insurance Services) Ltd having previously been Group Insurance Officer of C. A. Parsons & Co. Ltd and subsequently Group Insurance Manager of Reyrolle Parsons Ltd. His earlier insurance experience was with the Royal Insurance Group for a number of years. He is a Fellow of the Chartered Insurance Institute and is a past chairman of the North East Branch of AIRMIC.

J. T. Deprez (Contractors' all risks insurance) has over 30 years' experience in handling insurance matters with national contractors engaged in building and civil engineering, and as the Managing Director of insurance brokers specialising in the arrangement of construction industry insurances and claims handling. He is at present the Group Insurance Manager for the Wiltshier Group of Companies, and is a member of the insurance committee of the National Federation of Building Trades Employers. He is also Chairman of the Contractors Special Interest Group of AIRMIC.

H. F. Dillon (Insurance of liabilities) is Insurance Manager of the Nestlé Co Ltd. Mr Dillon is a Fellow of the Chartered Insurance Institute and worked in a tariff office and a firm of Lloyd's brokers before joining Nestlé.

D. J. Knight (Marine, aviation and transport insurance) is Group Insurance Manager of MAT International Group Ltd. This group is engaged in freight forwarding and surface transport activities. He has over 30 years practical experience of risk management in all modes of transport and carriage of goods.

Hugh R. Loader, ACII, ACIArb, FBIM (Insurance administration) is Group Insurance Manager for Tetra Pak, an international packaging company. His previous position was Group Insurance Manager for Associated Communications Corporation, and he is a past chairman of AIRMIC. Mr Loader is a frequent lecturer in the UK, Europe and USA on captives and risk management, and has contributed articles to insurance journals. He was also a contributing author to the CII risk management handbook.

J. M. Seatter (Theft and all risks insurance) is the Group Risk Manager of United Glass Holdings plc. His industrial insurance experience was gained in the building and civil engineering industries, following 15 years experience as an accident and contractors' underwriter with the Sun Alliance Group. He then became the Insurance Manager of Standard Telephones and Cables Ltd, before joining Alexander Howden & Co Ltd, the insurance brokers, as manager of their Contractors' department. He is a past chairman of AIRMIC, an Associate of the Chartered Insurance Institute and a BSc(Econ.) of London University.

T. E. W. Slatter (Insurance of personnel) is Director of Risk Management for Blue Bell, Inc. in the USA, having transferred from the position of European Insurance Manager for Blue Bell based in Brussels. He commenced his career in insurance with Edward Lumley and Sons Ltd, Lloyd's brokers, and from there entered the risk management field when he became Group Insurance Manager for Henlys Ltd.

John T. Steele (Principles of insurance law) is Head of Banking and

Insurance Studies at Glasgow College of Technology. A graduate of the Open University and a Fellow of the Chartered Insurance Institute, he worked in various capacities within the insurance industry for 18 years before entering full time education. He has contributed articles to the insurance and risk management press and has co-authored three books on insurance.

P. F. Talbot (Money insurance) is Group Insurance Manager of The De La Rue Company plc and has been engaged in insurance for 25 years, encompassing the insurance company market, Lloyds and industry. The majority of his career has been spent in risk and insurance management in industry. He is an Associate of the Chartered Insurance Institute.

Peter D. Whiley, FCII, ACIArb (Motor insurance) joined Fisons plc in 1966 as a Management Trainee and shortly afterwards moved into the Insurance Department where he completed his insurance studies. He was appointed Insurance Manager UK in 1980 and has maintained a keen interest in all aspects of motor fleet insurance. He is a Fellow of the Chartered Insurance Institute and an Associate Member of the Chartered Institute of Arbitrators. He is currently Chairman of the Special Interest Group of AIRMIC concerned with motor fleets.

PART I

COMPANY INSURANCE MANAGEMENT

1

Insurance and Risk Management

**R. L. Carter, Norwich Union Professor of Insurance Studies,
Department of Industrial Economics, University of Nottingham**

In a book concerned with the role of insurance in the handling of some of the risks which affect firms it may seem pedantic to begin by defining such a common word as risk. However, a short explanation of the nature of risk will provide a basis for understanding the role of risk management and in particular the part that insurance can play in the handling of a firm's risks.

Professor M. Haller (1977) defines risk as 'the possibility that positive expectations of a goal-oriented system will not be fulfilled'. Few things in the life of an individual or a corporate body are certain, and many uncertain events may disrupt the best laid plans. A company, for example, might suffer loss of production and of sales income due to fire, flood or strikes; it may lose business to competitors, or it may sell more abroad following a reduction in tariffs in its export markets; and the introduction of more stringent safety regulations may involve it in substantial additional expenditure. Some uncertain events are of such a nature that it is possible to obtain fairly reliable estimates of the chance of a particular event or outcome occurring. If all of the possible outcomes of an event are known, then the probability of a particular outcome occurring can be calculated by employing the mathematical laws of probability; to take a simple example, the probability of drawing one of the four aces from a perfect pack of 52 cards is 4/52 (= 1/13 or 0.077). However, few, if any, of the uncertainties confronting firms are amenable to such estimation, but in many cases past experience can provide a guide to future events. For instance, a company operating large numbers of delivery vans or electric motors may be able to obtain good estimates of the frequencies of vehicle accidents or motor breakdowns from its past records of such events.

One concept of risk, then, is the probability (that is, the chance) of loss. However, for an individual firm it is a concept of very limited usefulness because, as can be shown by the law of large numbers, the actual outcomes of uncertain events can only be guaranteed to approach the expected result (as measured by the probability value) in a large number of trials. Only if a firm controls a large number of exposure units (e.g. premises, vehicles, or employees) will past experience provide a reliable guide to future losses. For example, a trade association may calculate from details of losses supplied by its members that each of its 5,000 member firms has a 1/100 (= 0.01) probability of suffering a serious fire in any year. Therefore, provided that there is no change in conditions, it may expect that each year an average of 50 firms (0.01 x 5,000) will suffer a major loss. Moreover, although the actual number of serious fires in any year may vary, by calculating the standard deviation the association can be almost certain that in any year not less than 29 nor more than 71 firms will be so affected. However, there is no way in which an individual firm can tell whether or not it will be one of the unfortunate few, so that even with a reliable estimate of the probability of loss its future loss experience will remain in doubt. Therefore an alternative concept of risk is the objective doubt about the outcome of an expected event, with doubt being measured by the degree of variation in possible outcomes.[1] The measures of variation normally used are the standard deviation or coefficient of variation.

A further concept of risk, which is of particular value to a risk manager, is that of downside risk. At one extreme some losses are so small that they are hardly noticed, whereas at the other end of the scale a loss may be of catastrophic proportions. The size of loss which a company can tolerate without financial embarrassment will depend upon its cash flow, profitability, liquidity, capital reserves and assets that could be used to finance losses. Thus downside risk is measured in terms of the probability of an actual loss exceeding that tolerable size.

Therefore, in considering its risks a firm should pay regard to four factors: the probability of a loss-producing event occurring, the possible severity of loss, the size of loss it can tolerate, and the potential degree of variation in actual outcomes. All four are important in making correct decisions, though under normal circumstances it is arguable that loss severities are more important than the probability of loss.[2]

The great advantage that insurance companies possess compared with most firms is that generally they handle a large portfolio of individual units exposed to risk. Thus the law of large numbers operates in their favour in two ways: they possess a larger statistical base on which to estimate future loss potentials, and the larger the portfolio the more closely will their actual aggregate annual claims costs tend to accord with their expected claims costs. Therefore, with the additional backing of their capital and reserves, they can undertake with a high degree of security their business of accepting the transfer of risks. However, even medium sized industrial and commercial companies can often also enjoy some of the same risk evaluation and retention advantages, at least in relation to high frequency/low value losses. As a company grows, so its own loss experience will become more statistically significant and by combining the exposure units of the various parts of the organisation, it will be able to retain more of its own risks.

INSURABLE RISKS

Risks have differing characteristics and therefore may be classified in different ways.

A particularly helpful classification in the context of risk management is the distinction between speculative and pure risks. The former term embraces risks that may give rise to either profit or loss, such as the risk associated with the development of a new invention which may either generate abnormally high profits or end in financial disaster. Pure risks, on the other hand, are associated with events that can result only in loss. The so-called acts of God—fire, earthquake, hurricane etc—and the risks arising from human behaviour such as theft, fraud, or careless driving, are examples of pure risks.

Although the range of risks for which insurance can be obtained is constantly being expanded, insurance basically is concerned with providing protection against pure risks. More specifically insurance is a means of transferring to an insurer the financial losses which may arise from the occurrence of specified risks.

In order to be insurable a risk should ideally fulfil the following conditions:

1   The insurer should be able to calculate the probability and the severity of losses occurring; this means that there should be available to the insurer a sufficiently large number of such risks, all independently exposed to loss, for past experience to provide a reliable guide to the future.

2   So far as the insured person is concerned, any losses should be fortuitous.

3   Losses should be identifiable and capable of measurement in monetary terms.

4   The insurance should be economically feasible. This means that potential losses should be sufficiently large to merit the expense of arranging insurance. It is possible that with risks subject to a high frequency of occurrence but a low loss severity the cost of the premium, including the insurer's expense, contingency and profit loading, may well exceed even the severest expected losses.

Many of the risks which are insured fall short of these conditions but there are certain risks that insurers will not accept. Insurance is not available for speculative business risks like the possibility of a fall either in the demand for a product or the supply of essential raw materials caused by a change in market conditions or government policy. Likewise other risks where past experience provides no guide to the future, such as the success or failure of research projects, remain uninsurable. Insurers are hesitant too about insuring against uncertain events with loss potentials so widespread and of such magnitude as to threaten the financial stability of the local insurance market after allowing for any possible sharing of the risk with overseas insurers. Thus besides the difficulties that may be experienced in obtaining insurance against earthquakes, hurricanes and other natural perils in areas severely exposed to such disasters, in the United States the federal government had to intervene to prevent the complete withdrawal of riot insurance for urban properties following the race riots of the 1960s, and war risks are normally excluded except in marine and life insurance.

INSURANCE AND THE HANDLING OF RISKS

The economic costs of pure risks fall under three headings:

1 The cost of the actual losses that do occur.
2 The cost of handling the risk.
3 The cost of uncertainty itself.

Dealing first with actual losses, these include not only direct losses involving injury to persons and damage to property, but also consequential losses such as liabilities to injured third parties, loss of production, and additional costs which may be incurred in trying to minimise the extent of loss. Moreover, such losses often extend beyond the parties directly involved, affecting a wider range of firms, families and society at large.

Whatever methods of handling risks are employed there will be some costs involved. Such costs may take the form of actual monetary costs, such as additional expenditure on safety equipment or security patrols, or the opportunity cost of some alternative foregone, such as the revenue that could have been earned from a product which is abandoned because of the risks involved.

Among the costs arising from the mere existence of risk is the loss of goods which firms are deterred from producing because of the high risks involved.

Given the extent of the risks which confront every firm, a key test of an efficient management is whether it actively practises risk control. The idea is not new. Henri Fayol listed security as one of the six major functions of management as long ago as 1916 but for a long time it was a neglected area of management in most firms until the need for risk management became more widely recognised in America in the late 1950s and in the United Kingdom almost 10 years later. On the basis of Haller's definition of risk, the objective of a risk management programme could be expressed as being to:

> optimise the attainment of the corporate objectives. Thus it must take account of the impact of risk handling measures on both expected outcomes (i.e. the probability of loss × average size of loss), and the opportunity cost of resources that may be employed in handling the risks. (R. L. Carter, 1978)

Although a major objective will be to safeguard the firm from

7

losses which could imperil its solvency, and even to avoid financial inconvenience, the cost of security has to be taken into account too. It is paradoxical that a firm under financial strain that most needs the security against unexpected losses can least afford to buy it. Risk handling programmes have to be adapted to both corporate objectives (some firms are prepared to take more risks than others), and to financial circumstances (for instance, a firm that exercises tight cash budgeting cannot afford to retain as much risk).

The essential steps in implementing a successful risk management policy are set out in Figure 1:1.

Risk identification

The first task must be to ascertain all of the risks to which the firm is exposed. That involves both perceiving that there is an exposure to

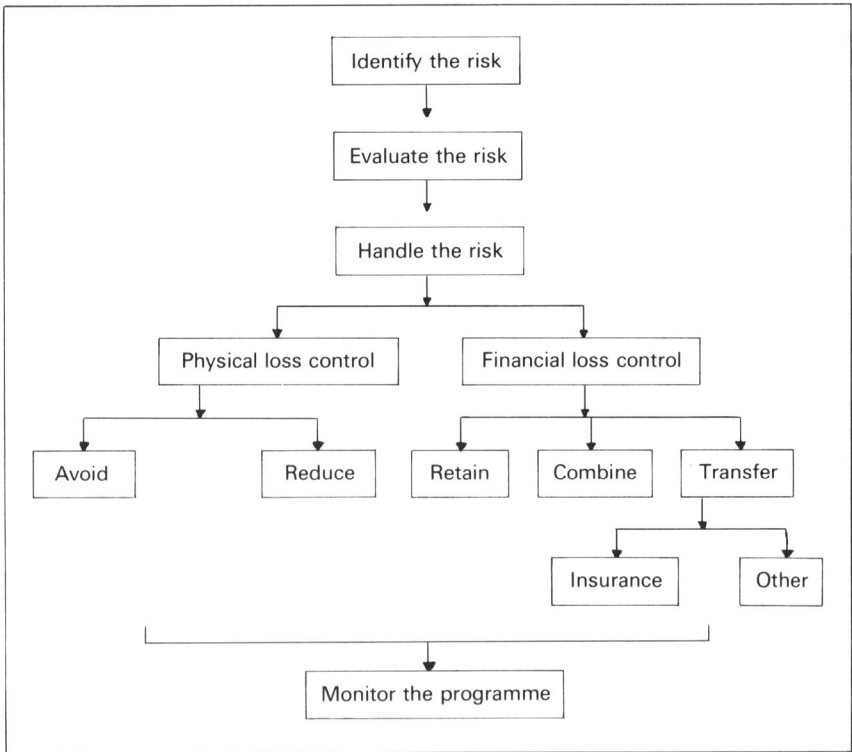

Figure 1:1 Risk management procedure

loss, and the identification of the operative cause or perils. The importance of this stage of the operation cannot be overemphasised because any failure to identify even one risk may leave the security of the firm still in jeopardy.

Whatever method is employed the essential principle is that the task is undertaken systematically, examining in detail every aspect of the firm's operations. The aim must be to know everything possible about all of the following factors which have a bearing on risk:

1   The firm: its products, processes, plants, premises, raw materials, suppliers, customers, consumers of its products, methods of distribution, and any other feature of its operations.
2   The social, economic, legal and political environment in which the firm operates.
3   The experience of other firms in the same and closely related trades.

Only armed with such knowledge and a good imagination will it be possible to identify not only the obvious but also the hidden risks.

No man can acquire such knowledge alone. He will need to draw on the knowledge and experience of experts both inside and outside his firm. This calls for good communications within the firm, and it also means that such knowledge cannot be obtained sitting in an office. Risk identification calls for both desk research and on-site investigation.

If the task is tackled by conducting a physical survey of the firm's premises and operations, it must be done methodically to ensure that nothing is overlooked. Ideally the survey should be conducted using checklists that set out all of the possible sources of risk, and the factors influencing the frequency and severity of losses. Another approach is to construct a flow chart of the firm's operations from the purchase of raw materials to the time when the end product reaches the final consumer, checking on possible risks at each stage. In either case it may help to consider in turn the following possible type of loss:

1   *Property damage* or loss resulting from fire, explosion, water, theft and other perils, including loss of or damage to goods in transit.

2 *Liability* for injury to third parties, customers and employees, or damage to their property, caused by the negligence, or other tortious act, of the firm, its agents and servants.

3 *Personnel losses:* the injury or death of key employees may involve a firm in extra costs or losses and it may wish to offer compensation to injured employees or their dependants regardless of any legal liability.

4 *Pecuniary losses* including:
   (a) loss of sales or additional expenses arising from business interruption due to property damage, denial of access or other cause affecting the firm, its suppliers or customers.
   (b) losses due to the misappropriation or theft of money and financial assets or of trade secrets.

Besides physical surveys and the study of flow charts, a wide variety of other risk identification systems have been devised, such as:

1 'Threat' analysis, where a list of events that could threaten the business is compiled (such as the loss of vital services, disruptions to the flow of supplies of components, damage to production facilities, etc), and then for each threat possible causes are listed, mitigating factors (such as the possibility of available stocks of components and/or finished goods, duplicate production facilities, etc) are investigated and loss assessments are made.

2 'Event' analysis which concentrates on possible loss producing events (such as fire, explosion, floods, machinery breakdown, etc) and examines in turn their possible causes and the various types of loss that may result from the event.

3 Hazard and operability studies undertaken at the planning stage of a new plant whereby the whole process is examined in an attempt to identify possible deviations from normal operating conditions, including their potential causes and results.

A risk manager needs to choose those methods which best suit his circumstances.

Finally, it must be remembered that firms operate in a dynamic environment so steps should be taken to ensure that knowledge once gained is kept up to date. This means adopting some system of regular follow-up.

Risk evaluation

After identification the risks must be evaluated in order to:

1 Arrange them in order of priority.
2 Provide information for deciding the most appropriate way of handling them.

The ideal would be to obtain a probability distribution of losses by size of loss (as shown in Figure 1:2) for each type of loss producing event, i.e. fire, storm, defective product, etc. It would then be possible to calculate such important data as the loss expectancy, the standard deviation and the maximum possible loss. Unfortunately rarely is that possible with any great reliability, even in the largest of firms. Not only is there usually little reliable experience regarding large losses from which to estimate the tail of the distribution, but also changing risk factors reduce the value of past experience as a guide to the future. Consequently it is often necessary to make do with a largely qualitative assessment of many risks. This may take the form

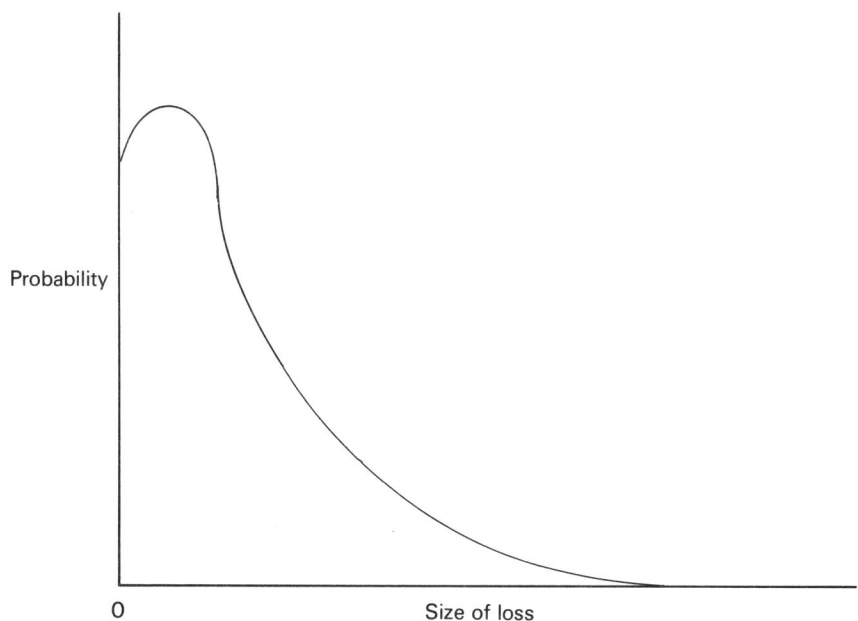

Figure 1:2 Probability distribution of losses by size of loss

of ranking risks according to degrees of (a) frequency of occurrence and (b) potential severity of loss.[3] In deciding upon the values to be attached to the differing degrees of severity—for example, small, moderate, severe and catastrophic—regard must be paid not only to the overall capital resources of the firm but also to its liquidity because even a moderate loss could cause financial embarrassment at a time of low liquidity.

Provided such a qualitative evaluation is made systematically, imaginatively and on the basis of all possible available information, the management of the firm will have a sound guide for making its risk handling decisions. Indeed it will be a better guide than inadequate statistics which may give a spurious impression of accuracy.

On the other hand the value of statistical tools should never be overlooked provided their limitations are fully appreciated.

Having completed the task of risk analysis, the firm can go on to decide how its risks shall be handled.

Handling risks

Nowhere are firms entirely free to decide how they shall handle their risks. In every country there are governmental and other official regulations regarding health and safety at work; fire precautions; hygiene; the construction and operating of vehicles, aircraft and ships; environmental pollution; food and drink; the handling and conveyance of dangerous substances; building codes; and many other matters relating to property, personal injury and other risks. Similarly most governments have enacted some compulsory insurance regulations, and in addition a firm may be obliged to insure certain risks under the provisions of leases, construction and other contracts. Amongst the member countries of the European Economic Community, the residents of the UK and the Republic of Ireland are subject to fewer compulsory insurance regulations than most: in Belgium, France, West Germany and Italy the list of compulsory classes of insurance is extensive. Failure to comply with both safety and compulsory insurance regulations may constitute a criminal offence, and may lead to the enforced closure of a plant or other establishment or the prohibition of the offending activity.

Thus if a firm wishes to carry on certain activities it must comply with official risk handling regulations relating thereto. There will remain, however, broad areas where it can exercise its own discretion regarding either physical or financial loss control.

Risk avoidance. Only rarely is it possible to avoid a risk completely. As Horrigan (1969) has said, it can involve 'either absurd inconvenience or drastic action', and generally risk avoidance is only feasible at the planning stage of an operation; for example, a particular site may be so subject to flooding that it is rejected in favour of an alternative situation.

Risk reduction. In many ways physical risk reduction (or loss prevention, as it is often called) is the best way of dealing with any risk, and it is usually possible to take steps to reduce either the probability of loss or its severity should it occur. Again, however, the ideal time to think of risk reduction measures is at the planning stage of any new project when considerable improvement often can be achieved at little or no extra cost. For example, when dealing with a new building or factory site it is far better to consult the architect, the insurer's fire surveyor and the local fire prevention officer regarding fire precautions in the early planning stages than be faced with essential alterations when the construction work is complete, usually at considerable additional expense.

The only cautionary note regarding risk reduction is that as far as possible expenditure should be related to potential future savings in losses and other risk costs; in other words, risk prevention generally should be evaluated in the same way as other investment projects. There are, of course, exceptional cases where on social or legal grounds every effort must be made to prevent injury or damage almost regardless of cost. Also sometimes a firm may prefer to spend money on reducing the probability or potential size of catastrophic losses even though a better return in terms of reduced loss expectancy could be achieved by concentrating on the smaller but more frequent small losses.

As can be seen from Figure 1:1, a firm can make provision for financing the losses arising from the occurrence of any remaining risk in three ways.

Risk retention. A firm can retain the risk itself when it can either:

1 Charge losses against normal operating costs as they occur.
2 Set aside regular contributions to a special contingency fund from which (exceptional) losses can be paid.
3 Borrow to cover the cost of any losses, repaying over an agreed period.

The funding method is often labelled self-insurance, but this is a misleading term because responsibility for the risk remains with the firm. If, when a loss occurs, the fund proves to be inadequate, or has been appropriated for other purposes, the firm is left to bear the financial consequences alone. Over the last decade many firms have progressed beyond internal funding by establishing their own captive insurance companies, often overseas in tax havens such as Bermuda, though in Europe the Isle of Man and the Channel Islands are increasingly attracting new captive companies for the same tax and insurance regulatory reasons. Not only does the formation of a captive provide its parent company with the tax deductibility of premiums (an advantage not enjoyed by contributions to internal contingency funds, other than in the Netherlands and Norway), a captive insurer also has access to reinsurance facilities and can provide other benefits too.

Risk retention has a useful role; it is the cheapest way of handling risks which regularly cause small losses because any insurance company would require a premium adequate to cover not only the losses but its expenses and profit too. However, care must be taken if there is the possibility of a serious loss occurring. The formation of a captive insurer considerably extends the possibilities.

Risk combination. Firms that control a large number of fairly homogeneous units all exposed to the same risk can, as mentioned earlier, reduce the overall cost by pooling the individual risks, thereby enabling total expected losses in any year to be predicted with a greater degree of accuracy. A common example of such risk combination is a firm which owns a large number of shops and centralises, at head office, the responsibility for damage to windows; as both individual losses and the risk of an accumulation of losses would be small, this is an excellent case of a risk which the firm could bear itself. When a firm is organised on the basis of separate profit centres, risk combination makes possible the retention of risks that may be too large for an individual profit centre to carry on its own.

Risk transfer. Finally, a firm can seek to transfer its risks. Although insurance is the main method of risk transfer it is not the only one. Sometimes it is possible to transfer the risk arising out of a particular operation by subcontracting the work to another firm. In other instances it may be possible to transfer responsibility for the consequences of a risk occurring; exemption clauses in contracts of sale or carriage, and repair clauses in building leases, are common examples. On the other hand, although the risk may be transferred, the ultimate cost may still lie with the same party; for example, a vendor faced with conditions of purchase that impose wider responsibilities for defective goods than is required by the law may raise his price accordingly. Also the tendency worldwide is for the courts and legislators to severely restrict the scope for contracting out of responsibility for losses. Indeed in relation to liability for injury and damage caused by defective products, the trend is to impose even more stringent liabilities on manufacturers and suppliers as, for example, proposed in the EEC draft directive on products liability.

The value of insurance lies in the financial security an individual or firm can obtain by transferring to an insurer, in return for a known premium, the risk of larger losses arising from the occurrence of a specified peril (or perils). Thus, insurance substitutes certainty for uncertainty.

Insurance does not protect a firm against risks occurring; it offers restoration, at least in part, of any resulting economic losses. Most insurances, apart from life contracts, are subject to the principle of indemnity which restricts the policyholder's rights of recovery to no more than the amount of his loss, though in practice the principle is substantially modified by the use of reinstatement covers and valued policies.

In comparing insurance with other methods of handling risks two points always should be borne in mind. The first is that insurance only offers compensation against economic losses; it can never, for example, comfort the family of the employee who is killed in any accident that could have been prevented. Second, the tax treatment of the various elements should be allowed for in the calculations.

Apart from risk avoidance, none of the forms of risk handling is mutually exclusive. Risk reduction measures may be a pre-condition to an insurer providing insurance, or they may entitle the firm to a reduction in premium. Also risk sharing is widely practised: large deductibles on insurance covers are now common, and increasingly the property and business interruption insurances of large, geographically spread companies are written on a first-loss basis where the sum insured represents the firm's estimate of its maximum possible loss, though both practices may prove disastrous. The aggregate retained cost of an abnormally large number of losses all subject to a deductible, or of major fires at two or more locations that together exceed a first-loss cover, could exhaust a firm's financial resources unless additional insurance provision is arranged to cover such contingencies.

RISK MANAGEMENT AND INSURANCE IN THE FIRM

Almost all large companies, public corporations and local authorities now employ full time experts to manage their insurances and to deal with fire and accident prevention, it being one of the requirements of the Health and Safety at Work, etc, Act, 1976 that companies designate responsible persons as safety officers. A few companies combine all responsibilities for the handling of risks into a single department under the control of a senior executive. The broadest view of the risk management function is that it should embrace not only pure risks which form the subject matter of insurance but also extend to the analysis and control of all risks arising out of the business of the firm. Although such a view is extremely unlikely to obtain board support, such an all embracing concept of risk management highlights the fact that most major business decisions have a bearing on the firm's insurable risks and may necessitate some rearrangement of its insurances, so that the official responsible for insurance must be kept fully informed of developments throughout the organisation.

Concentrating on responsibility for insurance within a firm, two surveys by The Association of Insurance and Risk Managers in Industry and Commerce (1969 and 1979) revealed that in most medium to large firms the company's risk or insurance manager was answerable to the company secretary or financial controller/chief accountant. This reflects two views of the function of insurance. On the one hand it may be seen as a means of discharging legal responsibilities to shareholders, creditors and third parties by protecting the assets and earnings of the firm from loss, and providing for the compensation of employees and third parties injured as the result of the tortious actions of the firm, its agents or servants. On the other hand insurance may be regarded as part of financial management being one element in the control of a firm's costs. In fact it fulfils both of these functions, and it is fruitless to argue where responsibility for it ought to lie in the management structure so long as it is recognised that although security should never be purchased regardless of cost, adequate arrangements for controlling risks, including the purchase of insurance, are fundamental to the continued survival of any firm. Therefore decisions whether or not to insure are far too important to leave to a junior employee, but must be taken at senior-management and sometimes board level.

If a company is too small to have a full time insurance or risk manager with responsibility for implementing the insurance programme broadly defined by the board, then the task should be undertaken by a senior executive, such as the company secretary or accountant, though some assistance will be necessary. A considerable amount of largely routine work is involved in assembling details and values of assets to be insured, providing information to insurers for the purpose of adjusting premiums, notifying details of changes affecting the insurance arrangements, and handling small claims. Technical advice and assistance will also be needed. Insurance is a highly specialised, complex subject which needs expert knowledge in order to avoid costly mistakes both in making the initial arrangements and subsequently in dealing with large claims. Considerable assistance can be obtained from insurance companies themselves, and even more from qualified brokers who possess expert knowledge of insurance principles, practice and market conditions. However, once it becomes necessary to employ a man full time on insurance matters there is much to be gained from appointing a trained insurance official to handle not only the detailed work of administering the insurance arrangements but also to advise senior management and the board in the formulation of the insurance programme. His role, however, should not be regarded as automatically replacing that of insurance brokers retained to place the business in the market; in many respects their roles are complementary.

Exactly what type of organisation is adopted to deal with insurance must depend to a large degree upon the size of the firm involved. As noted earlier and as confirmed by the 1979 AIRMIC survey of its members, in many firms the person responsible for administering the company's insurances also has executive or advisory duties in other related areas of risk management, such as risk assessment or loss prevention. Regardless of the precise range of the person's duties, two points must always be borne in mind. First insurance must not be treated in isolation from other areas of risk control; for example, it is essential to establish a close liaison between the risk/insurance manager and, say, the security and safety officers, even though the latter may be responsible to a different executive such as the chief engineer or factory manager. Second, the appointment of a risk manager or insurance specialist must not be regarded as relieving other managers throughout the company of various responsibilities in relation to the handling of risks and the insurance arrangements. The larger the company the more important it is that the risk/insurance manager be kept informed of the many factors having a bearing on insurance and other risk handling arrangements for which he is responsible—new acquisitions of buildings or plant, changes in distribution arrangements perhaps involving different methods of transport, the introduction of new processes or raw materials which may materially affect fire or other risks, incidents that may give rise to claims—the list is endless. Good communications are of the first priority, and any failure may have extremely serious consequences.

While it is essential that the person responsible for arranging a firm's insurance has the co-operation of colleagues he can also obtain considerable help, often at little or no extra cost, from external agencies. Besides helping with the actual insurance arrangements, insurance companies and brokers can advise on wider aspects of risk management. Both can draw on their experience of the ways in which similar problems have been handled in other firms, besides having a common interest in loss prevention.

The trend among both major insurance companies and broking firms is to widen the service they provide to cover not merely insurance but all other aspects of risk management. Also there are specialist firms of risk management consultants whose services are available on a fee basis. Finally help can be obtained from crime and fire prevention officers, and specialist security organisations.

FORMULATING AND CONTROLLING THE INSURANCE PROGRAMME

The insurance programme

So far insurance has been discussed purely in financial terms, the firm paying a premium and in return receiving the promise of recompense for any losses it suffers, subject to the limitations of the policy. The costs and benefits of insurance, however, are wider than this.

In comparing the cost of insurance with other methods of handling the firm's risks, due allowance must be made for (a) the expense of administering the insurance arrangements and (b) the impact on the firm's cash flow. Regarding (a) it is necessary for example to assemble certain data before insurance can be arranged —such as details of the property to be insured, its value and situation—and in an inflationary era property must be revalued and the sums insured must be revised regularly. Also when a loss occurs the firm will incur certain costs in preparing its claim. On the other hand such costs should not be overstated; much of the data would be required for accounting and risk control purposes regardless of insurance requirements. Likewise, measures required by insurers to reduce the risk of loss would be equally necessary, and indeed even more so, in the absence of insurance. As for (b), the firm will be called upon to pay the whole or at least a substantial part of an insurance premium at the inception of the period of insurance whereas losses and associated cash outflows will tend to occur later. Indeed payments for liability and some other types of claims tend to be long delayed so that funds set aside might earn considerable investment income which accrues to the insurer if the risk is insured. On the other hand the purchase of insurance will protect the firm's cash flow from unexpected outflows due to the occurrence of loss producing events.

Offsetting the additional costs are various benefits a firm can obtain by insuring, in addition to the basic guarantee of financial security and access to risk prevention advice. By purchasing liability insurance it will be spared the problems and possible embarrassment of defending claims brought against it by injured employees or third parties. Conversely the insurers can be left to make recoveries from third parties, such as carriers or warehousemen, for losses caused by their negligence. Brokers and insurance companies will advise on the terms of leases and other contracts having a bearing on the firm's liabilities and insurance arrangements. These are but a few of the potential advantages, and if evidence can be provided that adequate insurance protection has been arranged it will be far easier to raise loans and other external finance, especially from financial institutions. Indeed insurance companies, which are themselves major financial institutions, tend to look more favourably on requests for finance from their own clients than from other firms.[4]

Selecting the risks

Bearing in mind all of these factors, management must decide which of the firm's risks are to be insured and what limitations are to be placed on the cover provided.

First, the firm must comply with its statutory and contractual obligations. (As noted earlier, compulsory insurance regulations vary from country to country, so that care must be taken to check the requirements in each territory in which a firm operates.) Moreover, in many countries, including some in Europe such as France and Italy, all insurances relating to risks located within the country must be placed with locally-established insurers, unless special permission is obtained to insure abroad. Eventually such obstacles to the placing of multi-territory insurances should disappear within the European Economic Community: the Coinsurance Directive of 1978 was the first step towards creating the so-called freedom of services whereby eventually residents in one member state will be able to insure with an insurer established in another part of the Community.

Not infrequently firms have to accept certain contractual insurance obligations. For example, building leases often require the lessee to insure the property against fire and other perils in the joint names of lessor and lessee. Debenture and mortgage deeds generally include similar provisions, and many other contracts either place on one of the parties certain obligations regarding insurance, or modify the common law position regarding responsibilities for injury or damage arising out of the performance of the contract. In the latter case the firm should consult its insurance company because any waiver of rights of recovery against third parties could invalidate its own insurances.

Having met all legal requirements the management must decide, within the framework of its general risk management objectives, which of the firm's remaining risks to insure.

Dealing first with possible severity of loss, careful consideration obviously must be given to any risk which could jeopardise the solvency of the firm. However, even relatively minor losses cannot be dismissed entirely if there is a risk of an unexpectedly large number of losses occurring within a short period of time which in aggregate may seriously strain the firm's finances.

This introduces the question of loss frequency. At one extreme are those risks which cause small frequent losses, and which, as already explained, it probably will be cheaper not to insure especially if they affect a large number of individual risk units. However, if they could cause a large loss then the most satisfactory solution may be to insure subject to a deductible—that is, the firm itself will bear the first £x either of any one loss or of the aggregate of a number of losses caused by the same incident. So, for example, a firm running a fleet of vehicles may find that it will save overall by carrying a substantial deductible on its accidental damage insurance.

At the other extreme are those risks with a very low probability of occurrence but capable of causing a major loss—for example, fire damage caused by earthquake in Britain. Bearing in mind the fact that a low probability of occurrence carries no guarantee that the firm will be free from such loss for many years ahead, the question whether or not to insure is not simply answered. A great deal must depend upon the premium required and its opportunity cost to the firm—that is, the alternative benefits the firm could have by spending the amount of the annual premium in some other way.

The smaller the premium the stronger the case for insuring (if the firm places long-run survival high on its list of objectives). Whenever the decision is in doubt the balance must always lie with insuring risks which could ruin the firm; in any case this is a decision which should be taken at board level like other business decisions bearing on the firm's future.

Lying between these extremes will be a wide range of risks with varying degrees of loss probability and severity. Again in deciding which to insure, potential loss severity is of prime importance; the smaller and the more frequent the expected losses are, the stronger is the case for the firm carrying its own risk. When comparing quoted premiums against expected losses three additional factors should be considered:

1   The potential variation in losses, including the effect of inflation on future losses.
2   The cash flow implications, not least being the delays in the occurrence and settlement of claims during which time the insurer is holding premiums that are earning investment income.
3   Other possible benefits of insuring.

If restrictions on the insurance cover are considered in order to save on premium expenditure, then it is far sounder to exclude small losses from the insurance than to limit the insurer's liability for large losses, even though the probability of a catastrophic loss may appear remote.

Monitoring the programme

Having arranged an insurance programme the problem of insurance cannot be set aside for the next few years. Minor revisions probably will be required fairly frequently in order to keep the cover up to date following new developments within the firm, such as the purchase of new machinery or the introduction of new products, though the aim should be to incorporate as much flexibility as possible into the insurance policies. In particular while inflation rates remain high adequate provision must be made for the impact of rising prices and earnings on future claims settlement costs: even at an annual rate of inflation of 10 per cent, a claim that occurs twelve months hence and remains outstanding for another twelve months will cost 21 per cent more to settle than at today's prices. Constant watch needs to be kept too on legislative developments at home and abroad: new legislation may create new or more stringent liabilities and responsibilities requiring immediate action.

Policy covers should be reconsidered at each renewal, and at least every three or four years the overall insurance arrangements should be subjected to a full-scale review in the light of new developments both internal and external to the firm. Also it is desirable that the firm should carefully record not only premium expenditures but also its losses whether insured or not. This will provide a check on the costs of its risks, and indicate whether any changes should be made to its insurances or its physical loss reduction efforts in order to minimise the overall risk cost. Insured losses should be recorded according to the policy year in which they occur, and loss settlements (including any payments on account) should be analysed by date of payment in order:

1   To compare the cost of claims incurred in each policy year with the premium paid for that year.
2   To obtain estimates of the investment income earned on funds held to pay outstanding claims and also of the net cost of those claims for comparison with the premiums paid to the insurer.

Loss records also need to include details of causes, remedial action and so forth.

Risk management and insurance arrangements require a continuous effort to be fully effective.

NOTES

1   Readers interested in pursuing the subject in more detail may be referred to R. L. Carter et al, *Risk Management,* Tuition Service of the Chartered Insurance Institute, London, 1981 and G. M. Dickinson, 'Concepts of probability and risk', *Handbook of Risk Management* edited by R. L. Carter and G. N. Crockford, Kluwer-Harrap Handbooks, London, 1974 updated.

2 See R. L. Carter, 'Risk management in an adverse economic climate', *Handbook of Risk Management.*

3 See Parts 2 and 5 of the *Handbook of Risk Management* for an extensive treatment of these problems.

4 See Financial Facilities for Small Firms: A study by Economists Advisory Group directed by Dennis Lees (Committee of Inquiry on Small Firms Research Report No. 4) (London: HMSO, 1971), p. 109.

FURTHER READING

The Association of Insurance and Risk Managers in Industry and Commerce, *The Status and Techniques of Insurance Managers in Industry and Commerce* (AIMIC, London, 1969) and *The Status and Techniques of Insurance and Risk Managers in Industry and Commerce* (AIRMIC, London, 1979).

J. E. Bannister and P. A. Bawcutt, *Practical Risk Management,* Witherby & Co. Ltd, London, 1981.

R. L. Carter 'Risk Management: a British point of view', *Zeitschrift für die Gesamte Versicherungswissenschaft,* vol. 1/2, 1978.

R. L. Carter et al, *Risk Management,* Tuition Service of the Chartered Insurance Institute, London, 1981.

H. Fayol, *General and Industrial Management,* 1916, translated by C. Storrs, Pitman, London, 1974.

M. Haller, 'The aim of risk management', *Foresight,* June 1976.

W. Horrigan, *Risk, Risk Management and Insurance,* Withdean Publications, Hove, 1969.

2

The Insurance Market

A. P. Benson, Group Risk Manager, Arthur Guinness and Sons plc

MARKET COMPONENTS

There are four major elements that make up the insurance market. The principals to any insurance contract are the buyer (the commercial or industrial firm that requires insurance) and the seller (the insurer) who provides protection to the buyer in return for a premium. There can be two secondary participants, not necessarily involved in any particular insurance contract: these are the intermediary between the buyer and the seller, who may be a full-time professional broker or a part-time or full-time agent, and the reinsurer, whose role is that of the ultimate bearer of a part of the risk if the insurer decides that it is necessary to 'lay off' a proportion of his liability so as to ensure that he does not stand to bear too great a loss on any one insurance contract into which he may enter.

Associations

A variety of associations and trade bodies act in the market in the various interests of buyers, sellers, intermediaries and reinsurers. Some of them have considerable influence, and exercise profound effects on the way in which the market operates. Brief details of a few of the more significant of these are given below:

British Insurance Association

Founded in 1917 this body exists as the principal trade association of the British insurance companies. It represents the interests of the majority of the leading insurers (except Lloyd's, with whom it works closely), but it does not provide any guarantee of the solvency of its member companies. It has issued a recommended code of insurance practice for its members, but their compliance with this is not mandatory.

Sector associations

A number of bodies exist to represent the interests of insurers in matters relating specifically to the various major classes of insurance business. Their roles are by no means identical: they further their members' interests in a variety of ways, and these depend on the perceived needs of their members at different times. For example, the Fire Offices Committee establishes and revises agreed insurance rating bases for fire business, the Aviation Insurance Offices Association creates standard policy wordings, the Accident Offices Association is much concerned with the compilation of statistics for specified classes of business, and the Institute of London Underwriters sets out to promulgate and create a satisfactory climate in which its members can carry on their work on marine insurance.

British Insurance Brokers Association

At its foundation in 1977 this relatively young organisation incorporated the four previous significant but separate broking associations. Its membership of over four thousand is corporate, and extends from the largest to the smallest broking companies. Applicants are required to satisfy criteria relating to their financial soundness, their experience and their freedom from excessive insurance company dependence: they are also required to carry a minimum level of professional indemnity insurance in respect of their activities. However, no overall guarantee of solvency in respect of any of their member companies is provided.

Chartered Institute of Loss Adjusters

This is the professional Institute for this very important sector of the insurance business. It is greatly concerned with the maintenance and continuing improvement of the highest levels of professional competence and integrity in a field demanding the utmost probity and independence of mind of its practitioners.

The Association of Insurance and Risk Managers in Industry and Commerce

This body was founded in 1963: its membership is on a personal basis and it serves to bring together, for their mutual benefit, insurance and risk managers working in industry and commerce. It too is much concerned with the advancement of professional standards and, commanding as it does a very substantial collective buying power on behalf of members' employers, it has established itself in the market as an authoritative source of collective buyer opinion.

Insurance Ombudsman

In 1981 a group of leading insurance companies decided to set up this function, under the direction of a board drawn from insurance and consumer interests: there is no statutory basis for this appointment. His role is essentially to referee disputes between the group's private policy holders and their own insurers, and he has no remit to involve himself in any way in the affairs of commercial or industrial policy-holders.

Reinsurance Offices Association

Since its formation in 1969 membership of this body has grown to nearly four hundred companies worldwide, of whom about one hundred and twenty are authorised to operate in the London market. Its educational and advisory work is of considerable importance, and its members seek to improve the conditions in which they operate in international reinsurance markets: financial stability, adequate capacity and sound underwriting are of great concern to them. They do not exercise any formal supervision over or regulation of the affairs of their members.

Insurance Brokers Registration Council

This body was established by statute under the Insurance Brokers (Registration) Act 1977. It administers a system of registration for those who wish to describe themselves as insurance or assurance brokers, and its Council will investigate and act in any case relating to unprofessional conduct by an insurance broker. At law the description 'insurance broker' is now limited to those whose names are entered in the registers or lists established under the Act.

FACTORS AFFECTING THE MARKET COMPONENTS

Buyers

One of the basic aims of the insurer is to streamline his operations and to sell, wherever possible, a standard form of cover for each class of business that he writes. If a buyer wishes to obtain variations in this standard cover to suit his particular needs then he will obviously need to make an appeal to the insurer on commercial grounds, demonstrating that he can offer a more attractive proposition than can the average commercial or industrial concern upon whom the insurer can justifiably impose a standard form of policy.

Clearly, the buyer will find it helpful if he can identify for the insurer reasons for giving him special consideration. The following factors are among those likely to affect the buying power of an individual company.

Management efficiency

The responsibility for buying a firm's insurance may rest at board level or may be delegated either to the secretarial or the financial function. In every case it is important to the insurer that management competence is demonstrably applied to insurance matters. The policies must be properly and promptly administered, and recommendations for risk improvement must be seen to be fairly considered and either implemented or demonstrated to be unnecessary or not viable from the buyer's point of view.

The attitude of the buyer should clearly be that insurance is a protection against unforeseen contingencies and not a crutch to support the financial consequences of inadequate management. The buyer should make it clear that his basic concern is to reduce, and ultimately to move towards the elimination of, the risks against which he insures; in other words, loss prevention should be an integral part of the management function and the insurer should be made aware that there is a corporate policy directed towards this end.

Scale

As in most activities the size of the account that the buyer offers has an effect on the attitude of the insurer. An insurer who is offered all the business of a buyer will tend to be more co-operative when it comes to meeting particular requests or dealing with specific problems. The size of the account may appreciably reduce the insurance cost, and it may well enable the policies written to be tailor-made to the buyer's requirements. It may also serve to generate better service from the field staff, the underwriters and the claims departments of the insurer.

However, to give one insurer a monopoly of all the insurance requirements of the buyer may produce complacency on the part of the insurer and may also keep the buyer out of touch with market developments, particularly if a professional intermediary is not used. The buyer may therefore be well advised to concentrate his purchasing in the hands of two or three insurers, hoping that the effects of competition will be noted and will provide him with improved rating and service levels.

A further refinement in buying technique is to use specialist insurance markets for particularly unusual risks. Some of these may be open to direct approaches from buyers, but others (e.g. specialist Lloyd's underwriting syndicates), can be dealt with only through brokers. Examples of the type of risk best covered in markets of this kind include contingency policies, financial guarantee covers, defective title insurance, product withdrawal cover and retroactive covers for certain classes of risk.

Spread of risk

When the insurer quotes for business he is influenced by the maximum loss that he may incur if the event insured against does happen. Thus a fire insurer would much prefer to cover twenty shops that are each insured for £50,000 than one department store insured for £1,000,000. Similarly, a marine insurer prefers the business of an exporter who ships 10,000 relatively low-valued consignments annually to that of the firm that ships a hundred consignments a year each of which is of massive value. It should therefore be obvious that any steps that the buyer can take to reduce the single-risk exposure that he offers to the insurer should be reflected in improved premium rates and a better relationship.

Business potential

The insurer always like to obtain business which will develop over a period of time. In other words, he likes to be in on the ground floor for the insurance needs of an expanding concern. There is scope for goodwill here, and the dynamic, growth-oriented buyer should be able to establish a generally more helpful relationship with the insurer.

Insurers

Stability

It should be stressed at the outset that the great majority of insurance companies are financially sound. The Department of Trade has considerable powers to regulate the affairs of insurers and it would be wrong to make too much of the company failures (mainly in the field of motor insurance) of the 1970s. Nonetheless, it is prudent of the buyer to take whatever steps he thinks are advisable to satisfy himself of the stability of the company with which he insures, and this is certainly necessary when using the less conventional markets. Rapid growth may well be a danger signal, and this can be particularly true of new motor or life assurance companies.

Insurance is a cyclic business. At times of high interest rates the insurance market usually generates a considerable capacity, and this leads to fierce competition for business among insurers. When at the same time industrial activity is not expanding the scramble for insurance business becomes even more intense—premium rates are pared to the bone as insurers jostle to maintain their share of the available business, so as to generate investment income on the premiums which they receive. In times such as these security becomes of the greatest importance, and the prudent buyer may find that his safest alternative is to accept some marginal increase in premium costs over the minimum which he could obtain from less stable and less well-established competing insurers.

Size and market status

Is it better to be insured with a giant of unquestionable status or with a smaller, equally reputable office which may not be an innovator or trend-setter but which is perhaps more anxious to cultivate the smaller account? The giant insurer may bear a higher proportionate overhead cost than its smaller rival, may be less flexible in its approach and may be more inclined to adopt an arbitrary across-the-board line with all but the biggest clients. On the other hand, the service which the giant can offer may be substantially better than that of its smaller rival, particularly in the specialist fields such as engineering inspection or handling marine insurance claims. The choice is one for the individual buyer to make, and his past experience will undoubtedly have a significant bearing on the decision.

Service

From bitter experience the buyer will learn that service from the insurer does not depend only on the efficiency of the local inspector or contact man or on the goodwill of the branch manager or 'inside' staff of the branch of the insurance company with which he deals. Very often these people are governed by edicts from their own head offices which strictly limit their powers of independent action and which may compel them to refer back relatively minor points of accommodation to a remote and comparatively inflexible authority. From the buyer's point of view it is well worth knowing the level at which the branch of the insurer can make its own decisions: at best this can be significantly helpful and at worst it will often prevent misunderstandings if the buyer recognises that the representative of the insurer with whom he deals is often not a free agent in some of the less favourable decisions that are made. Day-to-day efficient handling of routine matters by insurers is not always found, and (particularly if one is dealing directly with the insurer) is almost certainly worth treasuring if it is discovered.

Intermediaries

The buyer must consider whether or not he proposes to use an intermediary and how he should choose his broker.

One of the principal reasons for using an intermediary for the purchase of insurance is to obtain the benefit of his professional advice and market knowledge. The part-time agent may have something to offer here but it is unlikely that he will be fully competent in every sphere of insurance work. The relatively small buyer may well feel that he is not adequately equipped to handle his insurance without outside advice and if this is so the criteria for selecting an intermediary become important.

Professional competence

Professional competence is undoubtedly a major factor: the broker's function will be to consider the business of the buyer in detail, to advise on those areas where insurance is required, to present the risks suitably to a chosen range of insurers, to handle the servicing and routine administration of the policies and to advise on changes in cover and improvements in wordings as the business develops or the insurance market changes. This is skilled work, and anyone choosing a broker must obviously take competence into account. It is difficult to test ability before employment: one method is to study competing presentations from different brokers, and another is to listen to the word-of-mouth recommendations of other buyers. Additionally, compatibility between broker and buyer has a considerable value.

Registration of the broker by the Insurance Brokers Registration Council means that he satisfies the criteria relating to professional capability laid down by that body, and similarly his membership of the British Insurance Brokers' Association indicates his willingness to conform to their code of practice vis-à-vis his clients.

Buying power

An intermediary's influence with an insurer may reflect the size of the overall account which the intermediary has and the professional competence which he can bring to bear in connection with it. Some of the very large brokers are multinational organisations, and insurers inevitably tend to be influenced by the weight of such massive accounts.

The smaller broker does not pose so significant a threat to the insurer: the size of his account is not so significant in terms of potential loss of business to an insurer if it is shifted elsewhere. Nevertheless some smaller brokers are able to strike up very satisfactory long-term relationships with some sectors of the insurance market, often to the considerable advantage of their clients.

Service

The best service obviously stems from a direct and intense interest in the business of the buyer by the intermediary, and here the relationship established between the two parties is of the greatest importance. The very large intermediary may well be less interested in the smaller cases on his books, although it is fair to say that a total annual premium of over £10,000 from an industrial or commercial concern will probably be of interest to even the largest broking firms. Naturally, the interest generated will amost inevitably be in direct proportion to the size of the account. It may be that a broker of moderate size can offer more to a small buyer than can a giant intermediary. Administration of business is expensive and eats into broker's profits; it can be very nearly as expensive to service a risk generating a premium of £5,000 as one producing a premium of £25,000 and this must to a certain extent govern the broker's attitude.

Flexibility and forward thinking

One of the great advantages of using a broker is that as he acquires further professional knowledge he is able to pass the benefit of this to all his clients if he so chooses. In this respect a large broker definitely offers advantages: his substantial portfolio of cases with their diverse individual needs will probably be spread over a number of insurers, and he will learn the idiosyncrasies of each, the particular points on which each insurer will alter policy wordings to suit him, and the insurers whose attitudes are most compatible with the needs of his various clients. A good broker can suggest improvements to policy wordings which he knows can be accepted by insurers, and he may well be an innovator in the development of better policies for a wide range of his client buyers. Although he lives by commission from the insurer he may be prepared to undertake specific work for the buyer on a fee basis, and this is particularly valuable if new enterprises or diversification are likely to occur in the business of the buyer.

Remuneration

Historically brokers have been remunerated by the insurers with whom they have placed the buyers' business. The method adopted has generally been to pay to the broker as commission a percentage of the premiums involved. This percentage varies according to the class of business being placed and sometimes according to the desire of the particular insurer to attract business from brokers at a particular time. Broadly speaking, the commission percentages conceded by insurers range between 10 per cent to 20 per cent.

Effectively this means that the buyer remunerates the broker (as the commission element is necessarily loaded on to the premium charged to the buyer by the insurer). The result here is often inequitable: for example, in times of relatively high inflation sums insured—and therefore premiums—increase quite rapidly, and brokerage therefore automatically increases if it is simply expressed as a percentage of the premiums generated by the business, but it should be remembered that at times of inflation a broker's expenses would also tend to rise.

Additionally, very large premiums can generate broker commissions which are disproportionately high in relation to the work involved if the conventional remuneration method is accepted. Many brokers, recognising this problem, are now prepared to negotiate their remuneration with the larger buyer on the basis that premiums net of commission are charged to the buyer with the broker taking an agreed fee from the buyer for his services.

CLASSES OF INSURER

There are two main groups of insurers in the United Kingdom. These are generally known as the 'company market' and the 'Lloyd's market'. The company market may be divided into: tariff offices, non-tariff offices, mutual and 'fringe' companies.

Tariff offices

Until relatively recently formal agreements about policy wordings and the rates to be charged for business in the fields of fire, business interruption (or consequential loss), engineering, motor, employers' liability and household insurance existed among a number of leading insurance companies. The agreements were known as tariffs, and offices subscribing to them were termed tariff offices. Numerous advantages, both for buyers and for insurers, were supposed to arise from the existence of the agreements: fundamentally, it was suggested that they prevented unrealistic competition which might lead to the failure of insurance companies and that they resulted in uniform cover at approximately uniform rates. However, in classes of business which seemed to offer relatively high potential profits the tariff offices suffered severe competition from their more flexible and sometimes more adventurous rivals who were not bound by tariff agreements, and over the past decade or so all the agreements have ceased to operate with the exception of those governing fire and consequential loss insurance rates and policy wordings. As a result of this, higher interest rates and over capacity arising from increased competition markets have been extremely volatile, and this volatility has spun off in such a way as to affect significantly cover and premiums for fire and consequential loss risks.

A report published in August 1972 by the Monopolies Commission on the supply of fire insurance called for the breaking of the fire tariff in the interests of free competition. This was opposed by the tariff offices at that time, and the recommendations of the report have never been implemented. To some extent the changing practices of the tariff offices (who now no longer necessarily adhere to their previously rigid rules) have rendered formal change less important, but in one respect the tariff insurers still place an impediment in the way of buyers seeking to minimise their insurance expenditures. By subscribing to what is known as the 'Competition Agreement' the tariff insurers bind themselves to requiring that not less than 65 per cent of any risk in which one of their members participates as a co-insurer (see p. 38) should be placed with tariff offices: the effect is to enable the buyer to achieve discounts from the non-tariff market on only the balance of 35 per cent of his risk.

Non-tariff offices

Although the phrase has less meaning now than it did, this description tends currently to be used to describe the limited liability companies that do not subscribe to the fire and consequential loss tariffs. Historically they have tended to follow tariff rates less a small inducement discount aimed at attracting business, and they are generally regarded as being more flexible than their tariff rivals. Some are extremely large and contribute significantly to the capacity of the insurance market. They are generally happy to participate in the larger-scale insurance covers which are needed by big business (see 'scheduled' insurances, p. 38). An increasing number of very large overseas (frequently American) insurance companies now operate as non-tariff insurers in London.

Mutual companies

As their name implies these are established on a joint-ownership basis, with every insured policyholder becoming a de facto member of the mutual partnership. They have always been non-tariff, and as they aim to be non-profitmaking and to return any profit element to their members they may present financial advantages in certain fields of insurance.

'Fringe' companies

There are a number of relatively small underwriting companies (some of whom are only approachable through broking intermediaries) which operate in London and which may be highly competitive for certain classes of business. Often they are so small as to be unable to take the whole of a large risk, and they then operate on a 'scheduled' basis (see p. 38). Their competitiveness is made possible by low overheads and continuing economies in operation. Similarly there are a number of underwriting agencies who take a proportion of a risk, generally on behalf of overseas insurers, and these are usually approachable only through brokers. Paperwork is cut to a minimum and the broker in fact handles the day-to-day administration of the policies.

The Lloyd's market

The individual underwriting members of Lloyd's are formed into syndicates. They have to make deposits and show sufficient capital assets to satisfy the Council of Lloyd's of their ability to meet their potential claims liabilities. The syndicates generally employ salaried underwriters (who may themselves be underwriting members with a share in their syndicate's fortunes) to conduct their business, and can only be approached through Lloyd's brokers. Each member has unlimited personal responsibility for his own liabilities (but not for those of other members), but a central funding system ensures that in the event of a member being unable to meet these the insuring public does not suffer financially. Lloyd's are noted for underwriting the more esoteric risks and also lead in the handling of marine business. They do, however, handle practically all classes of insurance (except long-term life assurance and financial guarantees). They therefore make a valuable contribution to market capacity generally, but they are now a relatively less significant force in the conventional direct non-marine insurance (as opposed to reinsurance) market than in the past.

In recent years Lloyds has not been entirely free of problems. A fundamental re-appraisal of its methods of functioning has resulted in final acceptance of the proposal that Lloyd's brokers will divest themselves of control of Lloyd's underwriting syndicates: a historic market link will thus be severed, and it remains to be seen whether the new arrangements will in practice enhance the image and efficacy of one of London's greatest insurance institutions.

Lloyd's rates are fluid and can be highly competitive: the system for placing business involves the broker's obtaining a 'lead' from an underwriter who specialises in the class of business concerned at a rate which he considers adequate, and then inducing other underwriters to accept percentages of the risk on the same basis. For industrial risks of any size it is rare for one underwriter to absorb the entire cover, and it is the broker's duty to ensure that the schedule of insurers is completed, and subsequently to deal with the payment of premiums, preparation of policies and collection of claims settlements.

COINSURANCE AND SCHEDULED INSURANCES

Every insurer fixes limits beyond which he does not wish to be exposed in respect of any one loss. He may arrange reinsurance protection for a particular class of business which permits him to underwrite covers considerably in excess of the limit which he retains for his own account, but even these may be inadequate to enable him to absorb 100 per cent of any large risk. There are therefore systems by which a number of insurers from any of the classes described in the previous section may combine to provide full cover for the larger risk, and this is usually done by insurers agreeing to accept varying percentages of risk on the basis of a policy wording issued by the insurer who insures the largest proportion. If insurers issue separate policies for their own percentage of the risk (using the same wording for each policy) the technique is known as coinsurance: if each company adds its name to the single policy issued by the leading insurer and shows on that policy the percentage of the risk in which it is interested then the policy is said to be 'scheduled' and the overall effect is the same. Both techniques may be applied in combination to a single risk, as, for example, when a number of tariff offices subscribe to a scheduled policy for a

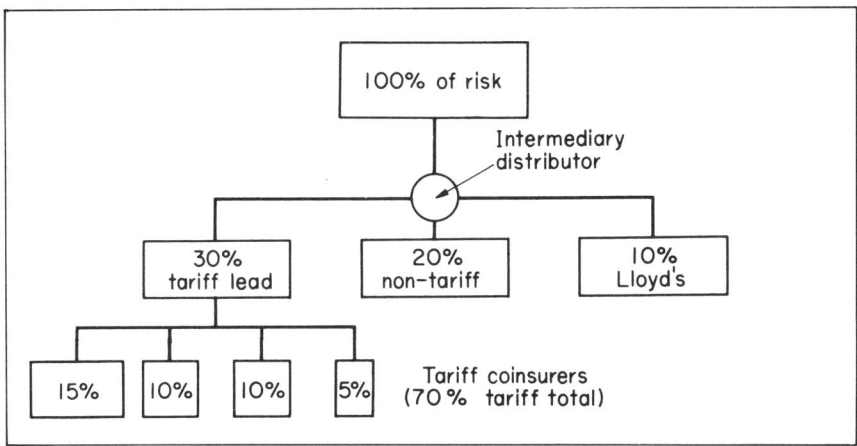

Figure 2:1 Distribution of Risk among Insurers on a Scheduled Coinsurance Basis

total specified percentage of the full amount at risk. A number of other offices or mutual companies issue their own individual policies each for their proportion and Lloyd's underwriters also issue a policy for the amount which they hold (see Figure 2:1).

As already mentioned on p. 36 there is an agreement among the tariff offices that if they appear as partial insurers for fire or consequential loss business they must collectively insure at least 65 per cent of the risk concerned. The effect of this is to limit the proportion of the business that can be placed more economically in the non-tariff market, thus potentially increasing the expenditure of the buyer if the risk being presented is larger than the non-tariff market can absorb alone.

Note that the leading tariff office often places the part of the tariff share of the risk that it is not retaining. Alternatively this business could be placed by the intermediary.

INTERMEDIARIES

A broker owes duties both to insurers and to buyers of insurance and, in varying circumstances, he may be held to be the agent of each. If he behaves negligently towards either party he may be liable in damages. He must also disclose to an insurer any information he has about a risk which may be relevant to it, particularly at inception or at renewal.

A buyer cannot afford entirely to transfer the responsibility for planning his insurance programme to a broker. He also cannot afford to leave a broker to deal with the fundamentals (preparation of proposals, arranging additional covers, increasing sums insured, etc.) of the insurances unsupervised. He should involve the broker to the fullest extent in the affairs of his business, keeping him in touch with changes, which are continuous in any non-static manufacturing or trading operation, and not relying on an annual glance at the policies at renewal to provide adequate insurance protection. If a broker is used, as is so often the case, as a shield for the ignorance of the buyer in insurance matters, the buyer must establish at the outset precisely what information his broker needs (and when he needs it) if the shield is to be of real benefit.

Much industrial and commercial cover is bought through the part-time agent, often a bank manager, solicitor or the like. Although in some cases there may be an overriding reason for employing such intermediaries it generally does not make good sense to do so. The part-time agent offers none of the skills of the broker, has not the range of market contacts and is usually no more than an introductory source for business for a limited number of insurers. The clearing banks have departed from their historical role and have set up professionally staffed departments aiming to provide a full broker service as part of their new packaged financial concept: it is still too early to say how these developments will work out, but they should not be confused with the old 'bank manager in his parlour' agency concept. However, buyers should be able to resist any excessive efforts by banks to compel them to utilise bank broking services.

Many buyers still retain what are termed 'own-case' agencies in respect of their own business. Such agencies are basically a fiction for allowing premium discounts under the guise of commission in return for the placing of the business with the insurer—the argument is that the insurer avoids acquisition costs which he would otherwise pay to an intermediary and which are taken into account in the calculation of his overheads and therefore of his rates of premium. If a buyer decides to deal directly with his insurers there is no harm done by seeking such an agency: indeed, a threat by the buyer to look for an insurer prepared to offer agency terms can produce a very prompt similar offer from the insurer presently holding the business! But the buyer should consider with some care whether the economies of direct dealing are worth the loss of the professional expertise that the broker can exercise on his behalf. At certain levels of premium expenditure the buyer may well find that he can continue to obtain the financial advantage of dealing directly with the insurer if he employs a competent insurance manager as a member of his own staff, utilising this manager's professional knowledge to ensure the adequacy of his cover and claims settlements.

Two other intermediaries often appear, but only after a loss has arisen. The more common of these is the loss adjuster, appointed and paid by the insurer to conduct an independent investigation into the loss to ascertain whether it is covered by the policy, what the level of claim settlement should be and what contribution, if any, is called for from the insured. Although appointed by the insurer the adjuster has a duty to act equitably in the interests of both parties; his professional integrity must be, and is, unimpeachable and his suggestions for the mitigation of loss and the quick rehabilitation of the business are often of immense value to the insured. There is no reason to regard the arrival of the adjuster with suspicion. Experience has led insurers to believe that, particularly in connection with the larger claims, his independent approach is welcomed by the insured in recognition of the contribution which he makes to just claims settlement and the preservation of good relations between buyer and insurer. In the insurance market the main opportunity that the buyer has to decide the true value of his purchase comes at the time of a claim, and the insurer cannot afford an intermediary at this point who creates antagonism and ill-will.

The second claims intermediary is the loss assessor, an independent consultant available for appointment at a fee by the buyer to negotiate his claim on his behalf with the insurer. Many see this as an unnecessary role: the broker or the insured himself can present the claim, and, if an adjuster is appointed, the buyer should not need an advocate to act on his behalf. However some buyers still find an element of comfort in claims situations from the presence of an assessor at their elbow.

REINSURERS

Reinsurers exist to make a profit out of the essential activity of levelling out the loss peaks in the claims experience of individual insurers in return for a proportion of the premiums that the latter are paid by buyers. Just as insurance consists in theory of spreading the losses of the few among the many, so too reinsurance enables the insurer to limit his loss per risk or class of business to an acceptable level, passing the excess over that level onwards and thus reducing the massive reserves that he would need if he was compelled to retain the chance of extremely high loss levels for his own account (see Figure 2:2).

Unless an insurer is operating at satisfactory overall loss levels, a reinsurer is unlikely to profit from his business. Thus if a reinsurer becomes reluctant to maintain his cover for an insurer, or demands a higher proportion of the premium to provide it, pressure would be brought to bear on that insurer to improve his profitability. Although reinsurance is long-term business, there are clear signs that this section of the market has suffered, perhaps disproportionately, in recent years, and that today its collective voice is being raised in warning to the direct insurers: the ultimate likely consequence is that higher premiums will be demanded from buyers, and markets may contract unless greater profitability is achieved.

Unless a healthy reinsurance market existed, buyers would find it very difficult to obtain reasonable cover at reasonable rates, and it is proper that this market should be adequately remunerated for its work. Its workings are often misunderstood by the lay buyer, on whom it has a greater influence than is generally realised.

FURTHER READING

'Self-regulation at Lloyd's'—the report of the Fisher working party, May 1980.

B. K. Doody, *Lloyd's of London: a detailed analysis of results for 1950–1977*, Lloyd's of London Press, 1979.

R. L. Carter, *Reinsurance*, Kluwer Publishing, 1979.

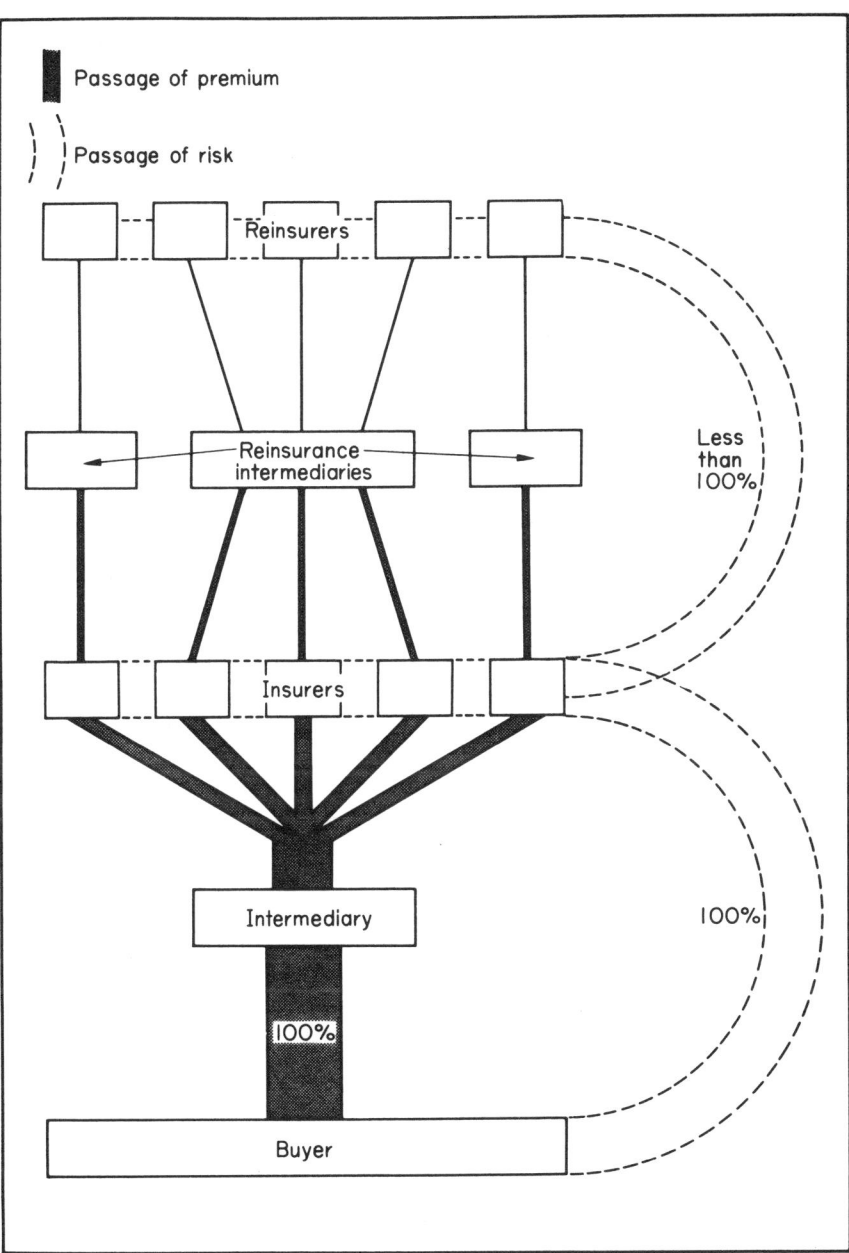

Figure 2:2 Transfer of Risk and Premium from Buyer to Reinsurer
Note the contraction of premium available to meet losses as a result of
retention of commission by intermediaries

3

Insurance Administration

H. R. Loader, Group Insurance Manager, Tetra Pak

COMPANY POLICY ON INSURANCE AND INSURANCE MANAGERS' RESPONSIBILITIES

Company policy should be laid down in a written statement along the lines indicated in Appendix 3:1. Reference to such policy and to the insurance manager's responsibilities is normally incorporated into the latter's job specification an example of which is given in Appendix 3:2. One of the objectives of the latter is to indicate to the insurance manager and other members of staff his authority and responsibilities. In a smaller company it may be necessary for another function to accept these responsibilities, in which case for a non-specialist a statement acts as both a reminder and guidance as to how they should be discharged. For greatest efficiency a single central manager is required to control a programme even though in a larger company there may be a local operating company or divisional personnel who carry out the daily routine tasks—it is only with central control that the greatest buying power can be exerted in the market which in turn enable cost savings and cover improvements to be maximised.

DEPARTMENTAL PERSONNEL AND ORGANISATION

The range of individuals responsible for the corporate insurance/risk management function can be expected to cover a spectrum from company secretary/accountant through insurance clerk/officer/

superintendent/manager to director, dependent on the size of the company and its insurable exposures and the importance which the company attaches to the insurance/risk management function. A common weakness in British based companies is the allocation of the title of insurance/risk manager without the delegation of responsibility and authority to commit the company, and this is noticable in terms of reporting structure.

Staffing levels for departments vary with several factors, but even major companies have been known to operate on a manager plus secretary basis and substantially sub-contract work to their brokers— such a decision is presumably taken for short term economic reasons as on a long term basis the direct employment of additional staff may well be more cost effective.

Premium expenditure is not a reliable guide to departmental size. A multi-million pound premium may be controlled by one person or require a twenty person department; similarly, a half million pound expenditure might need a department of four or five, although it would be an unusual situation that called for 4 people with premiums of only £100,000.

The organisation of a department will in fact be largely determined by such factors as:

1 Volume and nature of the business.
2 Geographical spread of risks.
3 Occupation of the premises (manufacturing, retailing, offices etc.)
4 Complexity of manufacturing processes or of services.
5 Degree of change inherent in the type of business. Is it continually developing or diversifying? Is it fairly static, or does it depend upon a number of contracts with others always emerging, as for example in a major building contracting company?
6 Volume of insurance work as determined by the classes of insurance cover e.g. a large motor fleet will bring much detailed work for the insurance department.

COMMUNICATION

If a company is organised by divisions, the insurance manager may deal only with one official of that division, such as the divisional secretary, or the divisional manager, through whom all information is transmitted to the insurance manager.

In other cases he may find that he is expected to deal directly with works or branch managers, or the company secretaries of subsidiary or associated companies. The nature and extent of all the links just described will depend on the circumstances of the particular company, its administrative structure, the nature of its activities (manufacturing, distribution, retailing, servicing etc.), and on the nature of the product or service. In all these matters the insurance manager must become well-informed, as he must also about any changes. He should, where appropriate, keep managers informed about insurances arranged within their area of responsibility. He must be prepared to 'interpret' insurance terms and expressions to them, and to explain the nature and scope of the cover arranged. He will usually need to give them firm guidance and advice on insurance matters.

He will often have to start all over again when successive managers are appointed.

Some companies find it valuable to issue an insurance manual. Such an internal publication can supply useful information under such headings as:

1   Corporate policy on insurance.
2   Responsibility for insurance matters.
3   Brief description of covers.
4   Procedure for notification of fires and accidents, including major incidents occurring outside business hours.
5   Claims procedures.
6   Staff insurance schemes.
7   Valuation procedures.
8   Maintenance of sprinklers and fire appliances.
9   Protection of important records.
10   Control of keys.
11   Definitions and explanation of insurance terms.
12   Claims examples.
13   Brief comment on other types of insurance not covered by manual which may vary by operating company.
14   Standard forms.

A useful and informative discipline is for the insurance manager to draw up an annual report for self evaluation on insurance which provides:

1   A classified list of insurances maintained or arranged during the year, together with the relevant premiums, including premiums outstanding.
2   A classified list of claims made during the year, showing the current progress.
3   A classified list of outstanding claims from previous years.
4   A classified list of claims settled during the year.
5   A comparison of premiums and claims for the year by type of insurance.
6   Significant developments and changes made in the insurance portfolio during the year.
7   Any other points of special interest.
8   Recommendations for the coming year.

A summary of this with comparisons for prior years and budget for the following year may be presented to higher management. This should be brief and free from jargon but contain all significant data.

PLACING THE RISK

Where a company employs an insurance manager it may be the practice to place a proportion of the company's insurances direct with the market on net terms. In this way the saving in premium may more than cover the cost of the insurance department, although in some cases brokers may argue that notwithstanding their receipt of commission they could have obtained a lower gross premium than the net premium obtained direct by the insured.

However, it is probably true that the majority of insurance managers place a large part, but not necessarily all, of their insurances through brokers, with a tendency to deal with not more than two.

The advantages of using brokers include:

1   Specialised knowledge and expertise available among brokers' staff.
2   Access to the Lloyd's and other specialist markets.

3   Assistance in negotiation of premium and conditions and in settlement of claims.
4   Wider knowledge of the insurance market.
5   Representation overseas.
6   Buying power.
7   Specialised services available from larger brokers e.g. surveys/ risk management/employee benefits/captive reinsurance/environmental health/computer services.

In placing insurance the insurance manager should look for policy wordings that are as simple as possible; he should aim to keep information and declarations required by the insurers to a minimum and he should recognise that his company will require his insurance arrangements to fit in with the company's administrative system.

VISITS AND SURVEYS

The insurance manager should aim to visit all premises of his company. The frequency of his visits must depend upon the nature of his company's activities and upon the number and location of premises, but a minimum of one or two visits per year to major premises is desirable. The value of these visits lie in the personal contacts with the people locally who are responsible for feeding the insurance manager with information and the knowledge of local circumstances which he needs to acquire, and which might not otherwise come to his notice. This will assist him in ensuring that the overall insurance protection remains satisfactory and is understood in the light of changing circumstances.

Surveys and inspections by officials from insurers and brokers will often be arranged by the insurance manager, who will ensure that responsible officials of his company are available to guide and inform the visitors. The insurance manager would normally find it advisable to accompany the party, not only for his own information, but also to act as linkman with insurers, and sometimes as technical interpreter between the officials of his own company and those of the insurers.

Later, when reports and recommendations are received from insurers or brokers, it will be the insurance manager's role to see that these are transmitted to the appropriate departments and that the necessary action is taken or, if the recommendations are not acceptable, to supervise negotiations.

He, or a member of his staff, will act in a similar capacity in connection with periodic inspections and tests of any sprinkler installations.

CLAIMS

The insurance manager should be given immediate notification of all incidents involving damage to or loss of property, accidents to employees or members of the public, and any other incidents for which the company may be held liable. The insurance manager will require full details of each occurrence, usually on standard forms, together with estimates of the cost of repair or reinstatement and also salvage estimates where appropriate. He will, with technical assistance where necessary, negotiate with insurers or loss adjusters for settlement of the loss.

In some companies the insurance manager may arrange for claims of a routine nature such as motor claims to be notified direct to insurers, with a copy of all correspondence to him.

In negotiating the claim he will serve a useful function as a middle man with his knowledge of the operations and requirements of both his own company and of the insurers. As a result of the claim records which he builds up he will be in a favourable position to draw attention within his own company to a run of claims which seem to need examination—for example, persistent claims under products liability may be capable of remedy; the production department may like to be reminded that engineering breakdowns are increasing so that they can enquire into the matter; an increase in the number of money losses may indicate that security needs improving or a run of motor accidents involving a particular driver may lead to the conclusion that he should be transferred to other work.

RECOVERIES FROM THIRD PARTIES

When loss of or damage to company property occurs for which a third party is considered to be responsible, but for which the company itself effects no insurance cover, it is often convenient to leave the question of recovery in the hands of the insurance manager, at least in the early stages. Later, if the claim has been questioned or rejected by the third party who is alleged to be responsible, the insurance manager may seek the advice of the legal department or pass the case to that department to take legal action. Except for simple routine claims it may be advisable for the insurance and legal departments to liaise from the start; but where standard initial letters for each kind of claim have previously been drafted and agreed between the two departments, these will usually be completed and despatched by the insurance department.

Claims of this kind may arise from damage to buildings and contents in cases where some perils are not insured—for example, those arising from impact by vehicles or from an overflow of water which finds its way into the company's premises from those of a neighbour. Much more common are claims for damage to motor vehicles for which accidental damage is not insured or where an excess applies. Apart from the cost of repairs or replacement, the claim may also include the cost of temporary hire of an alternative vehicle.

If a sizeable claim upon a third party is more than the amount of the excess under the relevant policy, it is best for the insurance manager to liaise with the insurers, who may agree to deal with the whole recovery.

When an employee is injured while travelling on company business, the insurance manager, together with the legal department may guide the employee in initiating his claim against the third party responsible.

GROUP PROGRAMMES

The use of a single insurer or panel of insurers to cover one class of insurance (e.g. fire, employees' liability) for a group of companies can be very valuable in exerting the maximum amount of influence on the terms and premiums for the group as a whole. Obvious examples of benefits include uniformity of underwriting standards, protection requirements and policy wordings. In the event of claims which may have to be negotiated the influence of the total support by an insured of an insurer on a specific class of insurance may introduce commercial judgment into a claim payment rather than just legal liability. In premium terms the grouping of business may allow sizeable discounts to be applied. These may require approval of the Fire Offices' Committee for fire insurance placed with a tariff office but this approval is applied for by insurers.

INTERNATIONAL

Two main alternatives are available to simplify administration of an insurance programme for a company with international operations. The first is a group programme with a single insurer or panel of insurers; in this way it is possible to develop a Master Policy in English (or other language) so that there is parent company or head office knowledge of the precise risks being insured and the applicable terms of cover.

The second alternative is to use a single broker operating worldwide and to impose upon him the obligation to ensure, so far as possible, a uniform standard of cover in each country. However, as some countries may not allow for sufficiently wide cover it may be necessary to arrange a *difference in conditions* policy in the head office country so that there are no gaps in cover, and in certain countries this policy may have to be on a non-admitted basis with premiums borne by head office and claims payable to them or other nominees. A major disadvantage of having claims paid centrally for overseas losses is the possible taxation implications—if the money is retained at head office it may be treated as an effective dividend payment by the subsidiary, whereas if it was remitted to the country that had the loss it could be treated as additional capital from the parent and subject to a capitalisation tax; also premiums may be ineligible for tax relief. In some countries, e.g. Brazil and Nigeria, insurance outside the country for local risks is prohibited and substantial fines could be incurred or even jail sentences imposed on local executives. Despite efforts towards free trade, in the EEC it is still not possible to insure in one country for activities in all EEC countries and have the insurance cover accepted and allowed in all of those countries.

Besides the methods described above, there are of course other options which may be more appropriate to particular circumstances.

Other basic considerations for overseas risks include currency exposures, particularly in relation to time constraints in obtaining import permits; any jurisdiction clauses contained in the policy both in respect of claims made by the insured and those made against the insured by third parties; (this is of particular importance if the company sells to the USA and the desirability to provide for waiver of rights of recourse against other group companies).

Different legal systems may provide for workers' compensation either instead of or in addition to Employer's Liability. Furthermore in the employee benefit area the insurance of temporary and permanent disablement may be common as well as the provision of substantial life insurance and retirement benefits.

STAFF INSURANCES

The insurance manager will be approached by employees of his company for advice and guidance in connection with their private insurances.

Help of this kind to senior members of the staff may win their co-operation when company insurances are under discussion. No such advantages will accrue from others, and such involvements are usually time consuming. A ruling should be made by management about whether the insurance department is to deal with such private insurance matters, and whether the employee, the company or even the insurance manager is to have the advantages of any commission earned. In a large company it may be necessary to allocate one member of the insurance department solely to this work. Alternatively, it may be possible to set up schemes (for private insurance, for example) whereby the employee will deal direct with the insurer or broker.

ACCOUNTING MATTERS

The insurance manager may be responsible for verifying accounts received and for authorising their payment. This would be normal practice in an organisation with central administration; however, with decentralised administration local operating companies might pay if premium levels have been advised by the insurance manager. Details of insurances debited must be checked as well as rates and calculations. For the centralised company the description of individual items may not be sufficient for the purposes of the accounts department, and the insurance manager may therefore need to add notes to make matters clearer, not only to the accounts department but also to operating areas or departments that may eventually be debited. For the same purpose it may be necessary to add a coding reference to each item. For block premiums the insurance department (or sometimes the broker) may have to break down the charge of many factories, companies or departments on varying bases such as turnover, wage bill, number of employees, area, sum insured and hazard.

Some companies will deal with insurance costs either as a central charge or will apportion them on an arbitrary basis. *Budgets* are another matter with which the insurance manager must concern himself, in common with his colleagues in other departments of his company. He will build up an estimate of the overall cost of insurance for the period required from past experience, from information of trends in insurance rates, from his knowledge of the current operations and projected developments within his company, and from proposed new sums insured and forecast sales and wage levels.

A system will be necessary to monitor future expenditure compared with the budget. This may be operated by the accounts department, which, perhaps monthly, will provide the insurance department with a statement of budgeted amounts compared against actual expenditure: or alternatively the insurance department may keep its own record.

Towards the end of the financial year, and possibly also at other times during the year, the insurance manager must prepare for the accounting department a list of costs incurred but for which premium requests have not yet been received. He may also be required to supply a summary of charges relating to the following accounting period, but which are included in accounts which have already been passed through to the accounting department for payment.

RECORDS, FORMS AND STATISTICS

Records, forms and statistics will differ from one company to another and no one company will use all those described here.

Records

1 Insurance register: this will record a brief description of subject matter, risks covered, sums insured, rates, discounts, net premiums, payment dates, policy numbers and special features, also name of insurers and brokers.
2 Separate and similar register of overseas insurances.
3 Claims register of insured and uninsured losses with provision for recording recoveries from third parties.
4 Master insurance manual: master version of that given to operating companies, divisions etc.
5 Record of any locally arranged policies outside central administration.

Forms

Most of the forms are used to report accidents or losses to the insurance department.

1 Fire report forms, reporting all fire incidents.
2 Accident report forms, reporting all accidents to employees or to third parties. Types of accidents may be coded for statistical purposes.
3 Motor accident report forms.
4 Drivers' record forms. One to each driver recording all accidents in which he is involved. (For reporting accidents, especially motor accidents, the insurers' forms are usually used).
5 Renewal information forms. These provide local management with a simple method of giving renewal details to the insurance department.
6 Declaration report forms. For reporting such matters as cash carried, stock levels, and wages paid. Often the insurers' own form will serve.

7   Premium payment advice forms. For advising insurance department that premium (deposit, actual or adjustment) was paid on a specific date.

Statistics

Examples of these are:

1   Comparison of claims against premiums.
2   Comparison of total premiums against turnover by the various companies of an industrial group.
3   Analysis of types and causes of fires, accidents and other incidents.
4   Budgets for management.
5   Tabulations of policies and premiums, analysed by classes of insurance and company divisions.
6   Tabulations of claims and uninsured losses, analysed in the same way.
7   Cash flow records for premiums and claims.

Miscellaneous records

1   Annual report.
2   Checklist. These are reminder notes for use when reviewing the insurance needs of new or existing companies.
3   'History book' recording important decisions, developments or changes over the years.
4   Insurance department staff records, including job specifications.

APPENDIX 3:1. ITEMS COVERED BY A COMPANY'S STATEMENT OF POLICY ON INSURANCE

Objectives
Protection of the company's assets and earnings against loss, including protection against legal liabilities, all at minimum cost commensurate with satisfactory cover.

Assumption of risk
Assume risk:
1 If the probable maximum loss is small and can be met from earnings.
2 If the probable maximum loss is small in relation to the insurance premium required, and there is a wide spread of risk.
3 If deductibles are possible, having considered the probable maximum loss, and the discount allowed on the insurance premium.
4 If funds or reserves can be relied upon to make good the loss.

Purchase of insurance

1 Consider whether to place insurance direct, or through intermediaries.
2 Insure all insurable exposures to catastrophe, unless they can at any time be met by available company funds, bearing in mind possible cash and overdraft positions.
3 Insure exposures where the probable maximum loss is too large for the company to bear.
4 Insure where the services provided by insurers make insurance an economical and convenient method. Such services are claims handling, engineering inspection, accident prevention etc.
5 Consider the financial stability of the insurers.

Administration

1 So far as possible administrative systems and methods must fall into line with those operating within the particular company or organisation.
2 Aim at simplicity by such methods as the amalgamation of

policies, the grouping of renewal dates, the placing of wide covers and by reducing the number of declarations to a minimum.

3 In major companies with many subsidiaries, branches, works, or divisions, weight the advantages of centralisation of insurance administration. Since insurance is a highly specialised business it is usually considered wise to have a professional responsible for the administration of a planned insurance programme, including the centralised purchase of insurance. This brings the advantages of expertise, balance, consistency and bulk purchasing, as well as relieving local management of a task for which they are not well equipped. Centralisation should reduce the possibility of duplication of covers, and conversely the chance of gaps in the covers.

4 In the case of international companies, decide upon a policy for the guidance of staff overseas who have responsibility for local insurance arrangements. Consideration should be given to the central purchase of insurance, so far as this is possible and desirable.

APPENDIX 3:2. EXAMPLE OF JOB SPECIFICATION FOR AN INSURANCE/RISK MANAGER

XYZ COMPANY LIMITED

Job title
Group Insurance/Risk Manager

Responsible to
Group Treasurer/Financial Director

PRINCIPAL OBJECTIVES OF THE JOB

1 To protect group assets and earnings and reduce potential legal liabilities by means of risk management and insurance, at optimum cost commensurate with adequate security.
2 To devise, implement and maintain a group risk financing programme in accordance with the corporate policy as laid down in the insurance manual and within overall corporate objectives.

SUMMARY OF MAIN DUTIES

1 Identification of risks within the group.
2 Provision of advice on self insurance and retained liabilities.
3 Arrangement of policies with insurers in the UK and overseas markets.
4 Liaison with brokers.
5 Conduct of renewal and other negotiations with brokers and insurers and liaison with group companies.
6 Undertaking claims negotiations with brokers and insurers on behalf of group companies.
7 Carrying out of periodic risk surveys and portfolio reviews, coupled with provision of advice to management on appropriate risk improvement measures.
8 Maintaining for the foregoing purposes all necessary records.

SUMMARY—THE SCOPE OF JOB

1   Knowledge and experience

   (a) A general knowledge of market rates, conditions and underwriting of Fire, Business Interruption, Marine Cargo, Accident, Motor and Liability Insurances.

   (b) Experience in risk management within industry.

   (c) Professional qualifications desirable, e.g. ACII.

   (d) Broad experience of both industry and relevant classes of insurance.

2   Responsibilities

   (a) To identify the various types of potential loss confronting the company and evaluating the financial impact of such losses upon the company. Position has the full authority for the selection of insurance companies and brokers and the negotiation and approval of the terms and conditions of all property, liability and group insurance contracts required to transfer risk which the company has decided not to retain.

   (b) The control of corporate premium expenditure.

   (c) For departmental staff.

3   Creative ability

   (a) To devise and negotiate suitable covers to protect special needs.

   (b) To maximise corporate profit by reducing the cost of risk through group and associated companies' insurance and risk management activities in UK and overseas.

   (c) To advise on insurance matters in such specialised areas as .... (any special areas of the business).

4   Relationships

(a)   To maintain contact within the group at all levels (as well as outside the group), in particular with the management of operating companies with a view to exchange of full information on local insurance and risk management matters.

(b)   To guide/advise corporate management on proper and adequate protection of group interests both with and without insurance.

(c)   To represent company at AIRMIC and present special interests and considerations where appropriate.

(d)   To represent company at professional and social functions within the industry.

4

Principles of Insurance Law

J. T. Steele, Head of Department of Banking and Insurance Studies, Glasgow College of Technology

The ordinary essentials of contracts such as offer, acceptance, consideration, capacity, legality, possibility and consensus apply to insurance as to other contracts. This chapter assumes that the reader has some knowledge of these aspects and concentrates on the principles which are peculiar to insurance.

CONTRACT OF INSURANCE

Definition

Insurance is a contract in which an insurer, in consideration of a premium, agrees with an insured either to indemnify him against loss caused by a risk insured against (such as fire or public liability) or to pay him an agreed sum on the happening of a specified event (such as an accident or death). The feature which distinguishes insurance from a pure wager is that the insured must have an interest in the subject matter of his 'bet' which is distinct from the 'stake' and this interest must be recognised at law; in other words, insurance guards against risks, while wagers create them.

Form

In common with other contracts, insurance is arranged by one party (usually the proposer or a member of the public) making an offer to enter a contract with the insurer who can accept or reject that offer. The offer and acceptance can be oral or in writing by letter or special forms. It is usual for the contract to be evidenced by a policy (marine insurance contracts are unenforceable if not).

Offer and acceptance

One can offer a risk to an insurance company by word of mouth, and where immediate cover is required by a proposer or intermediary well-known to the insurer, this offer may also be accepted orally. In many cases, however, a pre-printed questionnaire or proposal form is used to detail material information required about the risk. In the case of risks placed through brokers, proposal forms are not used on every occasion, but may be used in conjunction with a 'broker's slip', or the slip may be used on its own. The slip is a document detailing much of the information which is contained in a completed proposal form, and the insurer's acceptance of the offer (or a share of it), is confirmed by the signing of the slip by the insurer's representative, hence the term 'underwriter'.

Cover notes

Where a signed slip is not used to confirm cover, a letter, or more likely a cover note, may be issued by the insurers. The cover note is often for a fixed term, say 30 days, and is issued stating that cover is in the form of the insurer's standard form of policy wording for that class of risk. Any deviation from those terms must be noted on the cover note. During the period of this short-term contract, further investigation may be carried out by survey, or the proposal form received if it was not at inception. Assuming that after the final particulars have been received the risk is still acceptable to the insurer, an annual contract, the policy, will be prepared. In life or pensions business, the term of the contract may of course be for many years; such contracts are termed 'long-term business'.

Certificate of insurance

In the case of most classes of compulsory insurance such as third party injury liability under the Road Traffic Acts 1972 and 1974 and employer's liability insurance, the statutes require that an annual certificate of insurance be issued and a temporary cover note would incorporate such a certificate in the form designated by the appropriate statute.

The employer's liability insurance certificate must be displayed at each place of work. Non-compliance with this requirement of the Employers' Liability (Compulsory Insurance) Act 1969, leaves the employer open to a penalty of up to £50.

INSURABLE INTEREST

The subject matter of a contract of insurance is the insurable interest of the insured in the *subject matter of insurance* which is the property, life or potential liability mentioned in the policy. (Castellain v Preston (1883)).

Based on the case Lucena v Craufurd (1806) and Section 5(2) of the Marine Insurance Act 1906, insurable interest can be defined as a relationship, recognised at law, between the insured and the subject matter of insurance whereby he benefits from its safety, well-being or freedom from liability and would be prejudiced by its damage or the existence of liability.

Examples of relationships which can give rise to insurable interest in property are:

1 Full, part or joint ownership.
2 Mortgagees and mortgagors.
3 Executors and trustees.
4 Agents.
5 Bailees.
6 Spouses in the property (or life) of the other spouse.

On the other hand, it was decided in Macaura v Northern Assurance Co. Ltd (1925) that a sole shareholder, who was also a major creditor, did not have an insurable interest in the assets of a company. The company, as a separate legal entity owned the assets, not the shareholders. A mere expectancy does not constitute insurable interest. For example a beneficiary under a will cannot insure the property he may inherit nor the life of his benefactor (Lucena v Craufurd (1806)). If he were to sell his expectancy on condition that he would return the money if his expectancy was not realised, the purchaser could insure the beneficiary's life for the amount of the purchase price (Cook v Field (1850)). This interest arises out of the *contract* between them, even though the contract is based on expectancy.

The principle of insurable interest is an extension of the rules of capacity to contract as applied to insurance. By the Life Assurance Act 1774, any policy on the life of any person *or other event* in which the person for whose benefit or on whose account the policy is made has no insurable interest at the time of the contract, is illegal. The Act is not limited to life assurance as the words in italics show, but insurances on goods, ships and merchandise are specifically excluded from its scope. However, these insurances may be void under the Gaming Act 1845 and/or the Marine Insurance Act 1906 if at the time of the contract the insured had no insurable interest and no bona fide expectation of acquiring one. The Marine Insurance Act 1906, while allowing for a mere expectation of acquiring an interest at inception, provides that it must exist *at the time of the loss.* On the other hand, in the case of a life assurance contract, insurable interest need be present only at inception. If the value of the interest has reduced or indeed disappeared by the time of death of the life assured, the beneficiary can still recover the full interest that existed at inception (Dalby v The India and London Life Assurance Company (1845)).

Other insurances, being contracts of indemnity, require that insurable interest exists at the time of the loss, as otherwise there would be no interest to indemnify, *and* at inception.

Insurances as trustee for another's interest

Finally, in considering the nature of insurable interest, some comments are desirable on carriers, warehousemen and other bailees. They often insure goods up to their full value, although their own personal interest extends only to any loss or damage for which they are legally responsible to the owner. On the principles discussed above, one might think that this type of insurance could be attacked as unenforceable, but this is not so, because a person can validly insure for the benefit of others if that is found to be the real intention of the policy. It has been held that a policy taken out by a bailee covering 'goods, his own, in trust, or on commission' is such a policy, enabling the bailee to recover in full for a loss, and to hold any balance exceeding his own interest in trust for the owner. On the other hand, where the words quoted were followed by 'for which he is responsible', it was held to be covering the personal liability of the bailee only, so that in the absence of any legal liability for the loss on the bailee's part, there was nothing for the insurer to indemnify.

A person may even insure to protect the interest of others where he has no insurable interest of his own at all. In Prudential Staff Union v Hall (1947), it was held that a trade union could validly take out insurance against theft of cash belonging to its members.

ASSIGNMENT

The word 'assignment' is used in insurance to mean:

1   A complete transfer of all the rights and obligations under a policy—an absolute assignment.
2   A conditional or mortgaged assignment of the proceeds with or without direct rights accruing to the assignee.
3   A simple assignment of the proceeds with no rights accruing to the assignee directly.

Assignment of interest

In considering whether or not an insurance policy is freely assignable, one has to identify the nature of the relationship which the insured has to the risk being run. In certain types of risk, the probability of a loss occurring depends to some extent on how the insured manages his affairs; the motorist has a direct bearing on the likelihood of his car being involved in an accident; the factory owner, through bad management and housekeeping, can bring about fire or accident losses. On the other hand the life assured, unless he or she is suicidal, has little influence in the short to medium term, on his or her likelihood of death. The marine cargo owner, once his goods are on board ship, has no control over possible losses.

Non-life and non-marine contracts are therefore dependent on the *personal* attitude of the insured for their claims-free existence. The identity of that insured has been vetted at proposal stage by the insurer, and so a transfer of the contract to another person would be material to the insurer and cannot be carried out without the prior agreement of the insurer. Agreement to transfer of interest by will or operation of law is often given by policy condition. Other transfers of interest must be submitted to the insurer for approval, which need not be given if the insurer does not approve of the new proposer.

Life assurance contracts are freely assignable since the new assured is extremely unlikely to influence the death of the life assured. Under Section 50 of the Marine Insurance Act 1906, all marine insurances are freely assignable for the reason already mentioned, but it is the practice to require approval of the insurer to assignment of hull policies, since the nature of ship management and crewing is within the control of the shipowner.

Assignment of proceeds

The consent of the insurer to assign the proceeds of an insurance contract is not necessary since his interests are not altered or harmed in any way. The rights and obligations under the contract remain with the original insured. If he has a legitimate claim, it just means that he has authorised the insurer to pay someone else.

Any action on the claim must still be made through the insured. If the assignee wishes to sue on the contract in his own name, the assignment must be an absolute one for the entire proceeds and notice given to the insurer under the terms of Section 136 of the Law of Property Act 1925 or in the case of life contracts, the Policies of Assurance Act 1867. In the case of a mortgaged life policy, assignment can also take place under the latter Act with the assignee acting as trustee of the assured for any balance of proceeds above the amount of loan and interest.

Under Section 47 of the Law of Property Act 1925, vendors of property must hold in trust for the purchaser any insurance monies becoming payable after the date of the contract of sale, such monies to be paid to the purchaser on completion of the contract. This assumes that the contract has no stipulation to the contrary, that the consent of the insurers, if required, has been obtained and that the premium has been shared by the purchaser from the date of the contract. Most fire and householder's comprehensive policies have a 'purchaser's interest clause' whereby the insurers specifically give their consent in respect of building losses. The purchaser obtains no better rights than the vendor and would, for example, obtain no benefit if the vendor had broken a warranty.

GOOD FAITH AND WARRANTIES

Duty of disclosure

As well as the additional requirements of capacity to contract, i.e. insurable interest as already discussed, there are also extensions regarding the duties of disclosure. In all contracts, each party must observe good faith and must not *wilfully* mislead the other or perform any fraudulent act. The general rule is that of *caveat emptor*, let the buyer beware. However, in insurance each party owes the duty of *uberrima fides, utmost* good faith, to the other. This means that each must disclose all material facts to the other whether requested or not. An example of a material fact which an insurer would require to disclose, could arise in marine insurance, where, due to shipping intelligence services, an insurer may be aware of the safe arrival of a ship, while a cargo-owner wishing to insure a newly-acquired cargo, is not yet aware of the fact that the insurance is no longer required.

At the beginning of this chapter, mention was made of the use of proposal forms which elicit information about the more usual material facts. If there are additional material facts, about which the form is silent, the proposer must still disclose this additional information. A material fact is one which would influence the judgement of a reasonable or prudent insurer in deciding whether or not to accept the risk or what premium or terms to impose (Lambert v Cooperative Insurance Society (1975)).

In general terms, facts require to be disclosed if they would show that the risk of loss is greater than would normally be expected from a risk of the nature proposed, or that loss might be more severe. Previous losses, claims, imposition of special terms or of declinature by other insurers are also examples requiring full disclosure, although by the wording of proposal form questions or otherwise insurers may disregard certain facts more than 3/5 years before the date of the proposal. Certain facts relating to the moral hazard, such as a previous conviction for dishonesty, unless the conviction is now 'spent' under the Rehabilitation of Offenders Act 1974 must also be disclosed. Non-disclosure or misrepresentation of these facts would place the insurer at a disadvantage in assessing the risk since normally only the proposer will know all the material facts relating to the risk proposed.

Most legal liability insurances expressly exclude liability arising out of any contract unless such liability would have attached despite the contract. Even in the absence of this exclusion, the acceptance by the insured of an additional contractual liability of which the insurer had no notice (because it was not disclosed at the time of arranging the cover, and could not be said to be a matter of common knowledge), would increase the risk, and should therefore be notified.

On the other hand, certain material facts do not require to be disclosed, either because the insurer should be aware of them, for example facts of law, public knowledge, or which the insurer in the ordinary course of business ought to know, or facts about which the insurer does not enquire further after having been put on enquiry, or because they would tend to lessen the risk (and therefore not prejudice the insurer) such as the presence of alarm systems or sprinklers for combating fire.

The duty of full disclosure applies during the negotiations for a contract until there is offer and acceptance, at renewal of the policy, except in long-term business such as life assurance, and at the time of any alteration to the contract, if material to that alteration. Many policies contain a condition which requires the insured to advise the insurer of alterations which increase the risk during the period of the contract. Most proposal forms and renewal documents contain a reminder to the insured for the need to make a full disclosure, and of the effect on the contract if information is withheld.

Warranties and conditions

A warranty in insurance contracts is a vital clause which, in law, must be strictly observed or the insurer can avoid liability. Warranties usually relate to (a) some physical aspects of risk which if the facts were changed would worsen the risk but which were not present at inception and have not been charged for in the premium, (insurers will often delete such a warranty on request and then charge a higher premium), or (b) some aspect of good housekeeping, such as removal of waste, maintenance of machinery, etc., in good condition (such warranties will not be removed even at a higher premium, since they are fundamental to making the risk acceptable). While currently at law the insurer can repudiate liability for any claim if there has been a breach of warranty or condition, the majority of insurers are parties to one or other of two Statements of Insurance Practice whereby they undertake not to avoid liability if the breach was not material to the loss occurring nor to making it more severe than it would otherwise have been. In these Statements insurers undertake also not to repudiate a claim on the grounds of misrepresentation or non-disclosure where knowledge of the fact would not have materially influenced the insurer's assessment of the risk.

Compulsory insurances

Much of the force of compulsory liability insurances would be lost if the insurers were able to repudiate their liability under the policy by pleading that the insured had breached the policy conditions. To counter this, insurers of compulsory employers' liability and motor third-party risks are prevented by statute from avoiding liability by reason of something done or omitted by the insured after the injury occurs–such as his failure to notify the insurers within a fixed time.

Various other conditions are also made ineffective against third parties, including (in the case of motor vehicle cover) conditions about the age of the driver, the condition of the car, and the number of passengers. Likewise, regulations made under the Employers' Liability (Compulsory Insurance) Act 1969 prohibit insurers from making their liability conditional on the employer taking reasonable care to counter the risk of injury or disease to his employees.

It should, however, be mentioned that, after indemnifying the insured by paying any damages awarded to a third party, the insurer has the right to recover from the insured any monies which he would otherwise not have paid.

Use of agents

Many insurance contracts are arranged through the services of intermediaries of one sort or another. The knowledge of the agent will be imputed to the principal, and the wilful or negligent act of an agent will be held against his principal. Sometimes an agent or employee of an insurer will complete a proposal form for the proposer. In these circumstances, he is generally held to be the agent of the proposer for this purpose (Newsholme Brothers Limited v Road Transport and General Insurance Company Limited (1929)). Very occasionally, special circumstances may apply as in the case of an illiterate or blind proposer, or where the agent has been instructed by the insurer to complete the form, when he will be deemed to be the agent of the insurer (see Bawden v London, Edinburgh and Glasgow Assurance Company (1892) and Stone v Reliance Mutual Insurance Society (1972)).

THE LOSS

Insurance is a means of transferring the uncertainty of loss to an insurer. In non-marine insurance, if a contract was made and at that time, unknown to insured and insurer, the subject matter was already lost, the contract would be void because of mutual mistake. If the insured knew of the loss, the insurers could avoid liability on the grounds of fraudulent non-disclosure.

In the case of marine insurance, because interests may often be acquired when the vessel and cargo are on the high seas and neither party may know if a loss or partial loss has taken place, it is the practice to issue policies on a 'lost or not lost' basis. If the insured knew of a loss at the start of the contract and did not disclose it, then the contract would be voidable as with non-marine insurance. On the other hand, if the insurer knew that the subject matter had already arrived safely, the insured could avoid the contract and receive a return of premium, again on the grounds of non-disclosure and also frustration of contract.

To guard against these possible pitfalls, the insured would be well advised to obtain immediate provisional cover pending the issue of the policy.

Risks covered

The events insured against are detailed in the policy, together with any exceptions, or certain causes of these events may be excluded. For example, without special extension, a fire policy does not cover fire caused by riot or earthquake. If loss is brought about by the insured's negligence, this is not a bar to a claim, unless negligence is excluded which is unusual, but losses brought about by the insured's wilful misconduct are not covered. Losses caused by the wilful action of others, for example, an arsonist, would normally constitute legitimate claims, unless the subject of a specific exclusion (e.g. confiscation by government). Even if the insured accidentally committed a criminal act, such as manslaughter with a motor vehicle, he would be entitled to an indemnity. On the other hand, in a case where a man took a loaded gun to the house of another with the intention of frightening him, and the gun went off killing the householder, it was held to be against public policy for the man to receive an indemnity under his public liability policy, when sued by the widow (Gray v Barr, Prudential Assurance Company (Third Party) (1971)).

Many personal effects, business machines, computers and recently the whole buildings and machinery of factories can be insured on an 'All Risk' basis, but such contracts are still subject to exceptions such as wear and tear or inherent vice. Such policies cover 'loss or damage to property', and the meaning is clear if the 'loss' is by fire or if the property is stolen. When property is lost or mislaid, insurers usually allow a reasonable period for searches to be made before treating the property as lost and paying the claim. If the goods are subsequently recovered, they belong to the insurer. If due to a sudden change in market prices or to inflation, the value when recovered is higher than the amount of the loss paid out, the profit strictly belongs to the insurer, but in practice the insurer may retain just sufficient to cover the claim payment and costs of recovery (if any) and pay the balance to the insured.

On the other hand, if the insured did not receive an indemnity at the time of loss due to underinsurance or a first loss sum insured having been exceeded, he would be regarded as a coinsurer with the insurance company. In this event, any recoveries made would be shared between insured and insurer in proportion to the amount of the loss each had paid.

A distinction must be made as between property being lost where an owner is deprived of his car by a fraudulent auctioneer (Webster v General Accident Fire and Life Assurance Corporation Limited (1953) and where he wilfully parts with the car in return for a cheque which is not honoured by the bank (Eisinger v General Accident (1955)). In the former case, the insured has 'lost' his car and had a legitimate claim whereas in the latter case it was not his car which he had lost but the proceeds of the sale and so had no claim.

Causation

Inevitably, loss occurs at the end of a chain of events, and one of the principles of insurance law is that of 'proximate cause'. In establishing liability, it is essential to identify the efficient cause of the loss which may not necessarily be the last cause in time. The cause of causes is important because, insurance policies name certain perils as insured, some as excluded, and are silent about others. It is necessary to identify 'the active efficient cause that sets in motion a train of events' and to identify each link in that chain until the financial loss occurs. If there is no excepted peril in that chain then all damage from the operation of the insured peril onwards is covered. A fire policy does not mention smoke or damage from extinguishment water but damage from both of these perils as well as from the burning would be covered. If an excepted peril occurs before the insured peril in the chain, there is no cover.

Consideration of the following cases and their judicial decisions will make the operation of this important doctrine more clear.

1   An earthquake overturned a heater in a building which was thus set on fire. The fire in this building set fire to the one next to it by heat and sparks blown in the wind. The fire spread in a similar manner over some 500 yards to the insured's building. The policy excluded fire caused by earthquake, and since each link in the chain was a natural effect of the one before it, the direct or proximate cause of the fire was the earthquake, and the claim invalidated.

2   Fire weakened a wall and *a few days later* a storm blew it down. It was held that storm was the proximate cause since the fire was spent as a cause by the time the storm blew up. Compare this case with the following case.

3   Lightning weakened a wall and *almost immediately afterwards* storm blew it down. This time, lightning was held to be the proximate cause since the effects of the lightning had not had time to subside.

This element of a time lapse between events is important. If there is time to remedy the initial effects of a peril, e.g. shore-up or repair the wall, then the second event is deemed to be the effective cause of a loss. If there is insufficient time to do anything to safeguard the damaged property, then the original peril will be deemed to be the proximate cause.

Sometimes policy wordings overrule or amend the strict doctrine of proximate cause. An examination of the standard fire perils (see p. 71) will show that while spontaneous combustion is excluded, the spreading fire is not, since the exclusion of property refers to *'its own'* spontaneous fermentation. Accident policies sometimes exclude loss 'directly or *indirectly* caused by' some specified peril. In this case, it is necessary to go beyond the proximate cause and examine all causes no matter how remote.

INDEMNITY AND INSURERS' LIABILITY

Before a measurement of loss can take place, it is necessary to establish the nature of the contract. Property and liability contracts are basically contracts of indemnity, i.e. the insured is only entitled to be compensated for his loss and must not make a profit

(Castellain v Preston (1883)). Sometimes, as in agreed value policies, the parties agree in advance what the value will be in the case of total loss. However, certain types of insurance such as life and personal accident policies are not usually contracts of indemnity.

Life and personal accident

Individuals are deemed to have an unlimited insurable interest in their own lives or in the lives of their spouses. As such, the amount of insurance which can be bought is effectively limited only by the ability to pay the premium. When one is insuring the lives of others, as for example in the case of a creditor insuring the life of a debtor, or of an employer insuring the life of a key employee, it is permissible to effect cover only to the extent of the former's insurable interest (see p. 63). However, if that interest ceases after the inception date of the policy a claim would still be valid, (see p. 64) and so the contract is not necessarily one of indemnity.

Property

The sum insured in property policies is the maximum limit of the insurer's liability, but the amount payable within that limit is restricted to the value of the insured's loss, i.e. to an indemnity.

Total loss

In general terms, the measurement of loss is the market value of the property lost or destroyed. For many types of machinery and stock, this in practice means what it would cost *at the time and the place* of loss to replace the goods, less an allowance for depreciation, wear and tear, or betterment if the replacement goods would place the insured in a better position than he occupied at the time of loss. In other cases where there is a recognised secondhand market, e.g. in motor cars, indemnity would be the amount the insured would have to pay at the time of loss to replace the lost property with secondhand property of similar age and condition.

In the case of buildings, it frequently happens that the market value is somewhat less than the cost of rebuilding. If it is the insured's intention to rebuild, paying the market value would not indemnify him. In such cases he would be entitled to the rebuilding cost less an allowance for wear and tear and betterment (see Reynolds v Phoenix Assurance Company Limited (1978) and Pleasurama Limited v Sun Alliance and London Insurance Limited (1979)).

On the other hand, if the insured were intending to sell the property at the time of loss, the market value, if one can be established, less the value of the land, would represent indemnity (see Leppard v Excess Insurance Company (1979)).

Partial loss

The measure of indemnity will similarly be the cost of repair less an allowance for wear and tear or betterment.

Insurer's liability. After establishing the amount of indemnity, it is necessary to look at the insurance contract to establish the insurer's liability, which may be less than indemnity for one or more of the following reasons:

1 *Sum insured:* this may be lower than indemnity and as stated above, the sum insured is the maximum liability.
2 *Average:* in the case of partial losses, if the policy is subject to an average condition and the sum insured is below the total value at risk at the time of loss, the insured will recover only the proportion of indemnity that the sum insured bears to the total value at risk.
3 *Excess, franchise:* the sum recoverable may also be affected either by an excess clause specifying that the insured must bear the first £X pounds of any loss, or a franchise clause requiring the insured to bear any loss which does not exceed a stated percentage or amount but leaving the insurers liable to pay the whole loss (subject to (1) or (2)) if this amount is exceeded.

Contribution clauses

Where the insured has two or more policies covering a common peril which causes loss to common property, it is likely that each policy will limit the liability of each insurer to their rateable proportion. To obtain indemnity, the insured will need to claim from all his insurers, but contribution is a means of sharing a loss equitably among insurers who have all received a premium for the risk. The sharing of the loss among insurers should not prejudice the insured, who should still be indemnified subject to the limitations mentioned in (1), (2) or (3) above.

Reinstatement memorandum

Many policies on buildings and contents (other than stock) are extended to include the 'reinstatement memorandum' or 'new for old'. These policies pay the full cost of replacing the property lost, provided the insured actually does reinstate. If he does not, the settlement is on an indemnity basis. The difference between indemnity and reinstatement insurances is that the latter does not exclude wear and tear and depreciation or the effects of inflation on replacement costs between the date of loss and the date of completion of the reinstatement. Average may still apply if the sum insured is less than a fixed percentage (currently 85 per cent) of the full cost of reinstatement.

Agreed value policies

In some instances, where it may be difficult to establish value after loss, and for insurances on ships' cargo, valuables, vintage cars and the like, it may be possible to agree a value at inception of the contract, with the insurer undertaking to pay that value in the event of total loss. Such insurances are not a major departure from the principle of indemnity since the agreed value will usually take indemnity into account at that time. In the event of partial loss, the insured would recover such proportion of the agreed value as is represented by the depreciation in the actual value even if this is more than the cost of repair, although it is usual for policy wordings to modify this for partial losses, by stating that partial losses will be settled on an indemnity basis.

Liability insurances

The various types of liability insurance are also contracts of indemnity, which are measured as the amount of damages awarded or negotiated against the insured in terms of the cover under the policy (see Chapter 11) plus legal costs.

SUBROGATION AND SALVAGE

Subrogation

On occasion, a loss which the insured suffers is brought about by the fault of another. This could mean that someone else's negligence has caused the loss, or that a statute such as the Riot (Damages) Act 1886 or the Railway Fires Acts 1905 and 1923 has made some other party responsible in law for such damage. On other occasions, someone may have contracted to be liable for a loss which would normally fall upon the insured. An instance of the latter is where a full maintenance lease makes a tenant responsible for fire loss, but the landlord has arranged building insurance to protect himself in case of default by the tenant.

In all of these examples, an insurer, having paid the loss, can 'stand in the shoes' of the insured (or be subrogated to the insured's rights) and can recoup from the person legally responsible for the loss. The insurer can retain for himself only the amount he has paid, any balance belonging to the insured. On the other hand, if the insured himself has borne part of the loss himself, e.g. through the operation of an excess, he is entitled to be fully indemnified before any part of the recovery goes to the insurer.

Where the insured has made a partial recovery only, due to the operation of average, any recovery from a third party will be shared between insured and insurer in proportion to the average apportionment.

Subrogation is a corollary of indemnity whereby the insured is entitled only to one indemnity irrespective of the number of available sources of indemnity. Subrogation also arises out of equity, since it would be unjust for the legal 'wrong-doer' to escape his obligations because of the foresight of the victim in purchasing insurance. Subrogation does not arise in life and personal accident insurances since they are not contracts of indemnity. With these insurances, the insured or his executors can claim on the policies and recover from any third party who may be liable for the injury or death.

Third party rights against insurer

A kind of subrogation in reverse is found in legal liability insurances where an insured becomes insolvent or is compulsorily wound up. To prevent policy monies being treated as part of the general assets of the firm and the third party having to claim as a general creditor, the Third Parties (Rights Against Insurers) Act 1930 allows such third parties to recover directly from the insurer. In motor third-party insurance, this power of direct enforcement is taken a step further by Section 149 of the Road Traffic Act 1972 which, subject to various conditions, empowers a third party to recover direct from the insurers any damages awarded for compulsorily insurable injuries, whether or not the insured is insolvent, and regardless of whether the insurers are entitled to avoid or have avoided the policy (unless they did so before the accident). This enlarged right of direct enforcement has not been extended to compulsory employers' liability insurance.

Salvage

If an insurer settles a claim for the total value of property damaged but the remains of the property have some salvage value, the insured cannot claim to receive both a full indemnity from the insurers and keep the remains. The salvage therefore belongs to the insurers. In Holmes v Payne (1930), a necklace insured against loss disappeared and, despite a thorough search, could not be found. After the insurers agreed to replace it, it was found. It was held that (a) there was a 'loss' and so the insurers remained bound by their agreement to replace it, and (b) they were entitled to the recovered necklace as salvage.

INTERPRETATION OF THE CONTRACT

If there is a dispute that is brought before a court of law, oral evidence may not normally be given to contradict the terms of a contract that is in writing. Therefore, the written contract contained in the policy, plus the proposal form which is often incorporated into the policy as the basis of the contract, can alone (except in certain cases of ambiguity) be looked at to see what the parties intended. Words used are generally given their ordinary popular meanings; for example, 'fire', which in its scientific sense may include explosion, is confined to cases of ignition as understood in everyday language. All the same, words like 'riot' which have a technical legal significance and phrases like 'perils of the sea' are given their specialised meanings.

The contra proferentem rule

When the wording is ambiguous, certain rules of construction are applied: for example, the rule that a wording devised by an insurer to limit or exclude his liability is construed as far as possible against him. Thus in one case where a motor policy excluded liability if the insured vehicle (in fact a private four-seater) were used to carry a 'load' in excess of that for which it was constructed, and an accident occurred when six passengers were being carried, the court held that the exclusion clause applied only to lorries built to carry specified loads, and the insurers were therefore liable.

PROPOSED CHANGES IN INSURANCE LAW

The current law relating to insurance contracts is the subject of proposed changes from two quarters.

EEC

The Council of the EEC has proposed a Directive on the Co-ordination of Laws, Regulations and Administrative Provisions

Relating to Insurance Contracts in member states. English Law based largely on common law and precedent is, in many respects, out of line with the law of most of our European partners which is founded on Roman Law. The proposals largely uphold the French applications of Roman Law, and the purpose is to have a unified code of operations, service and law throughout the EEC. Such ideas have been floated since the EEC came into being but very little progress has so far been made.

One of the most fundamental proposals (from a United Kingdom point of view) is that Articles 3 to 6 of the proposed Directive introduce the concept of proportionality whereby misdemeanours in the duty of disclosure before and during the contract would warrant proportionally increased premiums, which if not acceptable to the insured, could mean that the contract can be cancelled, with a proportional refund of premium. Reductions in risk during the contract would warrant a proportional reduction in premium.

The Law Commission

A law commission was set up in 1978 to look at various aspects of disclosure and warranties in insurance law and they reported their findings in 1980 (Law Com. No. 104).

One of the matters examined was the EEC Directive proposals and these they found to be 'unsatisfactory and inadequate'. It was considered that in some areas they favoured the insurer too much, while in others they were more stringent on the insured than our current law. The proportionality idea they thought to be fraught with difficulties in practical application.

The Commission proposes changes in our laws of insurance which can be summarised briefly as follows:

1 The duty of disclosure (see p. 67) should be lightened by defining a material fact as 'one which the proposer knows or can be assumed to know and which *a reasonable man in the position of the proposer* would disclose. . . .'

2 Warnings in bold type on proposal forms and renewal notices should inform the insured of his duties as to disclosure and the insured should be given a copy of the completed proposal form.

3   To be effective, warranties should be material to the risk and to any loss. Claims should be paid if the breach of a warranty had no effect on the claim.

4   'Basis of the contract' clauses which make answers in proposal forms into warranties should have no effect with regard to past or present facts. If specific undertakings by the insured as to the existence of past or present facts are required by an insurer they can be introduced into the policy as individual warranties. Undertakings as to the future can be covered by a basis of contract clause insofar as it creates a promissary warranty.

Neither the EEC proposed Directive nor the recommendations of the Law Commission have been enacted at the present time. Some of the proposals of the Law Commission had already been suggested in 'The Fifth Committee Report' in 1957 without any changes being made, so it may be some time before any of the points become law. The United Kingdom insurance industry had introduced 'Statements of Practice' prior to 1980 which incorporated the point about warranties, for example, but the Commission felt that self-regulation did not give strong enough protection to the public.

FURTHER READING

Birds, John, 'Modern Insurance Law' Sweet and Maxwell, London, 1982.

Ivamy, E. R. Hardy, 'General Principles of Insurance Law', 4th Edition, Butterworths, London, 1979.

MacGillivray, E. J. & Parkington, M., 'Insurance Law Related to All Risks Other than Marine', 7th Edition, Sweet & Maxwell, London, 1981.

PART II

TYPES OF INSURANCE

5

Fire and Extended Perils Insurance

M. J. Angel,* Personnel and Insurance Officer, Flight Refuelling Ltd

The danger of fire is within the experience of all, and insurance against its effects is the most readily sought of material damage covers. Fire insurance has been available and in demand for three hundred years, because although proper fire prevention measures may reduce its likelihood, and proper contingency planning limit its effects in some measure, the possibility of a catastrophic loss from a fire is always there.

Fire wastage figures rise year by year, and no company can afford not to seek insurance protection against the loss of its assets by fire.

The fire policy can be extended either to delete some of the exclusions in the standard fire policy, or to provide cover against other natural or man-made perils. The need for these extensions will vary with the nature of the individual business.

STANDARD FIRE POLICY

Wording of the standard fire policy

Insurance companies have adopted a standard form of policy, covering the property insured against:

---

*The author is indebted to Mr G. N. Crockford for material retained from the previous edition. He also wishes to thank A. S. D. Cross for his help in compiling the chapter.

1   Fire (whether resulting from explosion or otherwise) not occasioned by or happening through:
    (a)   Its own spontaneous fermentation or heating or its undergoing any process involving the application of heat.
    (b)   Earthquake, subterranean fire, riot, civil commotion, war, invasion, act of foreign enemy, hostilities (whether war be declared or not), civil war, rebellion, revolution, insurrection or military or usurped power.
2   Lightning.
3   Explosion, not occasioned by or happening through any of the perils specified in 1(b) above:
    (a)   Of boilers used for domestic purposes only.
    (b)   In a building not being part of any gas works, of gas used for domestic purposes or used for lighting or heating the building.

The standard cover therefore includes damage by fire (with certain exceptions) and lightning. It also includes some non-fire damage caused by explosion, although this is so restricted that it is not of much value to the commercial or industrial insurance buyer.

The conditions of the policy exclude other types of explosion, nuclear risks (cover for which is the responsibility of licensed operators of nuclear establishments), property insured under a marine policy, and (unless specially mentioned as insured) goods held in trust or on commission, money, securities, stamps, documents, manuscripts, business books, computer systems records, patterns, moulds, plans, designs and explosives.

The Lloyd's policy wording

The Lloyd's policy form covers:

1   Fire and or lightning.
    (a)   Fire consequent upon explosion wherever the explosion occurs.
    (b)   Explosion consequent upon fire on the premises insured.
    (c)   Explosion of domestic boilers and/or of gas used for domestic purposes or for heating and/or lighting.

There are the following exclusions:

1 Damage to electrical appliances 'directly caused by short-circuiting, overrunning, excessive pressure or leakage of electricity' but this exclusion does not apply to damage to electrical appliances by 'fire resulting from such causes and originating outside the appliance'.

2 Nuclear risks.

3 Loss or damage directly or indirectly occasioned by, happening through or in consequence of war, invasion, acts of foreign enemies, hostilities (whether war be declared or not), civil war, rebellion, revolution, insurrection, military or usurped power, riots, civil commotions or confiscation or nationalisation or requisition or destruction of or damage to property by or under the order of any government or public or local authority.

4 Computer systems records.

The Lloyd's policy therefore gives slightly wider explosion cover, and there are fewer exclusions. In particular, fire caused by earthquake and subterranean fire is not excluded. The war-risks exclusion, however, extends to nationalisation and acts of public authorities.

BASIC CONCEPTS OF FIRE INSURANCE

Fire, for insurance purposes, implies actual ignition and, to be covered by the policy, it must be accidental in origin from the point of view of the insured. Damage caused by a fire lit for a specific purpose while it is confined within its own intended limits is not covered.

Arson is covered, provided it is not committed by, or with the consent of, the insured.

The policy cover includes damage to the insured property caused by measures taken to put out the fire, and through such associated occurrences as smoke, scorching or building collapse, but not consequential loss or damage to the property of third parties.

The onus is upon the insured to show, prima facie, that his loss was caused by fire. Once he has done so, the burden of proof that the loss falls within an exception rests with the insurer.

SPECIFICATION

Wording

A standard specification wording is in use by the tariff offices to identify exactly, as far as possible, the property covered. It lists:

1 The building, including landlord's fixtures and fittings therein or thereon.
2 Machinery, plant and all other contents therein and thereon, the property of the insured or held by him in trust or on commission for which he is responsible, but excluding landlord's fixtures and fittings and stock and materials in trade.
3 Stock and materials in trade, the property of the insured or held by him in trust or on commission for which he is responsible.
4 Rent (for a specified period).

This last item is sometimes included, although for business premises it is usually preferable for rent to be insured under a business interruption policy (see Chapter 6). Rent may be insured by an owner whose tenant is not obliged to continue to pay rent while the premises are unusable as a result of fire, or by a lessee or tenant who has such an obligation. The rental value may be insured by an owner-occupier so as to pay for alternative accommodation.

Other specific items of property may be added to the above list.

Memoranda

Three memoranda are attached to this specification to define more closely the cover given; viz. designation: 'all other contents' and rent.

Designation. By this memorandum the insurers agree to accept the designation under which property is entered in the insured's books as determining the category in which it shall be included in the specification.

All other contents. The second memorandum explains the term 'all other contents' as including:

1 Money and stamps (other than National Insurance stamps).
2 National Insurance stamps.

3   Documents, manuscripts and business books, but only for the value of materials or stationery together with the cost of clerical labour expended in writing up.
4   Patterns, models, moulds, plans and designs.
5   Employees' pedal cycles and other personal effects.

A limit is usually imposed for (1) and (2), a limit per item for (3) and (4) and a limit per employee for (5).

Rent. The third memorandum states that if rent is insured, the cover applies only if the building that is insured, or any part thereof, is unfit for occupation because it has been destroyed or damaged. The amount payable shall not exceed such proportion of the sum insured as the period necessary for reinstatement bears to the term of rent insured.

Clauses

Computer systems records. Because of the high value of computer systems records used in business today, and their susceptibility to fire damage, insurers require such records to be specifically insured. They are therefore excluded from the standard policy. If insurance is required, a special clause is added covering:

Computer systems records, but only for the value of the materials, together with the cost of clerical labour and computer time expended in reproducing such records (excluding any expenses in connection with the production of information to be recorded therein) and not for the value to be insured of the information contained therein.

The cover is subject to a limit selected by the insured. More extensive material damage cover as well as business interruption protection is available in the market if required. (See Chapters 7 Theft and All Risks, 6 Business Interruption and 13 Engineering.)

Professional fees. Architects' and surveyors' fees and legal fees incurred in reinstatement work on the building, and engineers' fees in respect of plant and machinery can be insured either by making an appropriate increase in the sums insured under the various headings, or by adding a separate item on professional fees to the policy. Professional fees incurred by the insured in preparing a claim are not covered.

Public authorities clause. Statutory requirements and those of local authorities, particularly in such matters as standards of construction and fire precautions, are becoming more and more stringent, and reinstatement of fire damage may be deemed sufficient alteration to premises for by-laws or building regulations, not previously enforced on the premises, to be applied. These requirements can add very considerably to the cost of reinstatement, and it is therefore usual for a clause to be added to the policy providing cover for additional costs incurred in complying with such enactments.

It is essential that the sum insured should be sufficiently high to include these costs.

Temporary removal clause. This clause extends the policy to cover property other than stock or materials in trade while temporarily removed for cleaning, renovation, repair or other similar purposes elsewhere on the insured or other premises, and in transit thereto or therefrom by road, rail or inland waterway in Great Britain, Ireland and Northern Ireland.

Trade extensions. To meet the requirements of various trades, insurers are prepared, usually at a slightly increased rate of premium, to include property, up to agreed limits overall and per location, while at, or in transit to or from the premises of processors and the like, sub-contractors and customers. The geographical limits are the same as for the temporary removal clause.

Debris removal. The cost of clearing debris of building and contents in order to carry out reinstatement work will be met by the policy, provided that the sum insured is adequate.

The *basic* cover does not, however, extend to the cost of debris removal that is not essential to the reinstatement work, such as its removal from premises outside those insured, or the removal for disposal of contents with no salvage value.

The policy may, however, be extended by the inclusion of the debris-removal clause, and increasing the sums insured by a suitable amount, or including a specific sum insured on debris-removal expenses.

For stock, specific debris-removal cover with a separate sum insured is essential. Stock residues may be difficult and costly to remove, and a sufficiently high sum insured, which may also include building and contents debris if so desired, should be selected.

Contract-price clause. A fire may destroy goods sold but not delivered and still at the insured's risk, and the contract for the goods may be lost as a result. To meet this situation, a clause may be added to the policy to provide that a claim for such goods would be paid on the basis of the contract price and not the market price.

PERILS COMMONLY ADDED

Explosion

While the standard fire policy gives cover for fire following explosion, the cover it includes for concussion damage brought about by the explosion itself is extremely limited. Explosion cover is therefore frequently added to the policy for an additional premium. Even this extension does not cover all forms of explosion damage, however, because explosions of non-domestic boilers and steam pressure vessels under the insured's control, which are considered to be the province of the engineering insurance market, are excluded, as are nuclear explosions, and war and riot risks.

In considering the advisability of this extension, the insurance buyer should bear in mind that it is not limited to explosions on the insured premises, and the explosive potential of dusts, chemicals, gases under pressure or other materials on his own and surrounding premises should be taken into account.

Aircraft

Non-fire damage caused by aircraft or by articles dropped from them may be covered by extension of the policy at a moderate rate of premium. This form of cover should certainly be considered by the insurance buyer because of the catastrophic loss which could be caused by this peril. Recovery from the aircraft operator is possible in theory, but it depends upon identification of the aircraft involved, which is not always possible in the event of falling articles.

War risks and damage by sonic booms are not covered, liability being accepted by the government.

Storm, tempest, flood and bursting or overflowing of water tanks, pipes and apparatus

Extension of the fire policy to include these 'water perils' is now quite common, demand for the cover having possibly been influenced by their availability in household insurances. Although frequently included by a single endorsement, they are two separate perils, either of which may, if so desired, be added in isolation.

Storm, tempest and flood

These terms 'storm' and 'tempest' have not been judicially distinguished, and are always used together, implying some form of atmospheric disturbance. The terms do not include wear and tear due to weathering.

Insurance could be effected against storm and tempest alone, but the difficulty which would be encountered, in cases of heavy rain and overflowing watercourses in distinguishing between damage by storm and tempest on the one hand, and flood on the other, make it advisable to couple the perils together.

The extension normally excludes damage by subsidence and landslip, damage to gates and fences, and to property in the open, and it is usual for the insured to be required to bear some part of each loss.

The situation of the insured premises, the presence or absence of nearby watercourses, the local climate and any history of flooding in the area, as well as the nature and susceptibility to water damage of the stocks of materials and finished products to be insured, must all be considered by the insurance buyer in deciding whether to add these perils to his fire policy.

Bursting or overflowing of water tanks, pipes and apparatus

Cover for this risk, which is of particular importance where the premises contain property highly susceptible to water damage or to changes in humidity, is readily available, subject once again to an excess. This cover excludes damage resulting from sprinkler installations which is normally insured separately.

Riot etc. and malicious damage

War risks on land are uninsurable, but cover is available at an additional premium for some of the other risks, excluded in the same section of the standard fire policy.

Riot, civil commotion, strikers, locked-out workers, persons taking part in labour disturbances and malicious persons acting on behalf of, or in connection with, any political organisation

Damage by fire, explosion or other causes, such as wrecking or looting, are covered by this extension. Compensation may be available, subject to a time limit within which damage must be reported, under the provisions of the Riot (Damages) Act 1886, and the Government Compensation Scheme Criminal Damage (Compensation) Northern Ireland 1977. Insurers therefore require especially prompt notification of claims under this extension and the Government Compensation Scheme Criminal Damage (Compensation) Northern Ireland 1977.

Malicious damage

The riot wording can be extended further to include other malicious damage, by deleting the words 'acting on behalf of, or in connection with, any political organisation'. The cover will normally be subject to an excess, and damage consequent upon theft, which can be insured under a theft policy, is excluded.

OTHER PERILS

Impact

Damage by impact of road vehicles, horses or cattle can be covered by extension of the standard fire policy but, despite the low rate of premium charged, insurance buyers will often consider it an uneconomic form of insurance for buildings of substantial value.

Where the vehicle causing the damage can be identified, recovery of the cost of reinstating the building can usually be made from the owners or insurers of the vehicle. Where the impact risk is insured, it is common for the building and vehicle insurers to share the loss in agreed proportion, irrespective of liability.

Damage caused by vehicles or animals belonging to or under the control of the insured is normally excluded, but in special cases it can be included at an additional premium.

Earthquake

Earth tremors are not usually severe in the United Kingdom, and the risk of earthquake damage is one, therefore, that the insurance buyer will often leave uninsured, on weighing the chance of loss against the premium that would be required. Cover is available, however, for all earthquake damage or for fire following earthquake or earthquake shock damage only.

Subterranean fire

This is another risk excluded from the standard fire policy for which cover is available at an additional premium. The term 'subterranean fire' includes fires in mines and oil wells, as well as those of volcanic origin.

Subsidence and landslip

Cover against these perils is normally only sought for premises with a high degree of risk, so that premium rates are likely to be high; an excess will almost certainly be imposed, and the cover will be stringently defined.

Spontaneous combustion

The standard fire policy excludes property damaged by its *own* spontaneous combustion. Thus, only the property in which the fire originated is excluded, other property damaged by the spread of the fire being covered.

Cover for spontaneous combustion of coal and wood blocks is frequently written back into the specification by endorsement for premises where these commodities are not part of the usual stock in trade.

Insurers are prepared to extend the policy to give cover for other property stored in bulk which may be liable to self-heating, subject to stringent requirements about storage conditions. Cover is not, however, usually given for agricultural produce on farms.

Hail

This extension will be of interest to farmers and growers, and cover may be obtained for specific crops and for glass in glasshouses.

The market for crop cover is a fluctuating one, and insurance is normally granted on a short-period basis, terminating with the harvesting of the crop. Rates depend upon location because insurers' statistics demonstrate that certain parishes are particularly liable to hail.

Changes in temperature

Cover for stocks of food subject to deterioration in the event of changes in temperature due to the disablement of heating, cooling, or refrigeration plant by fire or other insured perils, may also be added to the policy for an additional premium.

SUMS INSURED

Bases of insurance

Indemnity

The fire policy is one of indemnity, and in the absence of specific agreement to the contrary, the measure of the insured's loss will be the cost of restoring the damaged property to, or replacing it with property in, its condition at the time the loss occurred. Sums insured should therefore be calculated accordingly. The following values should be used:

Buildings. The cost of reinstatement, less reasonable depreciation, if any. Other bases, such as market value, may, however, be appropriate in certain cases.

Plant, machinery and other contents. The cost of replacement, less an appropriate allowance for normal wear and tear. Obsolescence may also be taken into account.

Stock. The cost of materials plus the cost of manufacture to the state in which the stock is at the time of the loss. The profit element in the value of finished goods is normally excluded, as it is usually covered by business interruption insurance (see Chapter 6), but, in certain circumstances, insurers may agree to a selling price valuation.

Rent. The rent payable for the period insured, or, in the case of an owner-occupier, the rental value.

Reinstatement

A development from the original basis of insurance has been the availability of 'reinstatement' cover on buildings and contents, by which the insured is entitled to receive 'new for old' without deduction for depreciation. The proceeds of a claim on this basis must be expended in rebuilding, not necessarily on the same site, or replacement of the contents destroyed.

Insurers will require an appropriate contribution from the

insured in respect of any improvement value resulting from reinstatement. For example, if more modern machinery, which costs more and is more efficient than the destroyed plant it replaces, is installed, then the insured must pay the *additional* cost. If more efficient plant can be installed at no greater cost than that of an exact replacement, the insured will not be called upon to contribute. If the insured does not wish to rebuild or replace, settlement is on the normal basis of indemnity.

For reinstatement cover, the sums insured must represent:

Buildings. The cost, at the time of reinstatement, of rebuilding in a similar form.

Contents. The cost of replacement with new plant, machinery and other contents.

Valued policies

For certain types of property, notably works of art, insurers may be prepared to issue a 'valued' policy. An inventory and valuation of the property is required and a value agreed with the insurers at the commencement of the period of insurance, which will be payable in the event of total loss. Partial losses are settled on the normal basis of indemnity.

Particular care must be taken in fixing the value if substantial appreciation is likely during the currency of the policy.

First-loss cover

The sum insured is set at a figure, less than the full value of the property, that represents the maximum value the insured considers vulnerable to a single loss. A declaration of the full value is required by the insurer.

First-loss policies are mostly associated with water damage insurances, but some non-tariff insurers are prepared to accept first-loss policies to cover fire and other perils referred to in this chapter. In accepting cover on a first-loss basis for these perils, particularly fire, the insured stands the serious risk of not recovering the whole of his loss if the limit chosen has been under-estimated, particularly if an unanticipated catastrophe causes a much heavier loss than was foreseen when the insurance was taken out.

Selection of basis of insurance

The type of claims settlement required will vary with the particular circumstances of each business and the insurance buyer should base his choice upon the action his company would be likely to take following a total loss of its premises.

Reinstatement policies are now more usual, but there are cases where such cover would involve unnecessarily high sums insured and therefore wasted money in premiums. There is, for example, no point in insuring on a reinstatement basis premises which would not be rebuilt, on the same or another site, in the event of fire.

Old buildings of massive construction may present difficulties if, in the event of total loss, they would not be rebuilt in the same form, because the operations they now house could be carried on in buildings of lighter construction, which would be cheaper to construct.

The sum insured must, however, take account of the fact that a partial loss could involve costly repair work to the building in its present form. Agreement on a suitable method of adjusting losses, and on the method of arriving at the sum insured should, in such cases, be reached with the insurers at the outset. In many cases the premium saving achieved will not be proportionate to the reduction in the sum insured because of the operation of a penalty rating scale by most insurers.

Some insurance buyers exclude foundations from the policy and thereby reduce the sum insured. If this course is adopted, care is necessary in defining the property excluded, as expensive piling or underground service installations, which might be damaged by fire, may inadvertently be excluded. Furthermore, it should be noted that if the value of foundations is excluded on a reinstatement-basis policy, the policy will include no provisions for payment of the cost of foundations if the premises are rebuilt on another site.

Valuation and inflation

The application of average in fire insurance policies makes the maintenance of adequate sums insured extremely important, and once fixed, they should be kept under constant review. In an inflationary economy, ever-rising replacement costs must be matched by increasing sums insured if underinsurance is to be avoided.

Many firms have a periodical valuation of their premises and equipment for insurance purposes carried out by professional valuers, and this is usually acceptable to insurers as a basis for the sums insured. It is, however, essential that the sums insured should be revised at regular intervals between valuations. The insurance buyer may be able to have the appropriate calculations done within his own firm, or he may prefer to base his revisions on one of the published building and plant costs indices which are available. Additions are always likely to be made to buildings and equipment during the currency of the policy. To make certain that they are covered from the time they become the responsibility of the insured, a 'capital additions clause' may be added to the policy. This gives automatic cover for all capital additions, but not for appreciation in value, up to an agreed level of, say, 10 per cent of the existing sum insured. Detailed notification is given subsequently to the insurers, and the premium and sum insured suitably adjusted.

In an inflationary situation an annual revision of sums insured is insufficient to keep pace with rapidly increasing values of property. A continuous adjustment to sums insured is needed to avoid under-insurance. It is not only necessary to provide for inflation during the policy period but also during the period required to reinstate major losses.

In recent years the insurance market has developed three methods of making provision for dealing with inflation all of which seek to avoid unnecessary overinsurance. The basis commonly used for smaller covers is known as 85% Reinstatement Average Scheme (AVC). No professional valuation is required and provided the sum insured is at least 85 per cent of the total value, average will not be applied. A second method: Valuation Linked Scheme (VCS) requires an annual professional valuation and a third method: Day One Basis is only available where sums insured exceed £5 million.

Blanket policies

For firms with extensive premises, or a number of separate places of business, the task of determining and maintaining separate sums insured for each individual building and its contents would be difficult and time-consuming. 'Blanket policies' have therefore come into use, which show only the total sum insured in each of the categories—buildings, contents and stock.

Insurers have found in recent years that grouping together a large number of buildings with differing degrees of hazard so as to calculate a single sum insured makes their assessment of the maximum probable loss at the insured's premises and the premium rate calculation extremely difficult. Although they continue to issue blanket policies, they are now likely to seek some indication of the value at risk in individual buildings or complexes.

Stock floaters and declaration policies

The 'blanket' principle is often extended for stock insurances, so that stocks at a number or all of the premises under the insured's control are covered by a single 'floating' sum insured, representing the maximum value at any one time. A maximum limit will usually be imposed for any one location, or different limits for specified premises. The locations may be listed or a general wording such as 'any warehouse in the UK occupied by the insured' may be used.

In both stock floaters and stock policies covering specific locations, provision is made for seasonal and other fluctuations by making the premium adjustable on the basis of declarations by the insured of values at risk at monthly or other agreed intervals.

The premium payable is calculated on the average value throughout the year, as revealed by the declarations. A proportion (75 per cent with monthly declarations) of the premium on the full sum insured is charged initially, and is adjusted by means of an additional premium or a return of part of the premium at the end of the year. A limit may be imposed to the premium return which may be made, in which case care should be taken to ensure that the sum insured, while it must be adequate to cover the highest foreseeable stock level during the forthcoming 12 months' period of insurance, does not represent excessive overinsurance.

Average

Average is now applied to nearly all fire policies. The maintenance of adequate sums insured is thus of prime importance to the insured. Average penalises underinsurance by reducing the amount payable, even for partial losses, if the sum insured is less than the full value of the property at the time of the loss.

Pro rata condition of average. This is the most common means of applying average. Its effect is to require the insured to bear a proportion of each loss equivalent to the proportion of under-insurance.

Special condition of average. Normally used for insurances on agricultural produce, this condition does not apply as long as the sum insured is not less than 75 per cent of full value. If there is greater underinsurance, average is applied in full.

Two conditions of average. The main use of this condition is in cases where the same property is both insured specifically and included in a floating cover. It lays down that the floating cover will only contribute to the loss if the specific cover is exhausted, and applies average separately to each type of cover, which underlines once more the importance of ensuring that every sum insured in the policy represents the value of the property covered.

First-loss policies. Average is applied to first-loss policies if the declared full value is less than the total value of the property at the time of the loss.

Participation by the insured

Apart from enforced participation through the imposition of average in the event of underinsurance, the insured may bear part of a loss through compulsory or voluntary excess, or coinsurance.

Compulsory excess or franchise. It is not the practice of insurers to compel the insured to bear the first part of each loss on the basic fire insurance, but compulsory excesses, which may in some cases be replaced by franchises (where the insured bears losses up to an agreed amount, but receives payment in full from the insurers for losses exceeding that amount), are frequently a feature of extensions of the basic policy to cover other perils.

Voluntary excess or franchise. In recent years, insurers have begun to allow a discount in cases where the insured is prepared to accept a voluntary excess on a fire policy. In this they have been influenced by market practice in the USA, and in consequence the American term 'deductible' is frequently used instead of 'excess'. Voluntary excesses or franchises above the minimum figure required by the insurers also earn a discount.

The acceptance of voluntary excesses by insurance buyers has been fairly limited in extent, as the discounts allowed are considered by many buyers as inadequate.

Coinsurance. In special cases, the insured may be required, or may elect, to be his own insurer for a proportion of the risk, meeting that proportion of all claims himself.

PREMIUM RATING

Rating system

For rating purposes, fire risks are classified into groups, each consisting of a trade or a part of a trade, and a rate is allotted to each classification reflecting the hazard it presents. This rate would be applicable to an average risk within the classification. From it, the rate for a particular building and its contents may be assessed by taking into account the individual features tending to increase or diminish the hazard, as compared with the average risk, revealed by the proposal, supplemented by the inspection carried out by the insurers' fire surveyors.

Discounts for fire-extinguishing appliances

A scale of discounts is allowed from the basic rate, according to the fire-extinguishing appliances with which the premises are equipped. The scale ranges from a small discount for simple first-aid fire-fighting equipment of an approved kind to a substantial reduction in the basic rate for the provision of automatic sprinklers.

Percentage adjustments

In recent years, insurers have made the rate for specific trades subject to a percentage adjustment, which is applicable to the whole trade classification to which the risk belongs. For some classifications it represents a reduction on the basic rate; for most an increase, ranging to several hundred per cent in hazardous industries.

Insurers are prepared to reduce the percentage surcharge drastically, or, in many cases, to remove it altogether and allow a substantial discount, if the premises are protected with an approved automatic sprinkler installation.

There is thus a very wide difference in the premiums charged for sprinklered and unsprinklered risks of the same type, and the installation of sprinklers is usually the most effective single action that the insured can take to reduce his fire insurance premium.

Non-tariff discount

Non-tariff insurers and Lloyd's underwriters are usually prepared to allow a discount from the tariff insurers' rate for a risk. The Fire Offices Committee, the tariff body for fire insurance, imposes a requirement that if a tariff office participates in a collective policy, not more than 35 per cent of the total risk may be placed with non-tariff insurers or at Lloyd's.

Long-term agreements

In return for a premium discount, the insured may bind himself to offer the risk to the same insurers annually for a period of three or five years. The insurer is not, however, bound to accept the offer each year. If an increased premium rate is required during the period of the term, the insured may either renew at the new rate or allow the policy to lapse.

COLLECTIVE POLICIES

If the sum insured is larger than a single insurer wishes to cover, it may be apportioned between a number of insurers. A common policy and specification is issued listing the insurers and the proportion each insures. The office with the largest proportion, known as the 'leading office', surveys the risk, administers the insurance, prepares the documentation, and can be regarded by the insured, for communication purposes, as the sole insurer. Coinsurers contribute to all claims in the proportions of their participation in the insurance.

Where a proportion of the insurance is placed with non-tariff insurers or at Lloyd's, separate policies are issued for the non-tariff and Lloyd's proportions of the risk.

RELATED INSURANCES

Sprinkler leakage

Where an automatic sprinkler system is installed, it is prudent to insure the risk of water damage caused by the accidental discharge of sprinkler heads or by accidental damage to supply pipes, valves, or any part of the sprinkler installation. The cover is rated on the number of heads, and may be arranged for the full sums insured on the fire policy, or as a first-loss policy. The latter method will normally be the cheaper, since although the premium rate will be higher than for a full-value cover, the sum insured will be lower. The policy excludes damage resulting from the operation of sprinklers through heat caused by fire (which is covered under the fire policy) and also from repairs or alterations to the buildings or the sprinklers, freezing if the premises are empty or disused, earthquake, subterranean fire, riot and war risks or explosion.

Private dwelling houses

Fire cover

The standard fire policy is not used for insurances of this kind, and wordings vary between insurers. It is normal to include in the basic cover many of the extended perils which may be added to the standard policy, so that in addition to fire, lightning and explosion, the cover will include damage by spontaneous combustion and earthquake (although shock damage is only covered for contents), and fire damage caused by riot or civil commotion (outside Ireland and Northern Ireland).

Householders' and houseowners' cover

It is nowadays more usual to insure a private house or its contents by means of a householders' or houseowners' policy, by which insurers seek to provide much of the basic insurance protection required by an occupier in a single policy. It therefore extends beyond the bounds of fire insurance to include elements of theft, all risks and employers' and public liability insurance. There is now no standard form of policy and rates and wordings vary from one insurer to another.

Buildings. The cover on buildings includes the following perils which can be insured under the standard fire policy and its extensions:

> Fire, lightning, explosion, riot, civil commotion and strikes etc., (outside Ireland and Northern Ireland), aircraft, storm, tempest and flood (for which special terms may be imposed if the flood risk is abnormal), bursting and overflowing of water tanks etc., earthquake, impact and subsidence and landslip.

Other cover granted includes loss or damage by theft, or leakage of oil from a fixed oil-fired heating installation, breakage or collapse of television and radio aerials, accidental damage to underground pipes and cables and accidental breakage of fixed glass and sanitary fittings.

Loss of rent is covered, usually up to, say, 10 per cent of the sum insured on buildings, and property owners' liability cover is also included.

Contents. The contents cover gives similar protection, although theft not involving forcible entry or exit in premises which are in part let or sub-let or separately occupied is not covered.

In addition the policy is extended to include servants' effects, employers' liability cover in respect of domestic servants, and tenants' liability cover.

Householders' policies frequently include personal liability cover and some limited personal accident cover for the householder and his spouse.

Property temporarily removed from the insured premises, other than for sale or exhibition, or to a furniture depositor, is also covered, subject to certain restrictions on theft cover.

Inflation and sums insured. In view of inflation it is imperative that insured values should be kept in line with current values. A recent innovation has been for sums insured in respect of buildings to be automatically increased during the currency of the policy by a percentage related to inflation. With regard to contents, cover can now be arranged on a 'new for old' basis provided that sums insured have been maintained at full replacement value.

Traders' policies

Many insurers issue combined policies for shopkeepers and other traders, covering the basic risks against which cover is needed. These may take the form of either a single policy with a number of sections, or a standard policy for each risk bound into a single document.

Such a policy might typically cover fire and theft (sometimes combined into a single cover on the lines of a householders' policy, but not so wide in scope), business interruption, employers' and public liability and plate glass insurance.

Buildings in course of erection

The responsibility for effecting cover on buildings in course of erection may rest with the owner or the contractor, according to the terms of the building contract.

Fire insurance may be arranged on a specified building being erected, in which case the premium will be based on the contract value. The rate applied will be a proportion, often 50 per cent, of the normal premium rate for the period of construction.

Where a contractor is insuring, fire cover will usually be included in a contractors' all risks insurance, but if fire cover only is required, it can be obtained either for specified buildings, as outlined above, or by a floating cover on the contract works, plant, tools and materials, adjustable on the contractor's turnover for various types of contract. This subject is dealt with more extensively in Chapter 14 (Contractors' All Risks Insurance).

INDUSTRIAL AND COMMERCIAL ALL RISKS COVER

Although 'all risks' policies covering industrial buildings and contents including stocks have been available to a very limited extent for a number of years from sections of the non-tariff market, particularly from Lloyd's and certain overseas companies, it is only since the Tariff companies in the United Kingdom entered this market in 1982 that this broader cover has aroused wider interest. This new approach offers cover not only against named perils as described earlier in this chapter, but against *accidental* loss or destruction of or damage to specified property from *any cause* other than those individually excluded in the policy wording. Thus, the insured is covered against accidental events beyond those which might be normally anticipated without having to specify them individually.

The new standard 'all risks' form of contract insures not only property but also earnings (i.e. the business interruption risk) in the one policy; special features affecting the latter are referred to in Chapter 6 (Business Interruption Insurance).

Exclusions

Although the contract basically sets out to provide 'all risks' cover the list of excluded perils and property is quite extensive. In addition to the usual exclusion of war, nuclear risks and the like, the following are typical examples of those exclusions:

Excluded risks

1   Faulty design or workmanship, inherent vice, wear and tear and gradual deterioration.
2   Explosion of boilers.
3   Collapse or cracking of buildings.
4   Corrosion, rust, changes in temperature, vermin, insects.
5   Fraud or dishonesty.
6   Inventory shortages.
7   Cracking or collapsing of boilers and the like.
8   Mechanical or electrical breakdown.
9   Certain kinds of subsidence or landslip.
10 Riots in Northern Ireland.

Excluded property

11 Property in course of erection, alteration or demolition, or whilst under process.
12 Property in transit.
13 Money, securities and the like.
14 Road or railway vehicles, watercraft or aircraft.
15 Land, roads etc.
16 Livestock, growing crops or trees.

Although certain of the exclusions cannot be deleted because insurers consider the particular risks involved as uninsurable, some of them may be cancelled by negotiation at an additional premium, e.g. it is possible to include cover for money, goods in transit, dishonesty of staff and engineering risks to avoid having to take out separate insurances for these risks.

Premium

Premiums are built up from an appreciation by the insurers of the appropriate rate for the main perils covered, to which will be added estimated amounts to provide for the residual risks, some of which may very well be potentially hazardous.

There is normally an excess imposed of say £100 (higher for subsidence risk) for all material damage claims, which can usually be reduced at an additional premium. Conversely insurers will allow a discount if the insured voluntarily accepts a higher excess. The policy is subject to average and the sum insured should be the full value of the property insured, although separate lower limits of liability might be agreed with insurers for certain perils such as storm, subsidence or other perils in order to economise in premium. The sum insured may be inflation index linked on an agreed basis.

The above comments describe in broad outline the current practice in 1983 adopted by tariff insurers for industrial and commercial 'all risks' covers. Similar contracts offered by non-tariff insurers may possibly vary, but are likely to be on the same lines. Insurers will doubtless proceed with some caution both in fixing premiums and deciding the extent to which they are prepared to vary their standard exclusions and conditions during the early days of development of this broader form of cover. Although 'all risks' insurances have been available for many years to cover more simple risks (e.g. jewellery, personal effects, computers and objets d'art) many more problems will certainly arise in offering such wide cover on industrial and commercial property, as well as on the earnings arising therefrom. The varying features applying to the diverse operations of industry and commerce require extensive enquiries by insurers concerning the implications of offering 'all risks' cover to ensure that they properly evaluate the individual risk and charge an equitable premium. Up to the present time insurers have very little statistical information on which to judge all the aspects of each risk, but doubtless, in time, a discernable pattern will emerge and the demand for 'all risks' policies will spread.

It is likely that policy wordings will be amended as more experience is gained in this new type of insurance and it is most important that the insured studies the precise terms of any proposed cover to ensure that it meets his expectations.

FIRE PREVENTION

Properly arranged insurance can do much to limit the financial disaster that fire would otherwise entail, but it cannot eliminate the interruption, the inconvenience or the human suffering that may result. Fire-detection and extinguishing equipment can help to check losses when fire breaks out. Insurers, therefore, encourage their installation. But only the management and employees of a firm can prevent the fire starting in the first place.

It is of the greatest importance that a proper programme of fire prevention should be instituted. The likely sources of ignition and the materials likely to be ignited within the premises should be identified, and separated as far as possible, and a constant check kept on the standard of housekeeping within the premises. Smoking should be prohibited in areas of any degree of hazard, and the prohibition should be enforced.

Pre-planning will help to limit the effects of a fire. Contingency plans should be drawn up for limiting water and smoke damage in the event of fire, and for salvage and rehabilitation work afterwards. Fire protection officers of local fire brigades, the insurer's fire surveyors and the Fire Protection Association can all give useful advice.

Even with the best fire-prevention system, fire is still a possibility, and adequate insurance cover is therefore a necessity.

FURTHER READING

T. Smith and H. Francis, *Fire Insurance theory and practice.* 6th ed. Stone & Cox, London: 1975, 156 pages.

F. H. Jones, *Property insurance underwriting and claims.* CII Tuition Service, London, 1981, 200 pages (apply to publisher).

Chas. E. Hall, *Property insurance: risk assessment and control.* CII Tuition Service, London, 1981, ca. 150 pages (apply to publisher).

6

Business Interruption Insurance

W. A. Chrzanowski,* **Group Insurance Manager,**
Rowntree Mackintosh plc

A business interruption insurance contract is one of indemnity. The subject matter is the business. The object is to restore the business to the financial position that would have been achieved had the event insured against not happened.

This form of insurance is complementary to the material damage insurances described in other chapters. Whereas the latter provide compensation for loss of assets, interruption insurance preserves the financial stability of the business by covering the earnings derived from the use of those assets.

Previously, insurance was limited in scope to dislocation of the business following fire or the perils commonly included in the fire policy, but much wider covers are now available.

Such insurances are also known as 'profits', 'loss of profits' or 'consequential loss' policies, but these terms are sometimes considered to be inadequate or misleading and the word 'interruption' is now more commonly used.

Interruption insurance can be obtained for almost every activity pursued for gain. Because this chapter cannot deal with more than fundamentals, frequent qualification to provide for special cases is avoided by using the term 'business' in the widest sense.

*The author is indebted to Mr H. H. Parker for material retained from the previous edition.

NEED FOR COVER

The need for cover exists when the possible maximum loss is either greater than the business can safely carry or when, for other reasons, management prefer to transfer the risk.

Although the reinstatement cost of fixed and current assets may be adequately insured against loss or damage, as described in other chapters, their loss may bring about a fall in revenue. Indeed, relatively small material damage frequently leads to a disproportionately heavy loss of net profit. A fall in income reduces net profit because:

1   The volume of business is reduced.
2   The ratio of fixed costs to revenue increases.

If net profit is reduced so far that a net trading loss arises then shortage of working capital may follow. A prolonged interruption may cause the financial state further to deteriorate with the risk of credit withdrawal and possible liquidation.

Interruption insurance covers net profit and fixed costs. If a business is not earning enough to pay any of its fixed costs then there is nothing to insure. If earnings are sufficient to cover only some of the costs, the need for cover may be greater than when a net profit is achieved because if the business was interrupted the increased continuing burden of fixed costs would aggravate the existing financial difficulties.

BASIS OF THE CONTRACT

Interruption insurance is based on three elementary principles:

1   Reduction in turnover is usually a reliable guide to the effect of an interruption on earnings.
2   The ratio to turnover of the sum of net profit and fixed costs is a constant although the proportions of fixed costs and profit may vary.
3   The effect on the business's finances of a reduction in turnover can accurately be measured by multiplying the amount of the reduction by the normal ratio of net profit plus fixed costs to turnover.

A standard form of policy wording giving effect to these principles, using turnover as the standard against which a reduction in business is measured, is most commonly used in the UK. Variations are made in cases where the standard form is not appropriate. For the various professions, advertising agents, estate agents, stockbrokers and the like, a policy covering reduction in gross fees is available. When no loss of income is expected but the possibility of increased expenses arises, a form relating to increased cost of working, removal costs to and from temporary premises and the cost of equipping them may be used.

An interruption policy is unusual in that the wording includes:

1 The formula by which the amount payable in the event of a claim is calculated.
2 Definitions of the terms used.

These definitions are worth study not only to understand the operation of the policy but also because the meanings given to the terms are slightly different from those used by accountants.

In practice, the application of the policy to an insured loss is in four basic stages which are covered in more detail in the remaining paragraphs:

1 Calculation of the loss of turnover and hence the loss of gross profit (i.e. net profit and insured fixed costs).
2 Addition of the amount expended because of increased cost of working.
3 Deducation of savings in insured fixed costs.
4 Application of average.

Material damage proviso

Before an interruption policy can operate, material damage must occur resulting in an interruption that affects the business. Unless funds are available to replace assets, reinstatement of the business will be delayed or impossible. A clause, fundamental to the contract, is incorporated in an interruption policy stipulating that it will not operate unless at the time of an interruption caused by a peril covered by the policy:

1 There is a material damage insurance in force covering the insured's interest:
   (a) In the property.
   (b) At premises specified in the interruption policy.
   (c) Against the peril which caused the interruption.
2 The material damage insurers have paid or admitted liability for the damage.

In view of these considerations it is a waste of premium to include perils in the interruption policy that are not also within the scope of the material damage insurances.

Other implications of this proviso are:

1 Interruption insurers do not need to investigate the validity of a claim.
2 There is no need to repeat all the conditions and warranties of the material damage insurances in the interruption policy.
3 Separate investigation by the interruption insurers into the cause of damage is unnecessary.

There are circumstances in which insurers waive application of the material damage proviso. Examples are:

1 In respect of an extension to include losses resulting from damage at premises not used by the insured, such as suppliers' premises and commission agents' stocks.
2 Where, as tenant, the insured has no control over the landlord's building insurances.
3 When minor material damage causes serious loss of business— for example, an explosion of minor steam piping.
4 When interruption policies cover loss of revenue consequent upon disease, food poisoning, epidemics, murder and suicide. Such policies are frequently arranged for hotels, boarding houses, restaurants, schools and nursing homes.

A stipulation concerning material damage insurance would be of little value unless some procedure existed for checking the adequacy of it. At the time of the proposal, interruption insurers enquire into the material damage insurances and may withdraw if an unsatisfactory position is disclosed. Thereafter the insured's duty of disclosure enables the insurers to repudiate a claim if, at the time, the state of the material damage insurances would have affected their decision to accept the insurance.

PERIOD OF INDEMNITY

The premium payable for the policy is calculated at a rate per cent on the sum insured. Except for the fact that it is adjustable annually on declaration to the insurers of the actual results achieved by the business, the premium is a fixed price, for which insurers will provide cover up to defined limits.

In addition to the financial limit, which is the sum insured, interruption contracts contain a time-limit, usually expressed in months, known as the 'maximum indemnity period', which normally commences simultaneously with the interruption. It is not to be confused with the 'period of insurance' which is the term during which the contract itself is in force. In the event of an interruption covered by the policy, compensation will continue to be paid as long as the business is affected by the interruption or until the expiry of the maximum indemnity period, whichever comes first, irrespective of whether the contract is renewed at an intervening renewal date.

The selection of an appropriate period of indemnity is for the buyer to decide in the light of his special and intimate knowledge of the business. To avoid a form of underinsurance it must represent the full estimated period during which the business might be affected following the most serious probable interruption. If the period is too short the effect of the interruption may continue after the time-limit has expired and the policy is no longer operating. It is prudent to be generous when estimating how long the indemnity period should be rather than to fall into the common error of reducing premium cost by selecting a short period that later proves to be inadequate. As will be seen later, an adequate period of indemnity is conducive to a full recovery of increased costs of working. If it is too short, such costs may exceed the limits laid down in the policy with the result that there is an uninsured loss equal to the amount of the excess. In practice, insurers do not like periods in excess of three years because the longer the period the more opportunity there is for extraneous factors to arise which obscure the accurate measurement of the effects of an interruption. In special circumstances it may be possible to cover periods up to five years.

Various factors require consideration when deciding what period to select. These vary from business to business but generally they include:

1 Time required to reinstate buildings and to replace machinery and plant. It is prudent to allow a margin for contingencies which may cause delay. Examples are:
   (a) Need to obtain planning permission.
   (b) Effect of local authority requirements and legislation.
   (c) Time required for planning and design, particularly if the opportunity is taken to erect buildings different to the originals or on a different site. Similar considerations apply if different or more modern plant is to be purchased in replacement.
   (d) Whether any item of plant is specialised and made to order.
   (e) Time required for erection, testing and running-in of plant and machinery.
   (f) Strikes affecting building, manufacture or transport.
   (g) Bad weather.
   (h) Shortage of essential materials.
2 Availability of suitable alternative premises, bearing in mind that if several businesses are affected, as might happen in cases of multiple tenure, there may be problems of supply and demand.
3 The extent to which the business is dependent on computers.
4 Time required to regain lost markets. In markets where competition is intense, shortage of revenue from this source may take a long time to recover. If the indemnity period is long enough then cover does not cease when full production capacity is available but continues until, at normal cost of working, turnover reaches the level that would have been attained had no interruption occurred.
5 Time needed to engage and train the required number of employees.

Frequently the mistake is made that because various alternatives are available by which the business can continue, although for a period at a reduced level, a shorter indemnity period is indicated.

This may be so but care is needed to distinguish between the factors which truly enable the business more quickly to reach the position it would have attained at normal operating costs had no interruption occurred, and those which simply reduce the overall loss.

SUM INSURED

The sum insured is the financial limit of the insurers' obligation under the contract and is used by them for the calculation of the premium.

Need for estimation of future earnings

An interruption policy covers net profit before taxation plus standing charges. Revenue from non-trading activities is not insured because it would not be affected by an interruption. Examples are income from investments and profit on sale of surplus assets.

This type of insurance is essentially forward looking. When an interruption has occurred the intention is to put the business into the financial position it would have reached during the ensuing months. It follows that the gross profit it is desired to protect is not that of the preceding financial year or even the current figures: an estimation of future earnings has to be made.

Because a policy is an annually renewable contract and the indemnity period may commence to operate on any one of the 365 days of the policy year, it is prudent to assume an interruption taking place just before the next renewal date of the policy, that is to say, almost a year ahead. The indemnity period will commence then and run on for the selected duration. It follows that to provide proper protection for the business it is necessary when estimating future revenue and profitability to look ahead one year plus the duration of the maximum indemnity period.

Trends, variations and special circumstances

Without some provision for fluctuations in business the policy would not succeed in providing an indemnity. Hence, the definitions contained in the policy relating to rate of gross profit, annual turnover and standard turnover are qualified by a stipulation that trends, variations and special circumstances affecting the business at the time of the interruption shall be taken into account so that the adjusted figures represent as nearly as possible what the results of the business would have been had the interruption not occurred. This is an important provision. A business could sustain a heavy loss should an interruption occur when the trend is toward expansion or when the benefits of reorganisation, capital investment or introduction of new processes are about to accrue. However, the benefit would be lost or diminished if the sum insured proved to be inadequate. Thus the estimation of future earnings must take trends and variations into account.

Addition and difference methods of calculating the sum insured

Generally, the accounts for the last financial year are used as the basis for estimating future earnings. For the purpose of interruption insurance, gross profit can be calculated in two main ways, both involving judgement and selection:

Difference method. Variable costs are identified and subtracted from turnover. The residue automatically comprises all fixed and semi-fixed costs and net profit or loss. (Variable costs are those which vary in proportion to output or turnover—for example, purchases of raw materials and packaging.)

The variable costs that are to be deducted are listed in the policy. It is important with policies of this type to ensure that only costs that really do vary in strict proportion to turnover are included in the list of variable costs; otherwise an uninsured loss might arise.

Addition method. Fixed costs are identified and added to net profit. If there is a net loss, it is subtracted from the total of fixed costs.

It is wise to insure all costs and expenses that do not vary in strict proportion to turnover; otherwise losses may be sustained because the sum insured is inadequate or because of the application of average (see p. 120).

The fixed costs to be insured are listed in the policy where they are usually called 'specified standing charges'. Any omissions from the list are not insured.

The difference method has the following advantages and a form defining 'gross profit' as turnover, after adjustment for stock, less specified variables is now commonly used:

1   Usually the sum insured is more easily calculated.
2   It is less likely that some semi-fixed costs will be omitted.
3   A list of variable costs is always shorter than a list of specified standing charges.
4   A short list of variable costs is more easily reviewed than a longer, possibly incomplete, list of fixed costs. Alterations in accountancy procedures may create new cost classifications and alter account headings. Unless a policy on the addition basis is regularly reviewed, the list of insured fixed costs may become out of date, with the risk of inadvertent underinsurance and difficulties over loss settlements. These problems do not arise when the difference basis is adopted. This is partly because variable costs are usually less affected by such changes and partly because they are the uninsured costs.
5   The difference method of arriving at gross profit is more akin to normal accountancy practice than the addition method and is less likely to cause confusion.
6   A simpler form of auditor's certificate is required for the annual declaration to the insurers for premium adjustment purposes. The actual amount of net profit is not disclosed.

Value Added Tax

It is to be expected that there will be amendments to the rates of tax, the forms of relief and the transactions to which VAT will apply. Of necessity, therefore, comments about the effects of the tax on interruption insurance must be of a general nature.

The nature of VAT, or for that matter other revenue taxes such as excise duty, is that it is an additional charge collected on behalf of the tax authorities and as such, not earned by the business nor a charge on it. The turnover figures used in the calculation of the sum insured by the difference method should therefore be net of VAT.

Both variable and fixed costs will contain an element of VAT and this element should also be excluded from the calculation. If variable costs were to be incorrectly inflated by VAT, the effect would be to reduce the sum insured calculated by the difference method with the result that average might apply. Conversely, the addition method could lead to unnecessary overinsurance resulting from taking into account standing charges at too high a level.

Should a situation be perceived where, in the event of an interruption, a balance of liability may remain chargeable on the business after any available tax credits have been taken, such balance can be included. It is important to notify the insurer of such an inclusion as policies specifically exclude VAT.

Average

The intention of a business interruption policy is to make good the whole loss of net profit plus contribution to overheads sustained as a result of an interruption whose effects may be felt throughout the maximum indemnity period. Because of this, the insurers require that the sum insured shall represent the whole of the insurable gross profit for that period.

Underinsurance is penalised by the application of average which in cases of proven underinsurance requires the insured to bear a proportion of every loss. The test of full insurance is to compare the sum insured with the amount produced by multiplying the turnover during the twelve months immediately before the date of an interruption by the ratio of gross profit to turnover calculated for the last financial year before the interruption, after adjustment for trends, variations and special circumstances. When the indemnity period exceeds twelve months the average proviso is amended to include an appropriate multiplier to be applied to the annual turnover. If the indemnity period is less than twelve months, however, the proviso is unaltered.

As will be seen later, the cover provided by an interruption policy includes increased cost of working. This part of the cover is also subject to the average proviso. The reasoning is that if because of underinsurance the insured bears a proportion of each loss of gross profit he should also share, in the same proportion, any increased expenditure which reduces that loss. Thus, the effect of under-insurance is not only to reduce the recovery of gross profit but also to reduce the extent to which increased cost of working is recoverable.

Sum insured related to indemnity period

The sum insured by the standard interruption policy is based on annual gross profit, adjusted for trends, variations and special circumstances.

This is convenient because it follows accountancy practice. Confusion and waste of effort would follow the use of a different basis solely for the purpose of interruption insurance. Annual profits are used because twelve months is the minimum period that truly reflects the effects of an interruption on a business.

Although the sum insured for all periods of indemnity up to twelve months is the annual insurable gross profit, the premium is charged at a lower rate to allow for the fact that a shorter period is covered. For periods exceeding twelve months, the sum insured is the estimated gross profit, after adjustment for trends variations and special circumstances, for the whole of the maximum period of indemnity. The premium is not a multiple of that charged for one year. Insurers assume that losses are heavier in the early months of the indemnity period and decrease as the business approaches normality. They know, too, that total stoppage of business for the whole of a long period of indemnity is a rare event. In consequence, the rate of premium is reduced for periods exceeding twelve months. (Although the premium increases because the reduced rate is applied to a higher sum insured.)

Return of premium

It will be apparent that proper protection can only be secured if:

1   An adequate period of indemnity is chosen.
2   The sum insured is properly calculated.

It is prudent to tend towards generosity in both factors. Insurers are aware that the calculation of an accurate sum insured which will avoid the application of average is difficult because of the number of variable factors involved. They encourage people to make generous assessments of the cover they require by incorporating, where appropriate, a provision in their contracts whereby, after the close of each policy year, they will refund a pro-rata amount of the premium paid if the actual results of the business show that there has been overinsurance. To obtain the benefit of the provision, the insured produces to the insurer a certificate prepared by the auditors quoting the actual gross profit (as defined in the policy) earned during the last financial year. The return of premium is normally limited to 50 per cent of the amount paid. In other words over-insurance up to 100 per cent is possible without payment of an unnecessary premium.

If the sum insured has been properly computed it will be based on the expected profit for the year or years after the period of insurance (see p. 117). The figure that is used to calculate the premium refund is the profit for the year of the insurance. Hence, in times of inflation or growth, it is a sign of a healthy interruption insurance that a sizeable return of premium is received each year.

INCREASED COST OF WORKING

The principle of utmost good faith applies throughout the term of a policy and requires the insured to take all reasonable steps to reduce loss. As a corollary, he cannot recover that part of any loss attributable to neglect to take such steps. The dislocation of business caused by fire or other peril inevitably leads to expenditure that is made simply to minimise loss of income. An interruption policy, being a contract of indemnity, provides compensation for it, subject to certain reasonable provisions:

1   The expenditure must be necessarily and reasonably incurred.
2   The sole purpose of the expenditure must be to avoid or diminish a reduction in turnover that would otherwise have occurred during the indemnity period as a result of the interruption.
3   The expenditure must not exceed the gross profit which would have been earned on the amount of the reduction in turnover that has been avoided.

This part of the cover is subject to the average proviso, as already explained.

As well as being subject to average, policies on the 'addition' basis contain a proviso that the amount of the increased cost of working that is to be reimbursed is the actual increase in cost multiplied by

$$\frac{\text{net profit} + \text{insured fixed costs}}{\text{net profit} + \text{all fixed costs}}$$

The reasoning is that because the expenditure contributes to all the fixed costs, the insured should bear a share of the additional cost if some fixed costs have been omitted from the insurance cover. This proviso is unnecessary when the 'difference' wording is used.

Following an interruption it may be expedient to incur an increased cost of working in excess of the normal limit of recovery. To provide for this contingency a supplementary item 'on additional expenditure' may be added to the policy. Because the sum insured is necessarily arbitrary, average is not applied.

INSURANCE OF WAGES AND SALARIES

The object of buying insurance is to provide adequate protection for a business. It is difficult to decide what protection is adequate for wages and salaries yet underinsurance could lead directly or indirectly to heavy loss.

It will be useful to restate the fundamental principle that to protect the net profit of a business it is essential to cover net profit plus the fixed costs that do not fall proportionately with a drop in revenue, together with the variable costs that it would be desirable to continue to incur in the interests of the business. For insurance purposes the latter are often referred to as 'optional charges'.

Generally, salaried staff are relatively permanent and form the nucleus of the business. They will undertake the task of reinstating the business and will be retained irrespective of the effect of an interruption on revenue. In that case their remuneration is clearly a fixed cost to be insured as part of gross profit recoverable so long as the business is affected by an interruption.

Wage earners are generally associated with production and may become in some degree redundant if production is reduced. Wages tend therefore to be a variable cost and come under the 'optional charges' heading referred to above. Insurance of wages is thus at the discretion of the buyer who will be influenced by many considerations, the first of which is need. Need may arise in various ways, for example:

1   During an interruption it is likely that the ratio of wages to revenue will increase.
2   Company philosophy and relations between management and labour may create a moral obligation to continue to pay wages in full or in part for as long as possible.
3   If employees are dismissed there will be a legal liability to make various severance payments under:
    (a)   Agreements with trade unions.
    (b)   Redundancy Payments Act 1968 Contracts of Employment Act 1972 and the Employment Protection Act 1978.
          Various provisions of this legislation have been reviewed and re-enacted in the Employment Protection (Consolidation) Act, 1978.
    (c)   Individual contracts of employment which impose financial obligations on the employer, payable during a period of interruption when the business is most vulnerable.

Additional factors that tend to make desirability rather than strict need the criterion for assessing cover for wages are:

1   The local availability of labour. This determines to what extent and how quickly staff can be built up again after a period of reduced numbers.
2   The cost in terms of time and money needed to train new staff.
3   The extent to which the processes used in the business will allow dismissal of staff.
4   The possible existence of local competitors who would employ dismissed employees in an effort to take over trade.

The condition of the policy relating to reduction of loss must not be overlooked. A typical condition stipulates that 'the insured shall with due diligence do and concur in doing and permit to be done all things which may be reasonably practicable to minimise or check any interruption of or interference with the business or to avoid or diminish the loss.' On the face of it the insurers will need to satisfy themselves that the continued payment of wages to employees for whom no work can be found is justifiable as being in the interests of the business or on grounds of expediency.

Having reached a conclusion about the need for wages cover some thought should be given to the various possible degrees of interruption and the labour requirements likely to be met in each. If this stage is carefully done it should be possible to arrange reasonably adequate cover at an acceptable cost.

The particular effects of an interruption are specific to each business but generally there are three broad possibilities:

1 Partial interruption causing a reduced level of business.
2 Complete stoppage for a relatively short period.
3 Complete long-term stoppage.

After each, following on reinstatement of the damage, there is usually a period needed to recapture lost custom or markets before revenue reaches the level which would have been achieved had no interruption taken place.

Irrespective of the severity of an interruption if reinstatement of the business is possible it is usually necessary to retain the services of some or all of the employees in the following groups:

1 *Key workers.* These employees are usually employed on supervisory duties. Although an interruption might reduce the number of employees for whose production they are responsible, their services would be needed to supervise the remainder and to implement management's plans for reinstatement of revenue.
2 *Administrative, distributive and maintenance workers.* Because these employees are not directly engaged on production their services are usually required even though the volume of business is reduced. This group includes clerks, warehousemen, skilled packers, storekeepers, checkers, quality control personnel, boiler- and power-house attendants, tradesmen, drivers, canteen workers, cleaners, liftmen, gatemen, nightwatchmen and the like.
3 *Skilled workers, operatives and craftsmen.* If such employees are

dismissed because there is no work for them to do they will seek employment elsewhere. It may be desirable to attempt to retain their skills by continuing wages. There is some risk in this because the better type of employee is not happy being paid for idleness and may find a similar job to retain his skill.

4   *Apprentices.* An employer may be bound by agreement to continue to pay wages to apprentices irrespective of the availability of work or training. Additionally, it may be prudent to do so with a view to their future employment as skilled men.

In addition, there may be a wish to continue to pay wages to long-service employees for whom there is often a special regard on the grounds that their past service has contributed to the well-being of the business.

Because the extent of an interruption cannot be known before-hand, insurance of wages must either:

1   Follow the insurance of gross profit by covering the total wage bill for the maximum indemnity period,
      or,
2   Be covered by some less extensive but more flexible method.

Insurance of wages along with gross profit is appropriate in the case of a small business which can return fairly quickly to normal after an interruption and in which it is impracticable to reduce staff. Wages are then regarded as a fixed cost and are included in the definition of gross profit. The rate of premium charged is the gross-profit rate.

The disadvantages of this method when applied to larger concerns and longer indemnity periods are that because it is inflexible it leads to overinsurance and it is relatively costly in terms of premium. Various alternatives have been devised in attempts to overcome these disadvantages:

1   To regard wages as a fixed cost but insure only:
      (a)   A specified percentage of the total annual wages, or
      (b)   Up to a specified amount, or
      (c)   Wages of specified categories of employees.
2   To include indirect wages as a fixed cost in gross profit and cover direct wages by a separate item for a specified number of weeks. This period should be sufficient to cover the legal-liability

payments and allow breathing space to assess the effects of the damage and for planning. The sum insured by the separate item will represent the wage bill for the specified number of weeks for all employees whose wages are not insured as a fixed cost in gross profit.

Dual basis

Whilst the above methods give a measure of flexibility, they are not as flexible as the 'dual basis' introduced by insurers in the 1950s. It is known as the 'dual basis' because during an initial selected part of the indemnity period 100 per cent of the total wage bill is insured. In the remainder of the indemnity period a preselected percentage is covered. There are minimum requirements which must be satisfied before insurers will give cover on this basis:

1   The maximum indemnity period covered by the policy must be not less than 12 months.
2   The initial period of 100 per cent cover must be not less than four weeks.
3   The minimum percentage for the remainder period is ten.

Under this method the sum insured by the wages item represents the total wage bill for the indemnity period (with a minimum period of 12 months). It is subject to average in the same way as gross profit and there is usually a rebate clause to encourage full insurance.

The maximum compensation payable under the wages item is the shortage in turnover multiplied by the ratio of wages to turnover for the previous financial year, after adjusting for trends, variations and special circumstances.

The dual basis contains two very useful provisions:

1   Any savings in wages during the initial period become available to increase the amount covered during the remainder period. This is the 'carry-over' provision.
2   On presentation of the claim to the insurers, the insured has the option to convert the dual basis into a single period of 100 per cent wages cover for a prearranged number of weeks. This is the 'option' provision.

Savings are 'carried over' as a lump sum. If they were used to increase the percentage applying to the remainder period benefit would be lost in proportion to the turnover maintained. In practice, such savings are often used to finance the expansion and training of the labour force in anticipation of commencement of production.

Payroll basis

Increasing complexity of remuneration structures in industry, of liability for payments under legislation and the accelerated rate at which changes can occur have in recent years increased the difficulty of assessing adequate sums insured. This difficulty has been recognised by the insurance market and the 'payroll basis' developed.

It is a derivation of the 'dual basis': ironically, and perhaps inevitably, the wheel has turned full circle in that this method allows the insurance of all remuneration within the gross profit item, without specific limits, for the full indemnity period. The virtually total flexibility thus provided is a major advantage to the insured, particularly the larger business; moreover the disadvantage of higher cost mentioned earlier has been removed, since the premium in most cases should approximate to that required for an adequate 'dual basis' cover.

Cover is simply effected by amending the definition of gross profit; in the case of the 'difference' method, wages are omitted from the list of specified variable costs; conversely, if the 'addition' method is still in use, an appropriate wording is added to the list of specified standing charges. It follows that wage losses are settled using the same formula as for gross profit.

'Payroll basis' is not available where the indemnity period is less than twelve months.

PREMISES

An interruption policy relates specifically to property at the premises used by the insured for the purpose of the business. These are listed in the schedule of the policy and it is important to make sure that none is omitted. Owing to the dependency of one business upon another, however, it frequently happens that damage at a supplier's premises causing a breakdown in the supply of an essential material, component or service, or alternatively at an important customer's premises which would result in a cancellation of orders may have as much effect on gross profit as damage at the premises of the business itself. A careful investigation into dependencies will disclose what extensions of the policy are required to avoid a significant gap in cover. Examples of typical dependencies are:

1   Suppliers, processors and subcontractors.
2   Public supply undertakings.
3   Major customers.
4   Trading estates and multiple tenancies where a central boiler and engine house supplies steam and possibly electricity to tenants.

AUDITORS' FEES

The fees normally payable for auditing the firm's books and preparing accounts are a standing charge, insurable as part of gross profit. Following an interruption, however, additional auditors' fees will become payable for the preparation of the information required by the insurers in connection with the claim. As these fees are not a standing charge and cannot be measured by the reduction in turnover, they cannot be insured under gross profit. Neither can they be regarded as an increased cost of working because the expenditure does not mitigate the reduction in turnover. Further, the policy usually stipulates that evidence in support of a claim shall be furnished at the insurer's own expense.

Auditors' charges for producing and certifying any particulars in the accounts can be insured by an additional item in the policy. The sum insured is necessarily an arbitrary one and is not subject to the average provisions. The fees for the annual audit are a reasonable indication of the amount to insure for a twelve-month indemnity period, suitably increased for longer periods.

Increasingly, particularly in the case of large companies with high sums insured, insurers are prepared to grant cover within the main sum insured and without specific limitation.

PROCEDURE FOR CLAIMS SETTLEMENT

The method of calculating the amount payable is laid down in the standard interruption policy. This formula is not rigidly applied and if in the course of claims investigation it is found that an alternative method will more nearly provide a true indemnity the insurers will usually agree.

Assuming that the material damage warranty has been complied with and that the peril causing the interruption is covered by the policy, the sequence followed is this:

Loss of gross profit. The reduction in turnover is calculated by comparing the turnover during the indemnity period with the turnover in the period corresponding with the indemnity period during the twelve months immediately before the damage. When indemnity periods exceed twelve months, each year or part year is separately compared with the turnover during the twelve months immediately before the damage.

The amount of reduction in turnover is then multiplied by the ratio of gross profit to turnover for the financial year immediately preceding the damage.

Adjustments are made to the rate of gross profit and turnover in accordance with the terms of the special circumstances clause (see p. 117).

Increase in cost of working. Additional expenditure necessarily and reasonably incurred is added to the amount calculated as loss of gross profit.

Under policies that use the 'addition' basis, it is possible that only a proportion of increase costs will be payable (see p. 123).

With either the addition or the difference basis, the policy may limit the compensation for increases in cost of working to the amount of gross profit saved by the extra expenditure.

Savings. If, as a result of the damage there are savings in the insured fixed costs these are deducted from the total amount arrived at so far.

Average. The final step is to check whether any reduction should be made for underinsurance by applying the terms of the average proviso previously described.

INSURABLE RISKS

The scope of interruption insurance is very wide. If a business can be affected by a fortuitous risk, the insurance market will usually provide for it.

Standard risks

Normally the most serious risk to which business concerns are exposed is fire. The perils most usually selected for insurance by an interruption policy are those covered by the standard fire policy with or without the optional extensions such as riot and civil commotion, aircraft, explosion, earthquake, flood, storm and tempest as described in Chapter 5.

Unlike a fire policy, however, an interruption policy automatically includes explosion of any boiler or economiser on the premises. To provide the necessary material damage backing to the interruption policy, a fire insurance must be supplemented by an engineering policy covering boilers and other pressure plant against explosion. If the latter policy contains the general damage extension, the standard interruption policy can effectively be similarly extended. It can also be extended to include other items of pressure plant covered by the engineering policy.

Epidemics, infectious diseases, murder and suicide

The effect of an event of this kind, happening on the premises or in the area, may be serious for all businesses connected with the tourist industry or holiday trade, meat and food manufacturers and to those employers who provide meals for their employees. It is usual to extend the main interruption policy to include these risks.

Theft

Loss of gross profit may result from theft of stock when there is no spare productive capacity or when further supplies are not available. The nature of the business may be such that theft of a particular article or piece of equipment, or the damage caused by thieves, could have a significant effect on turnover or on operating costs. Given the material damage cover provided by a theft policy, the standard interruption policy can be extended to provide protection for gross profit and increased operating costs. Frequently underwriters require a separate sum insured relating to the theft risk. When cover relates to stock, the estimated maximum quantity likely to be stolen at any one time is a guide to the potential loss of gross profit. If the effect on production is the main concern the factors to be considered are:

1 The extent to which production could be affected.
2 How easy it will be to replace the stolen property or repair damaged equipment.
3 The alternative measures available.

Transit by land, sea and air

Usually the need for cover relates to anticipated profit arising from the installation of new plant or equipment. Should it be lost or damaged in transit, during loading and unloading, in course of erection, testing and running-in there may be an adverse effect on anticipated turnover in one or more financial years. The market for this type of cover, which is usually provided by separate policies for each transit, is limited with the result that insurance is relatively expensive. Nevertheless, the cost is often small in relation to the potential loss which usually can be calculated with reasonable accuracy.

Breakdown of plant and machinery

There may be a case for interruption insurance if, because of the nature of the plant, repair or replacement is likely to be a lengthy business and effective alternatives are not available. Generally the policy used follows the standard form except that a franchise or excess, excluding the first 24 hours, is applied to avoid the uneconomic effect of numerous small claims.

Usually the material damage warranty applies so that a breakdown policy is needed to provide an indemnity for the cost of repairs or replacement. Engineering breakdown interruption insurance is expensive. It is a sound approach to anticipate the need for repair and replacement by provision of a reasonable stock of spares, relying on a proper maintenance system to reduce the incidence of breakdown. The residual fortuitous risk may be such that the business can safely carry it, or alternatively the improvement of risk may persuade the insurer to waive the warranty, either totally or subject only to stipulation that regular inspection is carried out.

Deterioration of goods in cold stores

When stocks are seasonal or not replaceable there is a potential loss of profit should they deteriorate as a result of change of temperature or contamination by leakage of refrigerant. If the risk is to be insured, the interruption cover must follow material damage insurance against the same perils. Both covers are usually provided by specialist engineering insurers and relate to breakdown of or damage to the refrigeration plant, failure of electricity supply and, if required, contamination by leakage of refrigerant.

Often the perils usually covered by the fire and fire interruption policies are excluded, in which event it should be confirmed with those insurers that should the refrigeration plant be put out of action by fire or other perils insured by those policies the subsequent deterioration caused by change of temperature will be regarded as directly flowing from the fire damages and covered by the policies concerned.

Frequently the quantity of stock in cold stores commences at a low figure, builds up to a maximum ready for a season about to open and then fairly rapidly declines to zero as the stock is distributed and sold. This pattern can lead to waste of premium due to operation of the 50 per cent limit in the rebate of premium clause because, for safety, the profit on the maximum quantity of stock at any one time would be the sum insured. This can be avoided by:

1 Frequent alteration of the sum insured, a cumbersome method likely to be overlooked.
2 Arranging with insurers to declare gross profit monthly at the same time as stock values are declared for fire insurance purposes. In this method the sum insured would be the profit on the maximum quantity of stock but premium would be paid on the average value.

The rates charged for this type of insurance usually provide for an indemnity period of twelve months. The franchise or excess normally applied to insurances relating to failure of electricity supplies is not normally applied to this cover.

Failure of public utilities and steam supplies

Interruption arising from damage by insured perils at electricity stations, gas works or water works and resulting in breakdown of supply, can be covered by an extension of the standard policy at an appropriate additional premium.

Wider cover is available under an engineering interruption insurance which provides for failure from any cause other than the deliberate act of the authority and the usual war and nuclear risks. Cover is usually limited to one month or less with an excess or franchise of 24 hours which may be reduced to 30 minutes subject to an increase in premium.

The extension covers the premises of public supply undertakings from which the insured obtains his supply. In the case of natural gas from the North Sea, cover only extends to land-based installations, those of the supply authority and those of the gas producer which are linked to the supply authority from which the insured obtains his supply.

Accelerated development of telecommunications and increasing reliance by business on the public networks may present a risk of interruption to some firms in the event of damage at telephone exchanges. This is not a risk which is always obvious and careful investigation of hazards and effects of breakdown on the business is recommended. Although cover is not normally advertised within public utility extensions, it is obtainable on request.

The policy may also be extended to include failure of steam supplies caused by accidental damage to steam boilers and steam mains on the insured's premises, the standard policy already covers explosion of boilers and economisers and may carry the general damage extension.

Denial of access

This cover, which is usually provided by extension of the standard policy, relates to premises in the vicinity which, if severely damaged, might interfere with the business by preventing use of or access to the premises occupied by the insured's business. The need for cover depends upon the sensitivity of the business to interruption of this kind, the location of the premises and the construction of the surrounding property, bearing in mind that even main streets may be closed for a time when fire-damaged buildings are in a dangerous condition.

Chimneys—collapse and accidental damage

Damage to factory chimneys may cause an interruption of business due to:

1   Loss of steam-raising facilities.
2   Damage to surrounding buildings and plant.

The standard fire and interruption policies will apply but the perils covered by them may not be sufficiently wide in scope to meet the requirements disclosed by an analysis of risk. The policies may be extended to include such perils as storm and tempest, which includes winds of exceptional force, but, if damage from any unforeseen cause is to be covered it will be necessary to effect a special policy to cover material damage to chimneys and also to effect complementary interruption cover. Insurers vary in their administration; some provide these special covers through their specialist engineering insurance departments while others use a form of all risks policy. Either way it is usual to exclude the perils already covered by the standard policies or which could be included by extension.

Whether interruption insurance is necessary against collapse and damage to chimneys depends on the circumstances of a particular business and location. It is impossible to generalise other than to observe that of recent years the occurrence of unusually violent storms seems to have increased in certain areas. It may be that in a particular business reduction of risk by regular inspection and maintenance by competent steeplejacks is an acceptable alternative to insurance.

Frequently, production can be resumed fairly quickly following collapse of chimneys by the erection of temporary metal ones or by the use of one or more mobile steam-raising plants, although output may be restricted by reduced steam pressure.

However, damage to surrounding property is potentially more serious, depending on the importance to production of the damaged areas. Loss of key plant which has a long delivery time may cause serious loss.

Exhibitions and displays

If a stand is taken at an exhibition or trade fair there is the risk of loss of:

1 The expenditure incurred.
2 Profit on anticipated orders.

If only the expenses incurred are to be insured probably the most convenient method is to effect a special 'exhibition' policy which includes the material damage and public liability risks. Cover for expected gross profit can be arranged by extension of the main interruption policy. Measurement of fall in turnover may present difficulties but experience of previous exhibitions would provide a basis for reasonable estimation. In circumstances like these the standing and reputation of the firm and its relationship with its insurers are important factors.

Displays are often arranged for seasonal goods. Should the patterns, samples or designs be destroyed by fire it may not be possible to replace them and find alternative premises in time to book orders for that season with the result that there is a considerable fall in turnover. The resulting loss of profit can be covered by including the display premises in the main interruption policy. In this case the material damage policy must also cover the goods on display although it is likely that the consequential loss will be out of all proportion to the value of the property destroyed.

Cover for advance profits

Delay in completion of a project, whether it is a new enterprise or an extension of an existing business, will postpone the date when a return on the investment is expected to begin. It is sometimes argued that interruption cover during the erection stage of a new undertaking is unnecessary because trading losses are expected during the early years of activity and an interruption merely postpones this situation. It may be desirable to arrange cover because delay in earning the revenue with which to pay fixed costs incurred during the erection and commissioning period might be financially embarrassing.

It is useful to identify the possible causes of delay and to consider those which are insurable. Such an analysis will indicate whether cover limited to fire and the usual perils will provide sufficient protection. A wider base, related to the contractors' all risks insurance applying to the project, may be indicated.

It is equally important to consider need for advance cover on specially commissioned equipment, during its manufacturing period at suppliers premises and subsequently during transit from places in this country or abroad.

There is a limited market for advance profits insurance and discussion with the insurers at a very early stage is advisable.

Confusion sometimes arises from failure to distinguish between the three phases of a new project:

1 The construction, erection and commissioning period during which advance-profits cover applies, ceasing on completion of the project.
2 The first twelve months of trading. The standard policy is appropriate, subject to amendment of the definitions of rate of

gross profit and turnover to take into account the result from the commencement of business to the date of the damage instead of earlier trading history.

3 The second and subsequent years of business for which the standard policy was designed.

Expansion of an existing business is one of the circumstances for which the special circumstances clause was designed. Provided that the insurers are fully informed about the alteration in risk and reviews are made of the adequacy of the sum insured, duration of the indemnity period and scope of the insured perils, the protection provided by the existing policy may meet requirements. It may be desirable to supplement it with interruption cover for equipment in transit.

Rent

Sometimes there is confusion about insurance of rent which can be covered by a material damage policy or by an interruption policy against the perils included in the scope of these contracts.

Recovery under a material damage policy is restricted to the period during which the premises are unfit for occupation and the amount payable is in the proportion that the reinstatement time bears to the period for which the rent is insured. Cover by an interruption policy provides a more satisfactory indemnity. Rent payable is included as a fixed cost and is recoverable during the indemnity period in proportion to the reduction in turnover in the same manner as other fixed costs. This could arise when there is a partial interruption of business due to a fire or other insured peril occurring either at the insured's own premises or at suppliers' or customers' premises (provided the appropriate extension has been added to the cover). In the latter case the material damage policy would not operate at all. When it is necessary to take alternative premises there may be double rent to pay or the rent on the temporary premises may be higher than normal. The cover for increased cost of working will apply to the amount of the excess rent but unless rent is included as an insured standing charge no recovery is possible for continuing rent at the damaged premises or for the normal ratio at the alternative accommodation.

Loss of income from rents receivable does not necessarily cease on reinstatement of the premises following damage. Some time may elapse before they are relet. In addition expenditure may have been incurred on such items as overtime payments to tradesmen, in an attempt to accelerate reinstatement, and on advertising. The indemnity under a material damage policy would cease on completion of reinstatement and would not include any expense items. Insurance by means of an interruption policy may cost more but the wider cover often more than justifies any extra expense. Some reduction in premium may be achieved when the terms of a lease provide for rent to be paid for some time after the premises are rendered unfit for occupation. In these circumstances the commencing date of the period of indemnity can be deferred until the date when the duty to pay rent ceases.

The rate of gross profit on rents receivable is almost 100 per cent. When the main business is manufacturing or trading it is wise to reach an understanding with the insurers that in the event of a claim for loss of rent receivable, turnover from the other activities of the business is not brought into the calculation, otherwise a lower rate of gross profit will be applied to the reduction in income. An alternative is to specify a separate sum insured on rents receivable as an additional item in the policy.

Computers

Underwriters differ in the manner in which they attempt to meet the insurance requirements of computer users. Like any other equipment, computers are automatically included in the cover of the standard fire and interruption policies (provided of course that their value has been included in the fire sums insured). Owing to the sensitivity of the equipment and the possibility of serious interruption losses, insurers usually require a high standard of protection based on the Fire Offices' Committee pamphlet, *Recommendations for the Protection of Computer Installations against Fire.*

A careful assessment of the possible sources of loss to the business arising from dependency on the computer will indicate the extent of the insurance protection required. Relevant factors are:

1   Use.
2   Available alternative facilities.
3   Whether tapes and disks are duplicated; where and how they are stored.
4   The procedure for updating records.
5   The type of programme media in use, whether duplicated and where and how stored.
6   The time needed to replace equipment and systems records.

The extent of the cover to be arranged depends upon whether a reduction in turnover is anticipated. If turnover can be maintained by expenditure on alternative courses of action it will be necessary only to consider insurance of such increased cost of working. Although the standard interruption policy automatically includes increased cost of working the cover is limited to expenditure necessarily and reasonably incurred solely to avoid or diminish reduction in turnover. It is necessary, therefore, to arrange either a separate item in the policy—on 'additional expenditure'—or to effect a separate additional increased-cost-of-working policy. If a reduction in turnover is likely, as might arise when production or distribution is directly controlled by the computer, there is a need also to cover gross profit. In that event all the factors previously explained relating to calculation of the sum insured and estimation of the required maximum period of indemnity need to be considered, together with appropriate wages cover.

Because of the material damage warranty, the perils required to be included in the interruption policy must also be among those covered by the material damage insurances. A standard fire interruption policy rarely provides cover of sufficient scope for computers which are susceptible to a wide range of perils. It is usually necessary to arrange supplementary material damage and interruption covers which are generally on an 'all risks' basis covering sudden and unforeseen damage however caused, excluding the perils covered by the standard policies.

Insurance cannot compensate for the disorganisation and diversion of effort caused by loss of the computer facilities. It is wise to arrange a measure of self-protection by duplication and separate safe storage of records so that in the event of serious damage in the computer area it would be possible rapidly to transfer to outside compatible equipment.

INDUSTRIAL AND COMMERCIAL 'ALL RISKS' COVER

The most recent development in business interruption insurance, and perhaps the most far reaching for the future, is the current availability of policies which not only tidy up many of the risks and perils described in foregoing paragraphs into one contract, but importantly for many businesses, broaden the scope of events insured almost beyond specific definition.

This new 'all risks' form of contract includes in one policy: a) *loss or destruction of or damage to assets* (property) and b) *loss of earnings* (business interruption risk) arising from such damage due to any *accidental* cause other than perils and events which are specifically excluded.

Thus the main advantages for the insurance buyer are:

1 A philosophy and approach which more closely reflects the buyer's perception of his risk, being the business as a whole.
2 Cover for those events which unlike fire or explosion cannot always be easily foreseen.
3 Simpler administration.

In this new approach of covering all accidental causes other than those excluded, a primary concern of the insured will of course be the precise exclusions which are quite extensive in scope. The broad intention of these exclusions is first to specify causes which in current practice are considered as uninsurable (such as war, nuclear risk and deliberate acts). Secondly insurers try to segregate those risks which they still prefer to consider separately, either by a specific extension to their standard policy wording, or by special individual policy. The exclusions apply to both the assets and earnings sections of the policy, and they are considered in some detail in Chapter 5 (Fire Insurance) which deals with the assets section of the policy. The exclusions may vary and it is prudent for the insured to examine each exclusion individually to ensure that it meets the needs of his business.

An important point is that whilst there may be no provision in the contract to reverse some exclusions, in particular circumstances cover may be negotiable on request. A good example is spontaneous combustion, which is usually excluded as inherent vice.

The following special perils extensions, certain of which are explained earlier in this chapter are not envisaged in the standard contract but are available at additional cost:

1 Failure of public utility supplies (p. 134).
2 Infectious disease in the premises or the general area of the business (p. 131).
3 Food poisoning.
4 Defective drains or sanitary arrangements. The accidental occurrence of a major defect which renders drains or sanitary installations unusable can mean total closure of business until the defects are remedied or until adequate alternative arrangements can be made. In the case of a hotel, or a large factory, it may not be too easy to arrange alternative facilities and the repair period may be long, leading to a serious interruption and loss of business.
5 Vermin or pests. As in the case of defective drains or sanitary arrangements, the occurrence of vermin or pests could lead to immediate cessation of operations for however long it takes to eradicate the cause. Moreover, stocks of product could be rendered unusable through infestation, which could lead to additional cost of working in producing replacements or even direct loss of sales through inability to meet delivery times.

Bearing in mind that the policy, as under the other methods previously discussed in this chapter, principally concerns itself with activities at the insured's premises, the following further extensions, already mentioned in full in earlier paragraphs, need to be considered for inclusion if appropriate.

1 Suppliers' premises.
2 Customers' premises.
3 Property stored in other premises.
4 Hindrance of use of or prevention of access to the business.

If the special perils extensions outlined above are being considered, it is of course important to assess the risks from such perils at these third party premises also.

Other provisions, procedures and definitions described in this chapter remain unchanged. Thus payroll and increase in cost of working are provided automatically and sums insured and limits of indemnity should be assessed and calculated as already indicated.

A minimum indemnity period of twelve months is a prerequisite. No excess is imposed, except for a time exclusion for engineering extensions. Discounts for voluntary excesses are available.

At the time of publication, the method was in its formative stage; whilst the basic approach of all insurers is the same, contracts vary in their detail, wording and treatment of extensions. Moreover, only time and experience will show how far onto a true 'all risks' plane the market will go. In this context it is important to bear in mind that the basic principles of interruption insurance, which this chapter has attempted to describe, will continue to be applied to the new contracts. It is probable that some events causing loss will only be decided as insured or not after careful consideration against the intention and general practice of this class of insurance.

FURTHER READING

Denis Riley, *Consequential Loss and Business Interruption Insurance and Claims,* 5th edition, Sweet & Maxwell, London: 1981.

G. J. R. Hickmott MBE (ed.), *Interruption Insurance,* Gower, Aldershot: 1981.

R. L. Carter and G. N. Crockford, *Handbook of Insurance,* Kluwer-Harrap Handbooks, London: 1974.

7

Theft and All Risks Insurance

J. M. Seatter, Group Risk Manager, United Glass plc

THEFT

Property owners or those responsible for property should consider the vulnerability of their assets to theft. This will depend upon:

1 The type of industry.
2 The nature of the raw materials and components employed in the industry.
3 The attractiveness of these materials and in some cases the finished products to thieves, and the ease by which these goods can be passed into receptive markets.
4 The quality of the security measures taken by the owners.

Similar considerations apply in the case of wider cover given by means of 'all risks' insurance which is available for property of high value at particular risk to theft or damage, such as jewellery, works of art, office equipment, vending machines, computers, and the like.

THEFT ACT 1968

The crime of theft is defined in the Theft Act, 1968 which became law on 1 January 1969, replacing Section 1 of the 1916 Larceny Act. Under the Theft Act a person is guilty of theft if he dishonestly appropriates property belonging to another with the intention of permanently depriving the other of it. The expressions 'thief' and 'steal' are construed accordingly. Also the word 'dishonestly' is used instead of such expressions as 'with intent to defraud', and 'without claim or right made in good faith'. 'Appropriation' is taken to mean 'any assumption by a person of the rights of an owner', but an appropriation is not 'dishonest' if:

1   The person appropriating believes he has a right in law to deprive the owners.
2   There is a belief that the owner would consent if he knew of the appropriation and the circumstances of it.
3   There is belief that the owner cannot be discovered after reasonable steps have been taken.

The crime of 'robbery' is now understood to be the action of stealing where immediately before, or at the time of stealing, and in order to do so, the person uses force, or puts a person in fear, or tries to do so. An act of burglary under the Act consists of entering a building as a trespasser with intent to steal anything in that building, or damage the building, or inflict grievous bodily harm. This interpretation replaces the earlier concept of 'breaking and entering'. To commit a burglary a person must be *intent* on stealing from or committing similar crimes at the premises he is trespassing on although he may not in fact commit such an offence.

Other sections of the Theft Act deal with such matters as taking a motor vehicle without authority, theft of mail, blackmail, handling stolen goods, etc., but these are not the prime concern of this chapter.

SECURITY

Before reaching any final decisions on whether any insurance against theft is required, a company should first examine critically the security measures already in force. Some degree of protection is normally a prerequisite to any cover being offered by insurers, but at the same time the existence of security may reduce a company's need to rely upon insurance cover. Naturally an insurer's premium rates will be dependent on the protection and security measures adopted by the owners of the property. Where the insurer is not satisfied with the security, he may insist upon adequate safeguards being introduced at the insured's cost before cover is granted. In some cases where protection is below average, or where the insured is unwilling to introduce the insurer's recommendations, the insurer may insist upon the insured accepting part of the risk by way of coinsurance. Where a high risk is present for only a short period then an insurer may not be so adamant on pressing for the adoption of extensive security precautions, but his single premium will be above average in cost. The following points should be examined when assessing the security:

1   In what areas of operations are there attractive concentrations of desirable property in the form of raw materials, components, semi-finished products, finished goods or valuable manufacturing plant or equipment? Are these areas dispersed throughout the business?

2   What systems of control have been instituted to eliminate pilfering, stock deficiencies and stealing on a small but continuing scale in these areas?

3   Have housekeeping standards been reviewed? Has the intruder alarm system been modernised? Has the cost of the physical security measures been compared with that of surveillance by electronic means?

4   Is a measure of inevitable loss acceptable and has some financial appraisal been made of what amount is acceptable? Has the cost of loss protection been compared with the estimate of loss? Is the investment in protection a viable and economic proposition when compared with the cost of purchasing insurance?

It is more of a requirement today that some loss protection measures should be adopted by the prospective insured before the theft underwriter is prepared to consider the risk for insurance.

Various industries can be quoted as examples in considering the above alternatives. The food warehouse, the tobacco store and the wine and spirits store where high values coupled with ease of disposal into waiting markets make extensive security essential to protect the premises and the property. The television and hi-fi manufacturer has a maximum exposure in his finished product store, whilst the motor manufacturer may offer a target risk in his raw materials or components store. The steelworks or the oil refinery may offer a target to thieves in the spare parts store or the cashier's office. Commercial premises these days offer some attraction to thieves where calculators, electric typewriters and personal effects are left in open offices.

INSURANCE COVER AVAILABLE

The insurance cover provided for commercial and industrial premises in the modern theft policy is that of indemnity against loss of or damage to property caused by theft arising from entry to or exit from premises by forcible and violent means and also by persons who are on the premises as trespassers. There would be a strict interpretation of this wording as, for example, actions of pilfering or shoplifting are not covered. Any damage to commercial or industrial buildings or property in the course of such theft or attempted theft will normally be included in the policy cover.

The risks of embezzlement and taking money under false pretences, as encountered in business and commerce, are normally provided for under fidelity or money policies, and the loss of wages and other funds retained on business premises is dealt with under similar policies especially drafted by insurance companies to meet such concentrations of risk exposure. (See Chapters 8 and 9.)

It should be emphasised that the risk of theft by employees is not included within the terms of the 1968 Act.

The intention of an insurer under any form of cover is to avoid acceptance of those inevitable shortages which can arise in business where stock control is lax.

What then are the alternatives open to a company seeking the most economical protection?

In a very large concern having many different locations throughout the country and involved in primary industry, the cost of insuring large items of plant that cost tens of millions of pounds and many tons of raw materials or finished stock that are uninteresting to thieves is so great, even at a nominal premium rate, as to be economically unacceptable. There will inevitably be certain areas, however, where high values will be concentrated: the precious metals store, the factory safe, the cashier's office, the open office and the canteen bar being examples of this. Certain types of raw materials used in industrial processes have become very valuable commodities in their own right and markets for their disposal are readily available. Individual insurance might be sought to cover these types of exposure situated anywhere within the company's premises and within specified limits of value at each location. Such insurance can be tailored to each site's requirements.

The cost of insurance can be reduced by the acceptance of excesses or deductibles in respect of each loss whereby the company is its own insurer for say the first £100, £250 or £1,000 or any other figure negotiated with the insurers. There are also occasions where the insurer may not be satisfied with the risk as presented, and only be prepared to carry 80 per cent or 90 per cent of the risk, leaving the insured to be a coinsurer for the balance. By these underwriting features the insurer feels that he has retained the interest of the insured in the risk, whilst the insured is satisfied that he has taken prudent precautions to avoid exposure to substantial losses. In some cases the insurer may also be prepared to reduce the effect of the excess by limiting the number of excess amounts accepted within any one period of cover.

Another method that can be adopted to limit the cost of theft cover is to arrange insurance on a 'first-loss' basis, whereby the insured assesses the maximum likely loss at any one of his several premises or departments and arranges insurance accordingly, not overlooking the fact that the degree of exposure present at each location can affect the level of risk and therefore the maximum likely loss. The insurer would still seek assurances on security, but his premium charge would be lower than for cover provided on the full value of the property insured at all premises.

This form of insurance would be used by, for example, a chain of grocer shops, supermarkets, TV shops or jewellers where a total loss of stock cannot be envisaged. The insured would, however, be expected to disclose the estimated total value of his stock at any one time and the insurer would normally calculate the total premium on a combination of total value of stock, the value of 'first-loss' suggested and type of commodity.

The principle of 'average' would be applied by the insurer, in the event of loss, if the actual value of the property insured at time of loss was disclosed as being greatly in excess of the estimated figure originally advised. This would mean that any settlement based on the 'first-loss' sum insured would be reduced.

An example will probably make this clear. If the first-loss limit chosen was £5,000 for each premises, against an estimated total stock value of £500,000 and at the time of loss the total stock value was discovered to be £1,000,000, then insurers would claim that the insured was underinsured by 50 per cent and would only be prepared to settle for 50 per cent of the first-loss sum insured—in this example, £2,500.

In a company where the product and its components are extremely attractive, management probably will hold the view that theft insurance is an essential part of its budget, combined with the implementation of a degree of security.

There are industries such as parts of the retail trade, or the warehousing trade, where stocks are constantly under the threat of a major theft, perhaps even on a large scale if security is relaxed for a single moment. As an example, a building contractor's employees left a bank's premises temporarily for an unauthorised tea-break, leaving the important connecting door unlocked. Some well-informed burglars took advantage of this temporary removal of the defences to enter and rob the bank of £27,000 during its normal working hours.

When security has been provided (with or without insurance) it remains essential to ensure by regular maintenance procedures that all the protective devices, installed at some expense, will operate efficiently when the emergency arises. Technical advances, and the introduction of new devices might make it essential to up-date the security installation periodically. In recent years central alarm systems have been established by security alarm companies, as the police authorities have shown less interest in retaining alarm lines in their own stations. This may have been prompted by the growing number of false alarms to which the police have responded. The company should also anticipate the trends towards more violence, the use of firearms and the involvement of electronic experts or engineers.

Insurance considerations

As with many other insurance covers a completed proposal form is the basis of the contract and all facts upon which a theft underwriter could be expected to base his judgement must be disclosed. As emphasised above, information relating to existing security will be of high priority. This area will extend to questions on:

1 The nature and quality of locks, bolts and window catches, especially on skylights.
2 Times of occupancy and unoccupancy of the premises.
3 Automatic alarm systems installed.
4 Extent of security guard mounted during periods of unoccupancy.
5 Nature of the business and property to be insured, and estimated values at risk.

In addition questions on past loss experience will be asked including details of all losses or damage experienced due to theft over the last three or five years. In proposals of high risk on large values, insurance companies are likely to insist upon selective surveys of the insured's premises and known target areas will always be surveyed before a quotation is submitted. Acceptance of the risk may also be subject to the insurance company's recommended security arrangements being adopted, either before the cover is given or within a stated period afterwards. It is becoming more common for insurers to resurvey target risks periodically to keep their underwriting information up to date. Most insurers will include a warranty in their policy that the burglar alarm installed at the premises be efficiently maintained.

Insurers will be reluctant to accept risks where selection is made against them and in these cases the premium cost may appear to the proposer too expensive against the probable risk of loss. Such action may prompt the proposer to increase the effectiveness of his security, even if further capital expenditure is involved over the short term, in order to reduce or avoid an excessive continuing cost for insurance.

Insurance of retail premises

In certain categories of merchandising where many retail outlets are at risk the problem may be twofold:

1 How to assess the company's exposure to theft and the other

losses associated with retail shops, arising from shoplifting and stock deficiencies, the latter risks not being a proper subject for insurance.

2   Whether the cost of regular theft losses is to be met from insurance, or accepted as another operating overhead in running the business. It is obvious that where a regular pattern of theft losses is experienced, the insurance company will, over a period of years, aim to balance premiums against losses and maintain a margin of profit for itself by increasing premiums whenever an adverse claims experience justifies this. The operation of an excess will eliminate small losses, but the insurer's premium will be at such a level as to cover all anticipated losses and still carry a reserve for the unexpected large loss and allow for profit as well as expenses.

Policy wording

This section describes some of the features that are customarily included. The premises where cover applies are described in the schedule to the policy. Where there are several, then all the addresses will usually be shown in the policy or lodged with the insurance company. Invariably, property stored in the open, or in any outbuildings not forming part of the premises will be excluded, unless special arrangements are made with the insurers.

The liability of the insurance company will obviously not exceed the total sum insured specified in the policy or schedule and a typical description of the items covered by a simple policy might read as follows:

1   Stock and materials in trade the property of the insured or held by the insured in trust or on commission for which the insured is responsible.
2   Goods, other than those described in (1) held by the insured in trust or on commission, for which the insured is responsible consisting of: (description of goods).
3   Trade and office furniture, fixtures, fittings, plant, machinery, appliances and other contents, the property of the insured, or held in trust for which the insured is responsible, but excluding

stock. The term 'other contents' is understood to include:

(a) documents, manuscripts and books of accounts but only for the value of the materials as stationery together with the cost of clerical labour expended in writing up the information contained therein.

(b) computer systems records but only for the value of the materials together with the cost of clerical labour and computer time expended in reproducing such records (excluding any expenses in connection with the production of information to be recorded therein) and not for the value to the insured of the information contained therein.

Where some importance is attached to the value of documents and plans, then occasionally an insurer is prepared to broaden the insurance cover offered under 3 by an alternative wording which will provide for the reinstatement of documents, plans and writings, even to the inclusion of the cost of obtaining evidence of the contents of essential documents which cannot be reinstated. The insurer's liability in respect of any one deed, document, book, plan, paper or writing would be limited to an agreed sum (say £50). Any wider interpretation would have to be clarified and negotiated with the insurance company.

Of course no insurance policy would be complete without exceptions and conditions but the former in a theft policy are minimal, and the latter follow the normal pattern of any insurance contract. The exceptions would generally exclude most of the following:

1 Any property specifically insured under any other policy—for example, in a department store valuable jewellery might be insured separately under an 'all risks' cover.
2 War risks, riot or civil commotion.
3 Loss or damage arising from fire or explosion or which is normally covered under a plate glass insurance.
4 Loss or damage occasioned by a member of the insured's family, any employee of the insured, or any person who is lawfully on the insured premises.
5 Loss of or damage to particularly valuable items unless they are specifically mentioned in the policy. In this category would fall rare manuscripts and books, money, trade coupons or vouchers,

jewellery, watches, furs and precious stones. If any of these items are required to be included, then obviously the insurers would expect to be advised of the values involved and the additional security measures adopted to safeguard them.

6   Loss of or damage to tobacco and cigarettes, wines and spirits (unless these are included up to a certain limit as shown on the policy schedule or specially rated by the insurer).

Most insurers will also insert a condition establishing that their policy will not cover any loss of or damage to property in Northern Ireland caused by or in consequence of:

any unlawful wanton or malicious act committed by a person or persons acting on behalf of or in connection with any unlawful association. (An unlawful association means any organisation which is engaged in terrorism and includes an organisation which at any relevant time is a proscribed organisation within the meaning of the Northern Ireland (Emergency Provisions) Act, 1973.)

The general conditions in the policy would normally include the following basic clauses:

1   Instructions on procedure to be adopted in the event of loss. It is customary for notice to be given to insurers immediately any loss or damage is known to the insured, followed up within a stated period of time, usually fourteen or thirty days, by a more detailed statement of the various articles and goods stolen or damaged, supported by some evidence of value. It is also an essential part of this condition that notice is given at the same time to the police authorities.

2   A contribution clause.

3   The insured must exercise reasonable care in the selection and supervision of his employees.

4   The insured must make and keep secure all doors, windows and other means of entrance.

5   The average clause.

6   Stating that all sums paid out as claims under the policy would serve to diminish the sum insured under the policy during the same period of insurance, such that the insurers would not pay

out in any one period of cover sums in excess of the total sum insured.

7   Provision is made for insurers to refuse renewal and during currency of the policy to give reasonable notice of cancellation to the insured should they so desire, with provision for a proportionate return of premium to the insured.

8   Insistence by the insurers that the insured should maintain proper records of goods purchased or manufactured, or sold, or otherwise disposed of, and that in the absence of such documentation being maintained, the insurer would consider the insurance cover void. In a similar manner the insurer would expect to be advised of any material increase in risk by the insured during the currency of the cover, and that the insurance would only be maintained if the insurers had assented to such an increase in risk.

In addition to standard exceptions and conditions common to most insurers, there would naturally be additional endorsements to allow for special circumstances and to deal with any cover limitations, such as excesses and additional security measures.

Premium rating

It is not feasible in this chapter to offer any guidance on premium rating, as insurers differ in their assessments of exposure and the methods adopted to reduce it. Operating conditions can change rapidly, as can the loss experience of this class of insurance business. However, in the minimum risk areas of industry and commerce rates as low as 0.15 or 0.2 per cent can still be found for first-class risks, while rates of 10 and even 20 times this can be encountered in areas of high risk. Premium to the underwriter when he is first judging the risk is not the sole criterion; it is the attitude of responsibility adopted by the insured in the safeguarding of his property, and his approach to the implementation of security measures, which are paramount. The underwriter will also wish to study and evaluate the loss experience of the risk over at least the past 5 years, or even longer where losses have been numerous and substantial. If he is not satisfied on these points then there may be no rate which will compensate for the substantial moral and physical hazards.

There are times in the cycle of profitability within the insurance industry when some underwriters may place more importance upon increasing premium income than risking the loss of new business by pricing themselves out of the market, e.g. a period when interest rates are high may well make it attractive for the insurer to increase his premium volume by competing for new business through offering low rates. Such markets to an insured may be volatile and the risk to him is that if he suffers a series of losses, the insurer may turn him away or offer much increased terms on renewal. It is a matter for judgment, therefore, whether the low premiums are sufficiently attractive in the short term, as against the need for continuity of cover at higher rates over the long term.

'ALL RISKS' INSURANCE

The term 'all risks' does not imply that every risk of loss or damage is covered but is simply a phrase utilised by insurers to convey that the cover provided by this type of policy is wider than the normal fire or theft contract.

It is more usual to find a wording which refers to cover for 'accidental loss of or damage to the property insured' although wordings embracing 'loss of or damage howsoever caused' or 'all risks of loss or damage' are employed. Later mention is made of the specific exclusions in the policy incorporated in order to limit the cover.

As this is the widest form of property cover provided by insurers, the policy normally includes the risks of fire and extended perils referred to in Chapter 5 as well as the theft and accidental loss or damage risks referred to above.

Type of property insured

The goods and articles of value which are commonly the subject of this insurance are antiques and works of art such as paintings, and vending machines, photographic equipment, valuable and portable items of machinery, office equipment such as telephones, video units, desk calculators, electric typewriters and similar items, and any item having a high value in relation to its bulk. In this category of goods the risk of accidental loss or damage is as important as the theft risk. It is often the case when hiring individual items of equipment that the hirer accepts onerous hire terms which make it necessary for him to consider protecting his responsibilities for any damage to, or loss of the equipment while it is in his custody or control, by means of an 'all risks' cover. The lease document will indicate the extent of the hirer's responsibilities. When the economy is in a recession, industry turns more and more to the purchase of equipment by means of leasing through the finance companies and the banks. A common item which is the subject of leasing is the office vending machine.

A particular extensive and restrictive insurance clause which is not uncommon these days could include the following conditions:

1 The goods throughout the leasing period must be comprehensively insured at full replacement value by the lessee. 'Comprehensively' means that the property is to be insured against 'all risks' of loss or damage, as well as in respect of the public liability risk arising from its use. The lessee is also instructed to maintain public liability insurance on his business operations.

2 The insurance is to be free of any excess or deductible.

3 The goods shall remain the property of the owner and the insurance policy is to be endorsed to that effect.

4 The 'owner' is to be given 30 days notice by the lessee or his insurer of any variation in the terms, or of any intention to cancel the cover.

5 Evidence of insurance to be produced by the lessee within 10 days of the goods being in his possession, or at his risk, with supporting policies or premium receipts.

6 The lessee shall not do anything, or give rise to an omission which is contrary to the policy's terms.

7 The lessee shall notify the owner of any occurrence giving rise to a claim and shall ensure that any claim is promptly made in accordance with the terms of the policy. No settlement shall be made without the prior written consent of the owner.

'All risks' cover is often provided for risks associated with the trades of jewellers and furriers where it is extended to include not only the insured's stocks, but also articles passed out on approval, and customers' articles received for renovation or repair. The insurance on furs and jewellery can be arranged on a first-loss basis with the broader cover of 'all risks' being sought, rather than the more limited theft cover mentioned earlier in this chapter. One of the problems with this type of property is to establish the value in the event of loss, especially where a customer's goods are concerned. Security will certainly receive the insurer's close attention, as is natural where high values in small and easily disposable articles are involved. In certain circumstances the 'all risks' cover can also be extended to include the risk of transit.

Security

An important issue where 'all risks' insurance is involved, is the need for security to safeguard the property and for adequate precautions to be taken to protect property from accidental damage. Any prospective insurer will normally seek information on these aspects, and will be most reluctant to offer terms for cover unless he is satisfied that the insured intends to act in a responsible manner.

In this context information may be sought on such questions as:

1 Type and age of safes and strong rooms.
2 Values or amounts of cash normally kept in them.
3 Safeguarding of keys or combinations by staff.
4 Types of perimeter fencing and entrance gates. Methods of securing exits and entrances.
5 Control of access to the premises including offices and computer suite and to any plant yard or other vulnerable areas by outside contractors or customers and other third parties.

Policy wording

That normally adopted is particularly wide and provides indemnity in respect of damage to, or loss of, the insured property subject to certain general exclusions of which the following may be said to be typical:

1 All cash and bank notes.
2 Loss or damage caused by wear and tear, mechanical or electrical breakdown or derangement or atmospheric and climatic conditions.
3 Breakage of articles of a fragile nature such as china, glass, etc.
4 Loss or damage resulting from war, rebellion, revolution, civil war, etc. (On certain policies riot and civil commotion risks can be included, dependent upon circumstances.)
5 Any consequential loss.

Average would usually apply should the total value of insured property exceed the sum insured by the policy. There would also apply some geographical limitation, should the underwriter and the premium rate demand it—for example, restricted to United Kingdom only, or to Western Europe. 'Worldwide' cover can be obtained, usually at a much higher cost.

Money is usually excluded from the cover because it is normally insured under a separate cash policy (see Chapter 8), especially if commercial and industrial risks are involved. The risk of mechanical or electrical breakdown again is a cover provided in certain circumstances under engineering insurance, underwritten by specialist insurance offices, (see Chapter 13).

Valuation

One of the most important requirements of an insurer underwriting this class of business is evidence of value and this is often sought when the cover is first arranged in order to avoid any grounds for dispute in the event of loss.

COMPUTERS

'All risks' insurance can be provided on computer equipment by some of the larger insurance groups specialising in this risk. The cover, providing indemnity against loss of or damage to such property, can be extended to apply to not only the computer but its ancillary equipment such as air-conditioning plant, tape libraries, discs and electronic switchgear. Policy wordings are often very detailed and various warranties may be introduced. The exclusion of any loss or damage due to wear and tear, or gradual deterioration due to atmospheric conditions, or rust or corrosion, as already referred to on p. 152, is usually incorporated and is of particular significance for this type of equipment. A common warranty often makes it essential for the insured to retain in force a full maintenance service agreement on the computer with the manufacturer. Cover in respect of loss arising from any electrical or mechanical breakdown on such peripherals as the air-conditioning plant, the tapes and the switchgear would also be excluded from the insurance.

Variation of these more specialised 'all risks' covers will often arise and be catered for by specially adapted wordings introduced after discussions between insured and insurers to establish the scope of cover required.

BUSINESS INTERRUPTION INSURANCE

This form of insurance is primarily associated with fire perils, but the insurance market may be prepared to underwrite special situations where loss of gross profit can arise as a direct result of accidental damage, loss of property, theft or even malicious damage. Computers are one such area where business interruption flowing from the effects of an insured peril, such as accidental damage can be insured. The serious damage, or theft of a consignment of fashion goods is another example of a risk where the business interruption loss can be assessed over the short term and insured.

PACKAGE COVERS

There is an increasing tendency for various perils to be written under one single policy for a commercial undertaking. Such risks as fire, theft, damage, transit, cash-in-transit and fidelity guarantee can be covered under the same policy and at one annual premium. This is attractive to an insured as it avoids the issue of several policies and sometimes can offer wider cover.

FURTHER READING

F. Jones, FCII 'Property Insurance Underwriting and Claims' Chartered Insurance Institute Tuition Services 1981—Study Course 250.

D. E. Brigg and C. Bridges, *Burglary Protection & Insurance Surveys*, Stone & Cox (Publications) Ltd, 4th Edition, 1982.

8

Money Insurance

M. B. Skyrme,* Director, Stewart Wrightson (Midlands) Ltd

MONEY

Loss of cash by theft is still increasing. There is, however, a growing public awareness of the need for greater preventative security measures, coupled with the sensible precaution of insuring against the risk of loss of money.

One of the largest growth industries in the United Kingdom since the second world war has been the security industry. Specialist cash in transit security carriers are now widely used for the movement of money and securities. This service both protects the businessman's money and removes the danger of injury by criminal assault to his employees whilst the money is in transit.

Whether or not a security carrier is employed, the modern form of money insurance provides very good protection for the prudent businessman and its structure is explained in this chapter.

SCOPE OF COVER

The most usual type of policy available will provide an indemnity against the loss of money belonging to the insured (or for which he is responsible) within certain situations and circumstances. It is

*Revised for this edition by P. F. Talbot, Group Insurance Manager, The De La Rue Company plc.

basically an all risks policy and the cover will normally include losses occurring e.g. in the following situations, each of which may be subject to varying limits of indemnity:

1   In the insured's business premises. Varying limits apply within and outside business hours with and without safe.
2   At any of the insured's sites of contract (during business hours); it is possible to obtain cover for cash on sites outside business hours, although insurers will insist upon its being contained in a locked receptacle and a low limit of cover is normally imposed.
3   In the residences of the insured's principals, directors or employees.
4   In course of transit.
5   In a bank's night safe.
6   In the hands of representatives and collectors.
7   In the hands of representatives when travelling abroad.

Items 6 and 7 are not automatically included: a special extension may have to be obtained.

The insurance normally extends to include the loss of or damage to safes or strongrooms belonging to the insured (or for which he is responsible) caused by theft or attempted theft.

Policy extensions

Dishonest employees

It is customary for a modern money policy to include losses of money caused by the dishonesty of employees unless more specifically insured. Such cover is not meant to be an alternative to fidelity guarantee insurance which is dealt with later in Chapter 9. This extension is subject to the dishonesty being discovered within a certain time-limit which in some policies can be as little as 48 hours or, in others, as long as 30 days (more in unusual cases). The most common time-limit is 7 days. This extension is normally incorporated in the basic policy wording and is taken into consideration in calculating the premium.

Injuries to employees

For the payment of a relatively small additional premium it is possible to extend the policy to provide financial compensation for employees injured by assault when carrying or in charge of cash or securities. The benefits can be designed in various ways but will basically cover:

1　An agreed lump sum in the event of death.
2　An agreed lump sum for injuries resulting in the loss of limbs or eyesight.
3　Weekly benefit for temporary or permanent total disablement from engaging in usual occupation.

Many policies also provide compensation up to an agreed amount for damage to or loss of clothing through assault.

Peak trading periods

Where seasonal trading trends produce substantial variations in the amounts of cash handled it is possible to design the policy in such a way that it automatically increases the standard indemnity limits at suitable periods. It is thus possible to avoid underinsurance at peak periods without having to advise the insurers at the time and without incurring more premium than is absolutely necessary.

POLICY RESTRICTIONS AND EXCLUSIONS

Some of the most common exclusions are summarised as follows:

1　Shortages due to error or omission.
2　Loss destruction or damage arising from dishonesty of any employee,
　　(a)　Unless discovered within seven working days (this period can vary between insurers) of its occurrence.
　　(b)　Insured under a fidelity guarantee policy.
3　Loss destruction or damage resulting from a safe or strongroom being opened by the use of a key or combination code left on the premises whilst closed for business.
4　Losses due to depreciation in value.

5 Loss destruction or damage caused by
  (a) Ionising radiations or contamination by radioactivity.
  (b) The radioactive toxic explosive or other hazardous properties of any explosive nuclear assembly.
  (c) War invasion etc.
  (d) Confiscation, nationalisation or requisition by any government or public authority.
  (e) Pressure waves caused by aircraft and other aerial devices travelling at sonic or supersonic speeds.

6 Losses arising outside the limits of Great Britain, Ireland, Northern Ireland, the Isle of Man or the Channel Islands (where required it is possible to extend the policy beyond these territorial limits).

7 Loss from an unattended vehicle.

8 The consequence of riot or civil commotion occurring in Ireland or Northern Ireland (it has been possible to have this exclusion removed in return for the payment of an additional premium).

All policies providing cover against loss of money also carry a standard condition requiring the reporting of losses to the insurer as soon as possible together with immediate notification to the police.

As in all policies of insurance the contract relies upon the insured providing complete and truthful answers to questions contained on the proposal form. Failure to comply with this requirement or any attempt to falsify a declaration or statement of claim will jeopardise the cover and could well make the contract of insurance voidable by the insurer. This of course is equally applicable to any subsequent material changes in the risk.

SECURITY ASPECTS

Although the use of security specialist companies and modern security equipment has helped to control the number and severity of cash losses, they are nevertheless on the increase. Through vigilance and development of techniques every effort must be made to keep ahead of criminal ingenuity.

If a security firm is used, many accept responsibility for the cash handled and consequently it is possible to negotiate a reduced rate with insurers. However, to guard against any possible dispute as to liability or the insolvency of a security firm at the time of a loss it is considered best to arrange for the money policy to deal with all claims and for recoveries received through security contracts to be repaid to the insurers. This would also overcome the problem of ensuring that there is no gap between the company's own policy and the extent of responsibility of the security carrier.

The choice of adequate safes is most important. Unfortunately safes claiming to be 'fire resisting' are not always a suitable deterrent to the criminal. Insurers have therefore become more particular over the selection of the type used and it is most important to seek their guidance before purchasing or replacing a safe.

In general, insurers have reached a stage in their approach to security measures where they may seem to be unreasonable but their experience has clearly shown that neglect in today's circumstances will almost inevitably lead to unwelcome losses.

In many cases insurers will impose specific warranties on their policies concerning security. A familiar example is the 'key warranty' which requires the insured to carry out proper routine security procedures relating to the safe custody of safe or strongroom keys. Failure to comply with such warranties might prejudice the cover and the payment of a claim could be refused.

The proper selection and supervision of employees is a standard condition of money policies and again any neglect of this duty could invalidate the insurance.

DEFINITIONS

The most important factor requiring definition is the term 'money' and policies usually include the following items and sometimes more: coin, bank and currency notes, cheques, Giro cheques, postal orders, money orders, bankers drafts, current postage and revenue stamps, used or unused National Insurance stamps, National Savings certificates, Luncheon Vouchers, premium bonds, credit card sales vouchers, trading stamps, VAT invoices.

Although it is desirable to include crossed cheques in the cover, arrangements can be made to exclude their value from the annual return made for premium calculation purposes.

If National Insurance stamps are still in use it is desirable to have a separate item for 'stamps affixed to cards' with an unlimited amount as the sum insured. This is particularly necessary where large numbers of cards are held.

It is always possible to have the definition extended in the event of such a list not being wide enough. Some insurers are prepared to agree a shortened but more widely embracing definition avoiding the use of specific descriptions.

'Business hours' is defined as the period during which the insured's premises are occupied for business purposes and during which the insured or his employees entrusted with money are on the premises.

POLICY RATING

Premiums are normally calculated on the total estimated carryings in the course of a year, the rate being charged at so much per £1,000 (per mille) carried.

Rates vary considerably and depend upon the size, nature and location of risk. Recent years have seen a rapid increase in these rates and it is desirable to obtain several quotations before effecting cover so that full advantage is taken of current market variations.

Adjustment of premium

This is usually undertaken once a year at the end of each period of insurance. The insured is required to declare the actual amounts carried or held during the immediate past year. The premium rating is then applied to this figure and an adjustment premium is calculated in favour of the insured or insurer as the case may be. In the event of a substantial increase being experienced in the annual figure due to a general trend in business the initial provisional premium charged at the beginning of the policy year may be increased appropriately. In this way the revised renewal premium more accurately reflects the annual value of the policy, is more reliable for estimate or budget purposes and minimises the size of the end of the year's adjustment premium.

9

Fidelity, Bonds, Guarantees and Credit Insurance

The late B. F. Conner,* Manager, Group Insurance & Risk Department, Barclays Bank Group

FIDELITY GUARANTEE INSURANCE

All employers need to consider the risk of loss through the infidelity of employees, particularly in respect of those personnel who have control of or access to wages or other monies, accounts or stock.

It is possible to introduce and develop checking systems which will actively discourage fraud or dishonesty but it is virtually impossible to eliminate temptation or opportunity altogether. There are many cases on record of heavy losses (tens of thousands of pounds) suffered through the dishonesty of relatively senior and hitherto trusted staff. Too many people in certain special circumstances are unable to resist temptation if discovery seems unlikely. History shows that the majority of claims arising under fidelity guarantee insurance relate to the activities of honest people who have succumbed to temptation under severe social or emotional pressures. Even the most humane and understanding employer cannot, however, conduct his business with the financial erosion introduced by such defaulters. Therefore, the prudent employer cannot ignore the protection afforded by a specific fidelity guarantee policy or, in the case of a bank or other form of financial institution a blanket bond, a wider insurance embracing in addition other operational risks, which will be explained later.

*The author was indebted to M. B. Skyrme for material retained from the previous edition.

Setting up the insurance

Some employers find it difficult to consider effecting fidelity guarantee insurance for fear of upsetting apparently trustworthy employees and creating an atmosphere of suspicion. However, explanation of the sound commercial sense behind the idea will invariably satisfy any indignant employees. In the long term it is probably best to advertise the decision widely as a demonstration of concern over security and control systems.

The fundamental principle of this form of insurance is that it represents a guarantee by the insurer. For this to have been offered it is necessary for the insurer to be familiar with the personal histories of those to whom the guarantee applies and for those histories to be of a satisfactory nature. Extensive enquiries are undertaken and the employment record is established from the employee concerned. This is verified by reference to previous employers, who may or may not divulge important and sometimes unwelcome information. Gaps in employment have to be explained satisfactorily. In certain cases, such as in blanket policies, the duty of obtaining suitable references is often transferred from the insurer to the employer.

Once the enquiries are complete it is usually possible for the insurer to reach a decision and either decline the application or offer the required cover.

In the event of a declinature where insurers have themselves taken up references they will not normally explain in detail why the proposal was unacceptable as the information they have received is confidential. However, insurers will normally indicate specifically their inability to bond a particular person if the refusal to provide cover is due to incomplete information. Then it may be possible to obtain alternative referees from the employee concerned in order to assist insurers in giving further consideration to the proposal. If an employee is not acceptable to insurers any further action is in the hands of the employer.

Unless the securing of satisfactory references is the responsibility of the employer, such as in the blanket form of policy, it is not normal for cover to apply until insurers have confirmed acceptance, and it might be advisable to take this fact into consideration when recruiting staff who are to be responsible for cash. It may be possible for references to be taken up in the period between engaging a new employee and the date he actually commences his employment, such employment being subject to satisfactory references.

An insurer's refusal to bond any particular employee will not prevent cover being offered for other more acceptable employees.

Scope of cover

The structure of a typical policy is quite simple. It will require the insurer to make good any financial loss incurred by the insured through the fraudulent or dishonest acts of the insured's employees. Such losses will cover both money and goods and will therefore include stock. Simple though the basic cover may be it is necessary to appreciate the following specific points.

What is covered

Modern policies will include cover not only for money and goods belonging to the insured but also for money and goods for which he is responsible (this is important for firms such as solicitors who hold substantial amounts of clients' money).

Discovery period

There are two particular periods to consider:

1 The period between the date of the misappropriation and the date of its discovery.
2 The period between the date of the death, dismissal or retirement of the employee concerned or the cancellation of the policy and the discovery of the misappropriation.

It is clearly desirable to secure a lengthy discovery period and this will be found to vary between insurers, ranging between six and eighteen months.

Prolonged defalcation

Many of the larger losses experienced are those which relate to prolonged defalcation; therefore it is important to purchase cover which does not limit losses to those sustained during the year immediately before the discovery date.

Reinstatement

It is customary to agree a financial limit of liability in the policy and it is usual, in the event of a claim, for the 'sum insured' to be reduced by the value of the claim until the next renewal date. However, it is possible to obtain an interim reinstatement to the full amount from inception and this may be particularly desirable for large diverse organisations.

It is unlikely that insurers will grant reinstatement of the amount of guarantee on individual policies for an employee who has already defaulted. Reinstatement normally applies only in the case of guarantees on a floating or blanket basis.

Types of policy

There are four main forms of fidelity guarantee policy issued by insurers: individual, collective, floating and blanket.

Individual. The policy is issued to cover one named employee with a specified limit of guarantee and is suitable if the number of staff to be bonded is limited.

Collective. If the number of staff to be bonded is larger, a policy embracing a schedule naming individual employees, their occupations and the amounts of guarantee is considered more suitable.

Floating. This is basically a collective policy but, instead of individual limits of guarantee, one sum is quoted and this is the total amount for which insurers are liable, however many employees or defaults are involved.

Blanket. The most modern form of policy is one where the schedule covers all employees or defines only the categories of staff to be bonded. No individual names are mentioned and the limit of guarantee operates on the same basis as in the floating policy.

Variations to the arrangements can be designed to fit particular circumstances although the theme will remain basically similar to the types described above.

For larger organisations, the blanket type of policy reduces administration by avoiding the need to declare individual staff changes. In such cases, however, insurers will expect the employer to take up references for specified periods for new employees in a manner affording a check equal to that undertaken by insurers for individual policies.

Variations and extensions

Sharing the risk with the insurer

The main variation to this type of insurance has been introduced to cater for employers (normally of substantial size) who elect to retain part of the risk to their own account. In such cases it has proved possible to effect what might be called 'excess of loss' cover, which will only be concerned with losses occurring within a certain financial band. A typical example might be where an employer prefers to carry his own risk up to £5,000 but wishes to effect the guarantee for losses between £5,000 and say £100,000 or more.

Although loss settlements become a little more complicated the savings in premium are clearly the principal attraction and some insurers welcome such an arrangement, which involves the insured more directly with the importance of good security measures.

Counter-indemnities

If the employment of an individual is subject to effecting an insurance guarantee and the employee is not suitable for bonding by the insurer, it is sometimes possible to effect the guarantee nevertheless. An insurer may be prepared to offer cover provided it is possible to find someone who, in turn, is prepared to guarantee the insurer's indemnity against any loss.

Such counter-indemnities may well be in the nature of deposited property deeds or other securities. In the exceptional cases an insurer may accept a purely personal undertaking but in all cases the insurer will have to be granted the power of realising on the additional security in the event of a claim arising.

The introduction of a counter-indemnity does not affect the position at common law in that it maintains the insurer's right of recovery against the offending employee.

Auditors' fees

Some policies include in their cover the cost of any special audit carried out, with the agreement of the insurers, for the purpose of establishing and measuring a claim.

Policy restrictions

These vary between insurers and depend, in some cases, upon the extent of security and control measures introduced by the insured.

A few insurers still include a prosecution clause in their contract requiring the insured employer to prosecute an offending employee should the insurance company so wish. However, it is now generally considered better to leave the question of prosecution entirely in the hands of the employer as he can then escape the unwelcome publicity accompanying legal proceedings and is able to respond sympathetically to cases in which the guilty person has been subject to particularly powerful pressures. The employer must nevertheless retain, and possibly demonstrate, his ultimate right to prosecute as a deterrent to others.

There are still a few policies which relate only to the misappropriation of money belonging to the employer and it is therefore important to select a cover that does not exclude loss of stock if this is required.

As in all forms of insurance there are standard conditions relating to the operation of a fidelity guarantee policy. These include the procedure required in reporting claims and a clause dealing with the withholding of material facts, breach of which will invariably void the guarantee. Similarly, it should be recognised that most proposal forms incorporate questions on the basic accounts and auditing systems and any variation introduced subsequently should be advised to the insurers to avoid possible invalidation of the policy.

Rating structure

The basis of rating is normally a percentage charged on the amount of guarantee. The size of the rate depends upon the amount of guarantee and the attractiveness (or otherwise) of the 'risk'. In the case of floating or blanket policies a per capita charge is made on the number of employees and is added to the basic percentage charged on the amount of guarantee.

Although there are quite extensive variations in rates these are only brought about by the differing nature and size of the risk. There is no question of increasing a rate to include an applicant with a doubtful background: he remains unacceptable at any premium.

The rating of individual policies is often higher than that for collective policies. Reductions in premium can be obtained by the employer taking an excess as described previously.

Limit of guarantee

Choosing the amount to be guaranteed can be a difficult task but is one which should be approached by assessing the following principal factors:

1 The size of the business, its complexity and the relationships between various subsidiary or associated companies.
2 The value of cash and cheques handled and the nature and value of stock.
3 The ability or otherwise of the auditors to maintain frequent and reliable check systems both in relation to cash or cheque handling and to stock control.
4 Consideration of the possibility of long-term defalcation.

It is not possible to indicate any reliable method of determining the correct amount but it should be appreciated that e.g. doubling the amount of cover would by no means double the cost, and this should encourage the fixing of sensibly high limits.

Although it is obviously of great importance to select the correct amount it is perhaps not generally appreciated that the most valuable aspect of this type of insurance is the careful scrutiny of the applicant by the insurer or, where required, by the employer.

Local government guarantees

These are wider in scope than the commercial fidelity guarantees discussed above and usually require the insurer to be responsible for the proper discharge of the employee's duties in addition to his honesty. Local authorities frequently find it necessary to obtain guarantees to cover their duties under legislation. An example of these would be the duty of supplying accurate and reliable information concerning road charges etc.

BANKERS' BLANKET BONDS

Banks and other financial institutions have money, securities and other valuable paper as their basic stock-in-trade and thus have special needs for the protection of their operations. Whilst these needs could be met in part by separate fidelity guarantee, theft and forgery policies, with separate policies gaps in cover could exist and it is therefore usually considered more advantageous to effect a bankers' blanket bond which combines, under one insurance, cover for the major risks involved.

Setting up the insurance

The insurers require full underwriting information and this is normally obtained through a completed proposal form. The various sections of a typical form seek the following details:

1   The financial structure of the bank or company, the nature of its operations and the number of customers' accounts held. Particular attention is paid to inactive accounts, which are usually defined as those having no movements in or out during

the preceding twelve months; such accounts offer temptations for the dishonest employee.

2   Number of staff and locations. Unlike for the fidelity guarantee proposal form, personal histories of the staff are not required as it is known that the banks and financial institutions place great importance on the selection and control of their employees.

3   Maximum values at risk at the various locations.

4   Limits of indemnity required, together with brief details of any existing blanket fidelity insurance and information on any previous declinatures or cancellations of such insurance and the reasons.

5   Loss experience for the preceding, say, five years, together with information on corrective measures taken to avoid the recurrence of any substantial loss.

6   Security. This is the largest section of the form and deals with procedures and controls, internal and external audits, physical security for premises, and arrangements for the protection of cash and valuables in transit. Special questions are asked in respect of any safe deposit installations.

The form when completed is required to be signed by three senior officials, the general manager, chief accountant and security officer.

Scope of cover

A bankers' blanket bond normally covers direct financial loss, as defined in the insuring clauses of the policy, sustained by the insured subsequent to a specified date (the 'retroactive date') and discovered during the policy period subject, of course, to the policy exclusions, limitations and conditions, the limits of indemnity and the amount of any deductible which the insured has agreed to bear.

There is a very wide definition for the property covered and this includes cash, bullion, precious metals and stones, securities, cheques and other negotiable instruments, documents, and the insured's books of account and other records. The cover applies not only to the insured's own property, and property in which they have an interest, but also to property for which they are responsible.

The usual insuring clauses are:

1 *Infidelity of employees.* Covering dishonest or fraudulent acts of employees committed with the manifest intent of making, and which result in, improper personal financial gain for themselves.
2 *Premises risks.* Loss from the insured's premises, or the premises of any other bank, through theft etc., false pretences and mysterious unexplainable disappearance, as well as damage, destruction or misplacement however caused. The clause extends to include such losses of property whilst in the possession of a customer when on the insured's premises.
3 *Transit risks.* Cover under this clause is restricted to loss of or damage to property whilst in transit in the custody of any employee or of any security or armoured motor vehicle company, subject to the contractual arrangements and any specific insurance arrangements made with the carrier.
4 *Forged cheques.* Loss through the forgery or fraudulent alteration of cheques, promissory notes and other specified negotiable instruments. The clause does not cover forgery losses involving items which are genuinely signed or endorsed but are false as to contents.
5 *Conterfeited currency.* Loss through the acceptance in good faith of any counterfeited or altered paper currency or coin of the country in which the insured's office sustaining the loss is located.
6 *Damage to offices and contents.* Damage to the insured's offices and loss of or damage to specified contents, caused by burglary etc., vandalism or malicious mischief.

It is possible to add further insuring clauses by endorsement of the policy. These may be standard printed endorsements, such as that which extends the forgery cover to include securities or written instruments, and the safe deposit legal liability cover, or specially negotiated extensions.

Policy limits and deductibles

Most banks and financial institutions find it difficult to decide on the levels of indemnity which will give them adequate cover. The policy is not subject to average nor a requirement that the sum insured shall represent the full value of the property covered and it is therefore necessary to fix the limits according to the exposures under the various insuring clauses. So far as premises and transit risks are concerned the exposures to loss are a matter of fact and the real problem lies with the fraud risk, whether this be through acts of employees or others. There is no definite formula but guidance on minimum requirements can usually be obtained from general past experience in the countries where the organisation operates. Bankers blanket bonds have fairly substantial limits of indemnity and it is therefore often necessary to structure them on a layered basis; with such an arrangement the top layers can be purchased relatively cheaply in comparison with the cost of the primary section of the cover.

The insurers expect the insured to share in the risks involved and will therefore impose a minimum deductible amount for each and every loss sustained. Such deductibles are often increased voluntarily by the insured to such an extent that the protection given by the bankers blanket bond is regarded as catastrophe cover.

Conditions and exclusions

The policy specifies various conditions precedent to liability which require the insured to observe certain procedures in the interests of risk control and loss prevention. These are measures which would already be taken by any prudent bank and include the dual control of cash and valuable paper, keys to safes and vaults, and codes, cyphers and test keys, and an annual internal audit, examination and review of internal controls. A further important condition is that each employee must be required to take an uninterrupted holiday of at least two weeks in each calendar year.

The general exclusions include items such as losses resulting from the act or default of any director of the insured, cashiers' shortages, credit or charge cards, and trading losses.

Loss of or damage to property in customers' safe deposit boxes is only covered as part of the employee infidelity insuring clause, or under a safe deposit legal liability insurance extension.

Two further important exclusions which should be mentioned are extortion losses and computer fraud losses. Extortion losses can be covered either as an extension of a bankers' blanket bond or by purchasing a specific policy for this purpose. The bond will only insure those computer fraud losses which fall within the scope of the employee infidelity insuring clause. However, an important change in the banks and financial institutions insurance market has been the introduction of computer fraud cover to complement the bankers blanket bond but underwritten as a separate policy.

Premiums

The bankers' blanket bond is a specialised form of cover provided by specialist underwriters who will base their premiums on their own requirements. The main determining factors are the general underwriting information presented by the proposer, including past loss experience, the scope of cover and limits of indemnity and deductibles, and general market experience.

OTHER BONDS AND GUARANTEES

This section deals with the diverse subject of other bonds and guarantees that are required both privately and commercially. Because of the large number involved and their individual complexity it is only possible to provide a brief explanation of some of the more familiar types normally available from insurance companies or surety companies etc. They are dealt with in alphabetical order.

Administration bonds

The Administration of Estates Act 1971 provided that, as from 3 January 1972, administration bonds (previously required where no will had been left or where it was defective) would not be required. However, in certain circumstances listed in the Non-Contentious Probate (Amendment) Rules 1971 (SI 1971/1977) a guarantee is required.

Auctioneers' bonds

Where an auction of property or estates has been directed by a court the auctioneer will be appointed by the High Court. A bond is normally required (and usually at short notice) to ensure that the auctioneer will account for purchase or deposit money and the amount of bond will vary according to the value of the property to be sold.

Bankruptcy bonds

The Department of Trade and Industry requires these from trustees and special managers in bankruptcy appointed under the relevant Acts. These officials have a duty to protect creditors' interests and are obliged to offer security (the bond) for the due performance of their duties.

Chancery guarantees

Receivers (or receivers and managers) appointed by the Chancery Division of the High Court are required to provide security to that Division in relation to an action in that Court. It might, for example, be necessary to establish the rights of different classes of debenture holders in a company. While the action is being decided it becomes the receiver's duty to safeguard the company's assets.

There are other types of guarantee given to the Chancery Division, one of the more familiar being that of a guardian dealing with the estate of a minor.

Cheque signing indemnities

Where a company uses a machine for cheque signing the bankers concerned will normally require an indemnity. Insurance can be obtained to cover this liability subject to satisfactory information on the security control exercised over the use of the machine.

Court of Protection bonds

Where a person suffers a mental deficiency or is of advanced age and unable to manage his own affairs the Court of Protection will appoint a receiver. The duties and power of the receiver are clearly laid down and the bond provides a guarantee of the proper performance of those duties and powers and is given to the Court of Protection.

Customs and Excise bonds

Merchants, shippers and traders are required to provide such bonds to HM Customs and Excise to protect the possible loss of revenue because of the improper use or handling of items which are subject to duty.

There are a large number of these bonds, which vary in relation to the commodity or goods handled. The bonds themselves are prepared by the Commissioners of Customs and Excise according to their own specification. The insurer will be concerned particularly with the financial standing and past record of the applicant.

Defective title indemnities

In the sale and purchase of land and property difficulties often arise through the vendor being unable to establish an acceptable title. Subject to satisfactory information, the matter can usually be resolved by the issue of an insurance indemnity.

Such problems are particularly associated with land when a purchaser has to rely upon a possessory title established by adverse possession. In considering the risk the insurers will require copies of plans, abstracts of title, deeds and other relevant documents, as well as statutory declarations which describe and confirm positive acts of adverse possession over a period of years. Where a possessory title has been registered at HM Land Registry copies of declarations sworn at the time of registration will also be required.

Forged transfer indemnities

These indemnities are issued in respect of transfers of registered stocks and shares issued by public companies and local authorities. If a transfer is made against a forged certificate and the holding is subsequently transferred again, the company or local authority is precluded from deleting from its register the name of the last transferee and must reinstate the name of the owner whose signature was originally forged. To rectify the position an appropriate number of shares must be bought and the cost is covered by a forged transfer indemnity.

The indemnity will also cover legal liability for errors and losses and damage relating to the register and security documents.

Missing beneficiaries indemnities

These indemnities protect executors, administrators or trustees who would otherwise be unable to discharge their duties in the distribution of a deceased person's estate or a trust fund owing to the inability to trace the whereabouts of one or more of the beneficiaries.

In considering an enquiry, the insurers will often seek legal advice in cases of doubt or difficulty and a proposer may be required to make a statutory declaration regarding the facts of the matter.

Those who will benefit by the issue of the indemnity are likely to be required to execute a specific agreement to refund to the insurers rather than the insurers relying on the exercise of subrogation rights.

Missing documents indemnities

Indemnities can be obtained in respect of documents such as registered share and stock certificates, life assurance policies and title deeds which have been lost or accidentally destroyed.

Performance bonds

Many types of bonds or guarantees could be described as performance bonds, but the most familiar is a form of guarantee that offers protection to an employer against the failure of a contractor to complete a contract.

It is no longer safe to assume that because the contractor's name is nationally respected he is immune from those difficulties causing the large number of financial failures experienced over recent years. Competition, spiralling wage claims, credit squeezes, high interest rates and failure of major subcontractors can all expose a contractor to the possibility of failure. The guarantee of proper performance is therefore of the utmost importance to the employer. The cost of the bond depends largely upon the type and size of the work undertaken and upon the reputation and standing of the applicant. Consequently, it is not possible to indicate the level of costs normally experienced.

If a bond is required by a subsidiary company it is frequently necessary for a counter-indemnity to be obtained from its ultimate parent company. This gives the surety more opportunity for control and the benefit of co-operation from the parent company should the subsidiary run into serious financial difficulties.

Further bonds can be obtained to protect against the failure of contractors to supply raw materials etc. or to guard against the deterioration of agreed standards of performance of machinery and apparatus etc.

Public Trustee bonds

In administering an estate the Public Trustee will often entrust local estate agents with the collection of rents etc. The estate agent is required to give security in connection with money or property which he has (or should have) received. The bond itself is prepared by the Public Trustee's Department.

Restrictive covenant indemnities

These indemnities are most commonly issued in connection with the sale or lease of property where particular clauses in the agreement may impose obligations and restrictions. Problems with restrictive covenants often occur, for example, with the sale of building land which by redevelopment would undergo a change of use. Such change might be prohibited by a covenant and if the position cannot be remedied by obtaining a release from the covenant the problem can usually be solved by the issue of an indemnity.

CREDIT INSURANCE

The main purpose of this form of insurance is to protect traders and manufacturers against financial losses caused by the insolvency or 'protracted default' of their customers, anywhere in the world, to whom credit terms have been granted either for the sale of goods or for the completion of work. ('Protracted default' is the failure to pay an admitted debt for goods delivered on credit terms within 90 days of the due date—excluding non-payment brought about by political causes.)

Policies traditionally require the insured to retain part of the risk himself, the more speculative the business the bigger the proportion which will remain at the risk of the insured. The usual amount covered by the insurer is between 75 and 85 per cent of the total risk.

Recent years have seen a considerable growth in the number of financial casualties in business and the demand for this form of insurance has consequently become well established.

Scope of cover

There are two main types of policy: 'whole turnover' and 'specific account'.

Whole turnover

As the title suggests this applies to the whole of the insured's business or alternatively the whole of his business in specialised markets when the business is of a diverse nature.

Policies are usually issued on a perpetual basis from an agreed date but notice of termination can be given by either party on the anniversary date (normally taking effect from the following anniversary date). Cover will apply to those deliveries made or work done on or after the commencement date but will not apply to any existing liability. The insurers will agree a limit of credit up to which the insured has complete discretion but should he wish to offer credit above that sum then approval must first be obtained from the insurer. Similar approval is required for new customers.

Specific account

This policy is more selective in that it is issued to deal with one or more named customers and in those cases where only a single credit transaction takes place.

The cover will apply to deliveries made, or work done, within a twelve-month period but it is not necessary for insolvency to take place during that period in order to establish a claim. A limit of credit is selected by the insured but has to be agreed by the insurer who, after enquiry, may even deny cover altogether. Although the insurer may cover fresh deliveries under established contracts he will never offer cover for deliveries made before the proposal was submitted.

Operating requirements

For whole turnover policies, a turnover declaration has to be made every three months. Single totals will be sufficient but separate totals will be necessary for each country outside the UK.

Written notice must be given to the insurer normally when an account is three months overdue.

Extended credit (beyond three months) can be given with the agreement of the insurer.

Variations and extensions

Variations to the two main types of policy mentioned above include:

Work-in-progress policy. This will cover losses on work-in-progress under a contract due to the insolvency of the party for whom the work is being done.

Anticipatory credit policy. This will cover the loss of money paid for goods to suppliers in anticipation of future deliveries, if the loss is caused by the supplier's insolvency.

Resale loss policy. This will deal with losses incurred on the resale of goods which were to be supplied to a customer on cash terms, but which cannot be delivered because of the customer's insolvency.

One of the principal insurers of this type of policy also offers a debt collection service in the UK for debts on which a credit insurance cover has been effected.

Policy restrictions and exclusions

Credit insurance policies normally contain a condition allowing the insurer to terminate or reduce the cover on any customer or country in the event of adverse information becoming available. This condition will not normally apply to deliveries made during the period of the policy under sale contracts that are binding upon the insured at the time he receives notice of termination from the insurer.

The following is a list of exclusions which will normally be found in a standard form of credit policy:

1 Deliveries to government departments, public authorities or nationalised bodies.
2 Deliveries to individuals.
3 Deliveries to customers whom the insurer will not insure.
4 Deliveries to subsidiary or associated companies of the insured company.
5 Deliveries that are paid for before or at the time of delivery.

Definitions

The following is a short list of the most frequently used terms requiring definition.

Insolvency will exist when any of the following steps have been taken either by the insured or by a court or when some step has been taken which, under the law of the court having jurisdiction, is equivalent to any of the following steps under English law:

1 Adjudication in bankruptcy against the customer.
2 Approval by the court of a composition or scheme of arrangement after a receiving order has been made against the customer.
3 Making of a valid assignment, composition or other arrangement by the customer for the benefit of his creditors generally.

4   Making of an order against the customer for a winding up by the court.
5   Passage of an effective resolution for the voluntary winding up of the customer.
6   Making of an arrangement or compromise that is binding upon the customer and all his creditors.
7   Appointment of a receiver on behalf of debenture holders or other creditors of the customer.

Protracted default exists when a customer, having accepted delivery of goods, fails to pay such part of any insured debt as relates thereto at the end of a period of 90 days after the due date or, if the original due date has been postponed, at the end of a period of 90 days after the postponed due date.

Salvage means moneys (including dividends paid or payable out of an insolvent estate), securities, indemnities, guarantees, rights of action, counterclaim or set-off, or other advantages held by the insured or otherwise available for the purpose of reducing the amount of any indebtedness of an insured customer which has not been paid at the date of the 'insolvency' or the date for notification.

Rating structure

It is not possible for insurers to quote rates without first having regard to bad-debt records, periods of credit taken by customers and the quality of customers.

In the 'whole turnover' policy the rate is charged on the turnover figure. The 'specific account' policy rate can either be charged in the same way or, in certain cases, the rate is governed by the time which the insurer is on risk.

It is normal for an insurer to request the payment of a minimum and deposit premium once the policy is issued.

Availability of cover

Unlike most insurances credit insurance is not widely available and in view of its special considerations the use of a reputable specialist broker is indicated to select the most suitable insurer from the short list available and to advise on any newer forms of cover. One of the leading insurers is the Trade Indemnity Co. Ltd, which has branches in several cities in England, Scotland and Australia and which has been transacting this type of business since 1918.

Export Credits Guarantee Department

In addition to the commercial risk of insolvency there are also 'political' risks that can threaten export trade. A government department, the Export Credits Guarantee Department, is the best known source of cover for the commercial and political risks. It operates on a profit-making basis although it does not cover the home trade (unless ultimately for export) nor does it cover risks that can be insured commercially or with other government departments.

ECGD will consider underwriting many specialised covers, particularly those which cannot be accomplished under standard policies, and it can perhaps be said that its purpose is to attempt to provide protection to any export transaction involving a return of payment to Britain. The following list represents some of the main policies that the Department issues:

> Consumer and engineering goods
> Capital goods and projects
> Small exporter guarantees
> Provision of finance
> Direct bank guarantees
> Financial guarantees

The Department has regional representation throughout the United Kingdom and full details of its services and facilities are available upon application.

New markets

New markets, including Lloyd's, are emerging for the insurance of political risks and the use of a reputable specialist broker for obtaining advice on the cover available is again indicated, as with the newer forms of commercial cover.

FURTHER READING

R. C. Howard, W. A. Dinsdale, *Fidelity guarantee & contingency insurance*, London: Stone & Cox, 1962, 297 p.

M. Roberts, *Credit insurance,* Cambridge: Woodhead-Faulkner, 1982.

ECGD, ECGD services: insurance facilities of the British Government's Export Credits Guarantee Department, London: HMSO. (Updated editions are issued periodically.)

10

Marine, Aviation and Transport Insurance

D. J. Knight, Group Insurance Manager,
MAT International Group Ltd

GOODS IN TRANSIT BY SEA, LAND AND AIR

Need for insurance

Goods in transit represent tied-up capital which is at additional risk while the goods travel from the seller's factory or warehouse to the ultimate buyer's nominated place of delivery.

Careful preparation and packaging by the seller or shipper can help considerably in minimising damage, but even so goods in transit remain susceptible to damage, destruction or partial or total loss from material hazards and other perils while they are in the hands of carriers (by land, sea or air), transit warehouse operators, stevedores and others.

The causes of damage or loss to goods are legion and may, or may not, be the fault of the carrier (or some other party in the transport chain), but to the parties to a contract of carriage insurance provides protection against financial loss.

THE TRADER

Although the option of no insurance may be open to the trader, the prudent trader should not rely on recoveries from carriers—for reasons which will become apparent later in the chapter—to compensate for loss/damage to goods in transit. Generally speaking the responsibility for goods as between seller and buyer, and thus the requirement for insurance, will be set out in the sales contract. Where it is not, any disputes will be subject to the provisions of the law where jurisdiction is founded. In the interests of clarification and standardisation, the International Chamber of Commerce has published a set of international rules for the definition and interpretation of trade terms, known as Incoterms, the latest, updated version of which is the 1980 Edition. Among other things, Incoterms define when responsibility for insurance passes from seller to buyer. Incoterms are finding increasing acceptance in international trade, particularly in trade where documentary credits tend to prevail.

Changes in international and transport techniques have brought a swing in certain areas of trade from the traditional FOB and CIF contracts towards newer forms of contract which reflect modern practice. Buyers and sellers should familiarise themselves with the different forms of contract of sale since it is in the interests of both parties that goods are adequately and continuously insured throughout the transit period.

When the seller is responsible for insurance throughout, the buyer should be certain the sales contract adequately defines the cover to be effected, where such insurance is not according to an established custom of trade. To enable the buyer to effect insurance in those contracts where it is his responsibility to do so, the seller must give sufficient notice, otherwise the goods remain at the seller's risk.

If the principal portion of the transit insurance responsibility rests with the buyer, the seller can, if he so wishes, effect a seller's interest insurance. This is a form of contingency cover and protects the seller against loss or damage to the goods where the buyer refuses to accept and pay for them. Seller's interest insurance is relatively inexpensive and is a useful protection where payment is not guaranteed at the time of shipment.

INSURANCE COVER AVAILABLE IN THE MARINE INSURANCE MARKET

The insurance of goods in transit has its origins in what, in years past, was the principal method of international transport, by sea. By the end of the 18th century the London marine insurance market was using a standard form of cargo policy—the original SG (Ship & Goods) form—from which today's insurance covers on goods in transit for all means of transport have evolved.

Goods being transported internationally by road, rail, air or sea, or a combination of these modes will all, if insured with marine underwriters or insurers operating in the United Kingdom, be covered on what are essentially marine policy terms. Indeed the latest Institute Cargo Clauses (Air) are headed 'For Use Only with the New Marine Policy Form'.

Since its introduction in the 18th century, the SG policy has formed the backbone of marine insurance and survived the intervening years by adaptation through the use of various standard clauses which were attached to amend, or add to, the original wording. The most recent version of these clauses, The Institute Cargo Clauses 1963, remained operative until recently but has now been phased out.

From 1 January 1982 a completely new policy form has been adopted which now applies to all business. The new policy form is a simple document containing no conditions, just the name of the insurer and a 'binding' clause. To operate with the new policy are new, up-to-date clauses. These are:

Institute Cargo Clauses (A), (B) or (C)
Institute War Clauses
Institute Strikes Clauses (Cargo)
} for use with surface modes of transport

Institute Cargo Clauses (Air)
Institute War Clauses (Air Cargo)
Institute Strikes Clause (Air Cargo)
} for use with sendings by air

In re-drafting the above clauses, the previously used FPA and WA forms of cover have been discarded. Although the 'A' cargo clauses offer cover similar to the old 'all risks' form, the 'B' and 'C' cargo clauses are not re-drafts of the FPA and WA clauses. The new 'B' and 'C' clauses provide cover for specified risks only in diminishing scope, i.e. 'C' clauses give less cover than 'B' clauses, which in turn are less than the 'all risks' of 'A'. The risks covered by each set of clauses are clearly defined, as are all exclusions including statutory ones. From the insurance buyer's point of view the new clauses are more readily comprehensible. No longer is it necessary to be conversant with the Marine Insurance Act (1906) and related legal precedents to ascertain what risks are covered and what exclusions apply. Inevitably the new clauses will give rise to differences in interpretation but even so they represent a considerable improvement in clarity on the clauses they have replaced.

An abstract of the principal features of the new clauses is set out in Table 10.1. Practitioners should consult the actual clauses concerned for more detailed guidance. It should be borne in mind that the new clauses are in a standard form and amendments to the risks covered, the operative exclusions and the duration of cover are still capable of being negotiated by agreement between insurers and insured and on payment of any required additional premium.

The special trade clauses (e.g. sugar, corn, timber and jute) and frozen food clauses are due to be up-dated in the near future. For the time being however, the various forms, with clauses which have been agreed with the relevant trade associations, will continue in their present shape. With these specialised insurances, the risks covered and applicable exclusions vary considerably according to the type of commodity being transported.

Premium rates and sums insured

Premiums are generally expressed as a rate per cent of the sum insured. Occasionally it is possible to negotiate a rate per transport unit, e.g. for each full container load with a maximum limit of indemnity, but this is the exception rather than the rule. Rates are not subject to a tariff scale, each contract being rated on the prospective insurers' assessment of its individual merits as a risk. Consequently for a given risk, differing rates may be quoted for cover on identical terms. The insurance buyer's choice will then depend on a number of factors, not least of which should be the standing of the insurer and the security thus offered. Previous experience of the service provided by that particular insurer, with particular reference to claims settling, will also need consideration.

War, strikes and riot risks are also rated at a percentage of the sum insured, but are subject to a tariff scale which varies depending broadly upon the current political stability, or otherwise, and/or the

Table 10.1

THE NEW INSTITUTE CARGO CLAUSES 1982 (ICC 82)

Title	Risks covered	Principal exclusions	Duration
Institute Cargo Clauses (A)	1 Total or partial loss arising from all fortuities. 2 General average and salvage charges. 3 Expenses reasonably incurred by the assured for the purpose of averting or minimising a loss arising from an insured peril.	Loss or damage caused by: i) wilful misconduct of the assured ii) ordinary wear and tear, ordinary leakage or loss in weight/volume iii) inherent vice or nature of insured goods iv) insufficiency or unsuitability of packing or packaging v) delay, even when caused by an insured risk vi) nuclear perils vii) unseaworthiness or unfitness of vessel, conveyance, container or lift van to which the Assured or their servants are privy viii) insolvency or financial default of shipowners ix) wars and strikes as covered by Institute War & Strikes Clauses (see below). Note: Piracy is *not* however excluded	From leaving the warehouse for the commencement of transit to delivery to the warehouse at the named destination, or 60 days after completion of discharge from the carrying vessel, whichever occurs first. (See transit clause, p. 197).

(continued)

Title	Risks covered	Principal exclusions	Duration
Institute Cargo Clauses (B)	1 Total or partial loss caused by: a) general average sacrifice b) jettison c) washing overboard d) entry of sea, river or lake water into carrying vessel, craft, conveyance, container, lift van or place of storage 2 Total or partial loss reasonably attributable to: a) fire or explosion b) stranding, grounding, sinking or capsizing of vessel or craft c) overturning or derailment of land conveyance d) collision or contact of carrying conveyance with any external object (not water) e) discharge at a port of distress f) earthquake, volcanic eruption or lightning 3 Total loss of any package due to loss overboard or from dropping while loading into or unloading from a vessel or craft 4 As (A) 2 5 As (A) 3	(i) to (ix) As (A) plus: x) deliberate damage or destruction by the wrongful act of any person xi) piracy (Note: This risk is excluded from clauses (B) and (C)	As (A)

Table 10.1 (continued)

		As (B)	As (A)
Institute Cargo Clauses (C)	1 As (B)/1 (a) and (c) only 2 As (B) 2 (a) to (e) only 3 As (A) 2 4 As (A) 3		
Institute Cargo Clauses (Air)	1 As Cargo Clauses (A) 1 2 As Cargo Clauses (A) 3	As Cargo Clauses (A) (i) to (ix)	As Cargo Clause (A) except that 30 days is substituted for 60 days
Institute War Clauses (Cargo) and (Air Cargo)	Total or partial loss caused by: i) war, revolution, rebellion and similar warlike acts ii) capture, seizure, arrest, restraint or detainment arising from (i) above iii) derelict mines, torpedoes, bombs and other weapons of war, plus iv) general average and salvage charges arising from the above, with Institute War (Cargo) Clauses only.	As Cargo Clauses (A) (i) to (viii), plus: ix) any claim based on frustration or loss of the transit	From time of loading on an overseas vessel or carrying aircraft until discharge from an overseas vessel or aircraft at the final port or place of discharge, or 15 days after the date of arrival of the carrying ship or aircraft, whichever is the sooner (60 days in the case of goods on craft between vessel and shore where loss is caused by mines and derelict torpedoes)
Institute Strike Clauses (Cargo) and (Air Cargo)	Total or partial loss caused by: i) strikes, locked-out workmen or persons taking part in labour disturbances, riots or civil commotion ii) any terrorist or any person acting from a political motive iii) general average and salvage charges arising from the above (Cargo Clauses only)	As Cargo Clauses (A) (i) to (viii) plus: ix) war risks (as covered by Institute War Clauses) x) loss, damage or expense arising from the absence or shortage of labour due to strikes, etc. xi) any claim based on frustration or loss of transit (Cargo Clauses only)	Strike (Cargo) as per Cargo (A) Strike (Cargo Air) as for Cargo (Air)

Table 10.1 (concluded)

195

labour record of a geographical area into or through which goods will pass.

The details required by insurers before quoting a rate of premium will usually include:

1 Description of the goods.
2 Method and/or type of packing, including any special loss prevention precautions being taken. Whether goods are to be unitised, palletised or shipped in containers.
3 Method of transport—sea, air or land—and type of conveyance.
4 The voyage or journey; where from and where to, whether trans-shipment and/or transit storage is involved, whether on or under deck, etc.
5 Perils to be insured (See Institute Cargo Clauses.)
6 Sum to be insured and/or basis of valuation.
7 Past claims experience, particularly with open or floating covers.

Policies can be arranged for each shipment as required. The disadvantage of this method is that there is no cover until terms have been agreed and accepted by insurers. Traders regularly insuring goods in transit are recommended to obtain automatic cover through a floating policy or open cover. The former offers cover up to an agreed total sum insured, the value of all shipments made being deducted from this sum until it is exhausted; the latter covers all shipments of a certain type or types, either for an indefinite period usually with a yearly anniversary date when terms are reviewed, or for a fixed period of twelve months. The choice between individual policies, an open cover and a floating policy will be governed, to a large extent, by a trader's pattern of exports or imports.

Increased value insurance

Sometimes after primary insurance is arranged a requirement arises necessitating an increase in the sum insured. Separate 'increased value' insurance can be taken out to cover the extra value required. In such cases the agreed insured value of the cargo is taken as the total amount insured under the primary and increased value policies and claims are settled in the same proportion as the increased value sum insured bears to the total amount insured.

Inception of cover

When cargo insurance is placed, the risk must commence within a reasonable time after the insurer accepts the risk. Undue delay could provide grounds under the Marine Insurance Act for the insurer to avoid the contract.

Transit clause

Under the Institute Cargo Clauses 1982 (other than War) cover attaches from the time goods leave the factory, warehouse, or place or storage named in the policy for the commencement of the transit. It continues during the ordinary course of transit, that is, without unreasonable delay, or delay within the control of the insured, and implies, unless otherwise agreed, that the transit is by the most direct route to the named destination. Cover terminates either on delivery to the warehouse at the final destination named in the policy, or on delivery to any other warehouse or place of storage selected by the insured at or prior to the named destination, or on the expiry of 60 days after completion of discharge at the destination port, whichever occurs first. If, for any reason, goods have not been delivered by the expiry of this time limit, cover will cease unless the insurer has agreed to an extension. As goods can be delayed in transit due for example to heavy congestion at ports, it is important to remember to monitor the time involved in order to make the necessary prior arrangements to maintain cover.

With the Institute War Clauses (Cargo), the duration of cover is limited to the time goods are waterborne. Cover attaches as and when goods are loaded into an overseas vessel and terminates either as the goods are discharged from an overseas vessel at the place of destination, or on expiry of 15 days after the vessel has arrived at its destination, whichever occurs first. A vessel is deemed to have arrived once it is anchored, moored or berthed at or off the intended port or place of discharge. Extension of the time limit in the war risk clauses can be negotiated, but because delay is not held covered, insureds should make application to insurers as soon as they are aware of any delay likely to exceed the 15-day limit.

Trans-shipment

Trans-shipment, unless it is necessitated by an insured peril, or by a liberty granted to the shipowner under the bill of lading, is not insured unless specially referred to in the policy or contract. It is normal for open contracts to include an automatic arrangement to include trans-shipment where required. An additional premium will usually be charged for any trans-shipment risk.

Craft risks to and from the ship and loading and unloading risks are covered by standard clauses.

Claims—forms of loss, damage and other allowable expenses

Before any recovery under goods-in-transit insurance is possible, the policy holder must be able to show an insurable interest in the goods at the time the loss or damage occurred. Then, subject to the risks covered and the exclusions of the particular policy, the insured can proceed.

The principal forms of loss which an insured is likely to encounter are as follows.

Actual total loss

This expression encompasses the actual total loss of goods through, for example, the sinking of the carrying vessel, their total destruction by fire, where the entire consignment is so severely damaged as to completely change its nature (for example if a consignment of foodstuffs is damaged by water and can then only be used as a fertiliser) or when the insured is irretrievably deprived of them.

Constructive total loss

This occurs if the cost of recovering, repairing, or otherwise dealing with damaged goods will exceed their value on arrival, or where the insured is deprived of the possession of goods and is unlikely to retrieve or recover them.

Partial loss

In marine insurance the term 'average' is applied to partial loss and there are two kinds of average.

Particular average is the partial loss (not arising from a 'general average' act) resulting in the complete loss of part of the goods, or damage to the whole or part, causing depreciation in value, or a combination of both.

General average is loss, partial or total, or damage, which is the consequence of a 'general average' act. General average is peculiar to carriage by sea—it has no equivalent with other modes of transport—and has its origins in very early maritime trade. It is not in itself in any way dependent upon insurance, although the Institute Clauses do provide the appropriate cover.

There is a general average act when, and only when, a deliberate sacrifice is made or expenditure incurred for the common safety of all the property involved in a maritime venture and has a successful outcome. As examples, part of the ship or cargo may be jettisoned, or damaged by water used to extinguish a fire on board, or expenses may be incurred in taking a ship into a port of refuge because it is in danger. The loss or expenditure so sustained is shared by everyone with an interest in the ship, the cargo and (where appropriate) freight, pro rata as regards both loss and contribution (to general average expenditure) according to the individual values saved. Because a general average can only occur during carriage by sea, the declaration of general average is in the hands of the sea carrier, who will usually decline to release cargo at the port of discharge until security is given by the cargo owner to cover the estimated general average contribution from each individual interest. This security can take the form of a cash deposit but, where cargo is insured, is normally provided by an insurers' guarantee or undertaking to pay in a form acceptable to the sea carrier.

The York-Antwerp Rules normally govern the adjustment of

general average. Eventually, when all the losses and expenses are finalised, a general average adjustment is prepared showing, inter alia, the final amounts payable as general average loss, damage or expenditure and due as general average contributions from each interested party. Deposits are adjusted and guarantees called in accordingly.

General average contributions are assessed on the arrived market value of goods, which means that where underinsurance exists the cargo owners will be required to pay part of the contribution and possibly, in the first instance, part of the deposit.

Salvage charges

Anyone who voluntarily renders services which result in the saving of a ship and her cargo is entitled to claim salvage services. The reward to the salvors (the salvage award) is based on the saved value of the ship and her cargo. When a cargo consists of or includes loaded containers and/or trailers, the value of the goods stowed in the container or trailer is taken into account as well as value(s) of the carrying container or trailer.

The amount of a salvage award may be determined by agreement between the various parties, by arbitration, or by a court decision. It is borne rateably between all the interests. Security in anticipation of an award is normally sought by salvors and may be provided by the methods described for general average. Salvage contributions are covered by all the ICC Cargo insurance forms subject to contribution by the insured if there is underinsurance.

Particular charges

This is the term applied to expenses incurred by an insured aimed at averting or minimising a loss arising from an insured peril. It is the duty of every insured to take all reasonable, necessary measures to save, protect or recover insured goods and insurers pay such costs, in addition to any loss under a policy.

Extra charges

Extra charges are those expenses reasonably incurred in substantiating a claim against insurers and are payable in full. They include survey fees or the fees of average adjusters employed to prepare a claim statement or adjustment.

Proximate cause

A claim is only recoverable under an insurance policy if one or other of the perils insured is the proximate cause of the loss. This rule is of particular significance in maritime insurance. Usually the cause of a loss is obvious, but there may be occasions when a number of causes operate successively or consecutively, and one or more of those causes may not be insured perils. The proximate or dominant effective cause must be determined. It may not necessarily be the most recent cause in time. If there has been an unbroken sequence of events it will be the originating cause of that sequence which counts. The interpretation of the rule may sometimes be both difficult and frustrating. It is of particular significance in determining whether the loss is caused by inherent vice of the goods or delay in transit (see following paragraphs).

Inherent vice

An inherent vice is a quality inherent to a particular commodity or kind of goods which may result in them becoming damaged through deterioration without the assistance of an extraneous cause. Such damage is likely to occur due to some natural characteristic of the commodity or goods. Some naturally lose weight due to evaporation of the water content, others are readily susceptible to internal heating due to bacteriological or other action, or to spontaneous combustion. There are many different forms of inherent vice, which is not covered by any type of marine policy unless the policy specially so provides. It is worthwhile becoming familiar with the properties and characteristics of goods or commodities to be insured in order to appreciate the extent of the application of the inherent vice exclusion, as, in a number of instances, it may be possible to negotiate the inclusion of certain specific additional perils which could lead to damage.

Delay during transit

Losses proximately caused by delay in transit are not covered. Subject to the provisions of the transit clause (see p. 197), loss or damage by insured perils during delay is covered. Thus, if a ship suffers damage and the goods are unloaded at a port of refuge and deteriorate during the delay by reason of their nature, the resultant damage is not recoverable. If they are damaged by fire during that time, the loss is covered.

Shipment on deck

Goods carried on the deck of a ship are not normally covered unless by general custom of the particular trade, or unless specially agreed by insurers. If so agreed, the perils insured may well be restricted, but it should prove possible in most cases to include jettison or washing overboard.

Insufficiency of packing

As will be seen from Table 10.1 loss or damage caused by insufficiency or unsuitability of packing, which expression includes stowage by the insured in a container or road trailer, offers grounds for repudiation of a claim by insurers. Packaging is becoming increasingly expensive but in considering this cost the consequences of a repudiation by insurers should not be overlooked. Where special packaging is utilised, this should be brought to the attention of insurers as it may be possible to negotiate a reduction in the premium as a reflection of the potential for fewer claims.

Claims procedure

Prompt notice should be given to insurers, or to insurers' nominated representatives, if loss or damage to goods is evidenced or suspected. This is particularly important where the potential damage or loss is of sizeable proportions, enabling insurers if they so wish to appoint surveyors to assess and quantify the measure of loss or damage. The insurance policy or certificate will indicate what has to be done and traders should familiarise themselves with and follow these instructions. When surveyors are called in by insurers the precise extent of the loss or damage should be agreed with them, as insurers will negotiate settlement of the claim on their findings.

The insured must protect the insurers' rights of recovery of losses against carriers. A clean receipt should not be given if goods are received in bad order, but the delivery document should be appropriately claused and a copy retained. If damage or loss is discovered after delivery, immediate notice should be given to the delivering carrier. In every instance a letter (or telex) holding the carrier responsible should be sent as soon as possible.

In submitting a claim upon cargo insurers, the early provision of full documentation will facilitate settlement. Delay in the settlement of a claim will almost certainly ensue unless insurers' requirements are met. The documents should include:

1 Insurance policy or certificate.
2 Bill of Lading, CMR or CIM Consignment Note, or similar evidence of the contract of carriage.
3 Commercial invoice.
4 Evidence of loss or damage (e.g. Lloyd's agent's or surveyor's report or claused delivery note).
5 General average and/or salvage deposit receipts (if appropriate).
6 Copy communications to carriers, etc. holding them responsible for loss/damage.
7 Any other relevant document or documents.

An insured should remember that damage or loss can occur which does not have its origins 'in transit'. For example, a shortage from a container carrying the seals originally placed on it by the shipper, or sender, may well be repudiated by an insurer on the grounds that the loss occurred before the transit commenced. Damage caused by insufficiency of packing will also be rejected by insurers. An insured's recourse is then limited to his rights as a buyer against a seller.

Genuine claims upon insurers should be pursued vigorously if necessary. An initial repudiation may be based on an incomplete evaluation by insurers of the circumstances, etc. of a particular loss. Although it is not essential to present a claim through the insurance brokers who arranged the cover, in practice there can be distinct advantages in so doing. Not only are they familiar with the background of the insurance arrangements in question, but through their business they can often marshal sound arguments to support a claim which are not readily available to an insured.

Loss prevention

Although shippers and consignees have little or no control over the safety of goods in transit, loss and damage can be minimised by using sound and satisfactory methods of packaging and of packing. What has proved suitable for the home market may be completely inadequate for overseas sendings which can frequently involve a greater measure of handling and be subjected to unusual and violent movements in transit. Expert advice upon packing can be obtained from professional packers and cargo surveyors. It is often available from insurers' own advisers if so requested.

The increasing use of trailers and containers brings its own problems, not all of which are immediately apparent but which need to be guarded against. Shippers stowing and packing trailers or containers should carefully examine the equipment to see if it is watertight, clean and free from odours, contaminants and infestation. Stowage should be adequate to prevent damage in transit due to the possibility of crushing and collapse of a stow caused by the movements and shocks which may be encountered on a normal journey. The risk of condensation, particularly in a closed container, should not be overlooked and precautions against pilferage and theft must be carefully considered.

Consignees or receivers have an obligation to take all necessary steps to minimise the effect of transit damage discovered at destination. Prompt advice to insurers or insurers' local representatives will invariably result in the early intervention of a surveyor whose recommendation will be designed to contain, and if possible reduce, losses. Even so, consignees/receivers can often do much before a surveyor's arrival to inhibit and prevent further or more serious loss and should take all reasonable and practicable steps in this regard.

LAND TRANSITS—TRADERS' AND CARRIERS' COVERS AVAILABLE IN THE NON-MARINE INSURANCE MARKET

Where transit of goods is restricted to movement by land it is more usual to arrange cover under a non-marine 'goods in transit' type of cover rather than a marine insurance contract, and the remaining comments in this chapter are concerned with such non-marine contracts.

Carriers' insurance

The carrier and others who handle goods in transit, like the trader, should be certain their interests in the safe carriage and handling of goods are properly insured. The insurances effected by carriers (and others handling goods) must be structured to protect them against their full potential range of legal liabilities. There are many first-class standard policies which will provide adequate cover for a standard form of transport/carriage activity. The terms and conditions of such insurances should be carefully examined to ensure the risks to which the business is exposed are, in fact, fully covered. If not, it is frequently possible to obtain insurers' agreement to delete certain standard exclusions (such as those referred to under traders insurances below), or provide supplementary cover on payment of an appropriate additional premium, thus widening the scope of the basic standard policy.

The policy should, in particular, extend to include the carrier's liability for goods carried by his subcontractors, and insurers will probably require that all subcontractors operate on conditions that are at least as wide as those of the insured carrier, so that the subcontractors cannot avoid claims for which the carrier himself is liable to the trader. Thus the insurers' subrogation rights against the subcontractors are properly protected. Subcontractors' carriage conditions should therefore be clearly established before employment is offered to ensure compliance with the carrier's insurer's requirements.

As a further safeguard it is recommended that carriers check that their subcontractors are themselves properly and adequately insured in respect of their liability. Periodic re-checks are also advisable to verify subcontractors' policies subsist.

Where a company is engaged in a number of different activities which may, or may not, be related to one another, several separate liability policies may be required, or better still one single composite cover negotiated. The diversification of the transport industry has prompted a number of insurers to offer composite covers which can be adapted to suit individual business requirements and which will often show economic advantages in premium terms over separate insurances. The composite insurance also reduces the problems associated with interfacing separate policies which can lead to serious and unsuspected loopholes in cover.

Traders' insurance

The carriers' insurance, however wide its apparent terms, will not normally cover the trader for any losses for which the carrier is not responsible under the carriage conditions, and the former should therefore arrange his own cover. This will usually be on an 'all risks' basis, although in the case of non-hazardous goods a trader may be content with cover against specified perils, such as fire, theft, collision or overturning of the vehicle. Insurers will exclude from their standard all risks policies the risks of war, riots, strikes, mildew, vermin, inherent vice, defective packing, radioactive contamination, and consequential and indirect losses. The policy should include the risks of loading, temporary housing en route, and unloading, and normally applies to transits anywhere in the United Kingdom (including, where required, Northern Ireland).

The policy can apply to goods on carriers' vehicles and/or on the trader's own or contract hire vehicles as appropriate.

The trader's insurers will have subrogation rights against carriers for any losses for which the latter are responsible under the carriage conditions, or at common law if no conditions are applicable.

Hazardous goods

Standard policies for traders and carriers exclude cover on certain vulnerable goods such as bullion, cash, valuables, dangerous goods and livestock. Due to unsatisfactory claims experience over recent years, most insurers have added to the exclusions such goods as spirits, radios, and tobacco. If such property is to be included an additional premium will usually be required.

Packaging and covering

Tarpaulins, ropes, pallets, and other equipment on vehicles may be covered similarly to the goods carried.

Machinery and plant

Machinery and plant in transit may present special insurance problems in loading and stowage on the vehicle, especially when carried unpacked. The trader may also require cover not only during the transit, loading and unloading, but also during the operations of dismantling and/or erection on the site. In that event, if the additional cover is to be included in the transit insurance, the cover may have to be with specialist insurers.

Household furniture and effects

Standard furniture removers' conditions absolve the removers from liability for loss or damage to the goods except under very limited circumstances. The removers may offer to arrange insurance for a householder's interests at the latter's expense. Alternatively, house-holders may arrange their own cover, either by extending their existing householders' policy covering the contents of their house, or by effecting a separate transit policy. Either way, the insurance would normally be required on an 'all risks' basis. A small excess may apply, and the policy will normally be subject to average.

Risks while temporarily in furniture store may be included by special arrangement, which may not include fire and explosion risks for property stored at a rental.

Refrigerated goods

Such goods are subject to the additional risks of deterioration due to breakdown of the refrigerating plant on the vehicle, especially during temporary housing of the vehicle overnight. Traders should check the extent of refrigeration cover provided under their goods in transit insurance even if the cover is on an 'all risks' basis.

Travellers' stocks

Special policies are issued to insure samples and other goods while in the care of sales representatives, not only while in transit, but in hotels or elsewhere during their journeys.

Warehousing risk

Although both traders' and carriers' insurance usually cover goods during temporary housing en route (whether on or off the vehicle), such cover may be restricted in time (for example, to 72 hours in all).

Premium rates, sums insured and underwriting factors

It is usual for policies to be issued on an annual basis to cover all goods transported in the period. Limits of indemnity will be incorporated and may be expressed as one or more of the following:

1 A limit per conveyance, accident or occurrence.
2 A limit per location (to cover the possibility of more than one load being housed temporarily in one place during transit).
3 A limit per article or package.

All limits should be adequate to cover the highest possible value which may be at risk under each heading, particularly as any of the limits may be subject to average.

Premiums may be calculated in a number of different ways, e.g.

1 *On the total annual freight charges (turnover),* which is the most common formula for carriers' liability covers. For most carriers and others handling goods this is the only feasible method because they will be unaware of the value of goods passing through their hands. A provisional premium is paid on inception based on the anticipated turnover, which is adjusted on expiry on actual turnover, probably with a minimum retained premium.

2   *On the total value of goods transported* during the year, a provisional premium being paid on an estimated value, with adjustment on expiry on the actual figure, again probably with a minimum retained premium.
3   *On the total maximum value at risk at any one time* on all vehicles, which is usually calculated by multiplying the maximum value to be carried on each vehicle by the number of vehicles (taking into account the varying capacity of different types of vehicle).

The rate of premium which is applied to the totals referred to above to produce the premiums payable will be influenced e.g. by some or all of the undermentioned factors:

1   Kinds of goods carried.
2   Methods of effecting carriage.
3   Perils to be insured (all risks, specified perils, carriers' liability only).
4   Nature and type of operations contemplated.
5   Geographical areas of operation.
6   Indemnity limit or limits selected or required.
7   Conditions of carriage/business, contractual or statutory.
8   Extent to which subcontractors are employed and their conditions of carriage (in the case of carriers' liability insurances).
9   Precautions taken to minimise losses in transit.
10 Claims experience over previous three to five years.

Proposal forms are usually required and the insured should retain a copy so that any material alteration in the information supplied can be advised to insurers.

Policies are also issued for individual sendings, or on a declaration basis, the latter operating similarly to floating policies as described on p. 196.

Excesses and coinsurance

Excesses are often applied to goods in transit insurances and may vary from a nominal £10 to as much as £100 or more. Alternatively to improve loss prevention measures insurers may stipulate that the insured bears uninsured a fixed percentage of all claims arising under certain cirumstances (perhaps 10 to 25 per cent).

Cancellation of cover

Cancellation conditions vary. When cancelling, insurers may be required to give from 7 to 30 days' notice with a return of premium. On the other hand cancellation by the insured during the currency of the policy does not always bring a similar return of premium and may entail the loss of the unexpired proportion.

Claims procedure

The policy conditions will normally detail the claims procedure to be followed by the insured. Particular cognisance should be paid to time limits for the notification of claims, as late notification could lead to a repudiation by insurers. All insureds are recommended to keep claim records in order to check the reasonableness of premiums. Such records can also serve to highlight those parts of the business, or areas of operation, where there is a heavy claims frequency and where remedial action to reduce such losses may be possible.

Loss prevention

Losses under goods in transit insurances having increased during recent years, insurers are insisting on better loss prevention measures being taken, for example:

1   Adequate vehicle maintenance to avoid accident. Vehicles not to be overloaded. Proper sheeting to be provided for open vehicles to avoid damage by bad weather conditions.
2   Vehicles not to be left unattended at any time en route, or alternatively to be locked or otherwise protected by an alarm.
3   Limiting the parking of loaded vehicles overnight.
4   Fitting recognised anti-theft devices to vehicles.
5   Carefully taking up new drivers' references by the insured to reduce the risk of theft through drivers' possible collusion.

Further action which can be taken to minimise losses includes:

1   Improving the standards of packaging vulnerable goods.

2   Varying the routes taken where loads of valuable goods are regularly sent between two points.

3   Correct loading of the vehicle and protection by adequate tarpaulins, ropes, etc.

4   Careful choice of route for unusually awkward loads (plant, machinery, car transporters) to avoid damage by low or narrow bridges, or passing through narrow streets.

APPENDIX 10:1. THE LIABILITY OF CARRIERS AND OTHERS IN THE TRANSPORT CHAIN

All carriers are, in general, responsible for the safety of goods entrusted to them. The liability of a carrier for loss or damage is not, however, absolute and can vary considerably dependent upon the mode of transport being employed, whether the journey is international or domestic and whether the contract of carriage is regulated by common law, statute or by contractual terms, or a combination of the foregoing. Even where uni-modal transport is governed by international convention, national enabling legislation can introduce local variations through differing interpretation of the terms of the convention. Also, international conventions are rarely truly international in application, with the result that the same type of goods being transported by the same mode of transport can be subject to different regimes of liability simply because of the route over which they are travelling.

While most carriers take out insurance to indemnify themselves against compensation paid in meeting a legal liability for loss of or damage to goods, more often than not there is no legal requirement for insurance. A liability for loss or damage rests with the contracting carrier, not his insurers, and is not directly affected by the existence, or otherwise, of insurance. In practice the ability of the carrier to satisfy large claims may depend upon his liability insurance, which must, of course, be extant if a claimant is to obtain the redress he is seeking and to which he may be entitled.

Common carriers

The common carrier in the United Kingdom is a disappearing category of carrier, rarely encountered today. The common carrier is liable for any loss of or damage to goods during carriage, except when caused by:

1 Act of God.
2 An act of the Queen's enemies.
3 The fault of the consignor or owner of the goods.
4 The inherent vice of the goods.
5 Fraud of the consignor or owner of the goods.

In practice, carriers now usually operate on written conditions which embody provisions which classify them as private carriers and which, inter alia, define the extent for which liability will be accepted.

Carriage by sea

The first international convention relating to the carriage of goods by sea was the Hague Rules 1922, brought into force in the United Kingdom by the Carriage of Goods by Sea Act 1924. Over the succeeding years the Hague Rules gained widespread acceptance but the limit of liability, fixed in 1922 at £100 per package or unit, gradually lost much of its value. In 1950, in an attempt to modernise the Hague Rules limit, the Gold Clause Agreement was introduced, with a £200 limit per package or unit being voluntarily applied by all subscribers to the Agreement.

The technological changes in transport eventually ushered in the Hague–Visby Rules in 1968, enacted in the UK by the Carriage of Goods by Sea Act, 1971, which was brought into force in 1977. COGSA 1971 remains the legislation applicable to the carriage of goods by sea from the UK. However, the Hague–Visby Rules are still only applied by a handful of nations, the majority—for various reasons—adhering to the original Hague Rules.

COGSA 1971 applies to all goods shipped under a bill of lading, or non-negotiable document specifically incorporating the Rules, if the bill is issued in the UK, or carriage is from a UK port, or the contract evidenced by the bill provides for the application of UK law.

Under the Act, the carrier by sea is obliged to properly and carefully load, handle, stow, carry, keep, care for and discharge goods entrusted to him. The carrier's duty is a strict obligation which must be exercised throughout a whole voyage and is not modified by the exercise of due diligence, as applies to other obligations imposed upon the carrier. The initial burden of proof in relation to stowage rests with the claimant, who should therefore utilise the services of accredited cargo surveyors when damage is first discovered to try and establish the necessary facts to support this proof. The Act does not give cargo owners, or their representatives, specific permission to board vessels for this purpose. On the other hand it requires the 'carrier' and the 'receiver' to give all reasonable facilities to each other for inspecting and tallying goods.

The sea carrier having received goods under a clean bill of lading is prima facie liable if the goods out-turn short, in bad order, or in damaged condition. The Act offers the carrier a number of exculpatory provisions from responsibility for loss or damage. These are:

1   The negligence of the master or servants of the carrier in the navigation and management of the ship.
2   Fire.
3   Perils of the sea.
4   Acts of God.
5   Acts of war and of public enemies; restraint of princes; quarantine; strikes; riots and civil commotions; saving of life at sea.
6   Act or omission of the shipper.
7   Inherent vice.
8   Insufficiency of packing.
9   Latent defects not discoverable by due diligence.
10 Any other cause without fault on the part of the carrier or his servants and agents.

The exemptions available to the carrier by sea are among the most generous afforded by statute or international convention. Their interpretation has created, much legal authority and precedent which can vary in emphasis from one jurisdiction to another. But generally courts throughout the world have tended to construe the exemptions very strictly, so restricting their scope of application.

Where liable under the Hague–Visby Rules, carriers are permitted to limit their liability to 10,000 gold Poincaré francs per package or unit or 30 gold Poincaré francs per kilo of gross weight, whichever is higher. In the United Kingdom the sterling equivalents of the gold francs specified in the Rules are fixed by HM Government Order. They are currently about £400 and £1.20 respectively, the latter producing a limit per tonne of approximately £1,200. When goods are consolidated into a container, or on to a pallet or similar article of transport, such article of transport is taken as one package or unit for the purposes of calculating liability, unless the number of individual packages making up the container or pallet load is separately enumerated in the bill of lading.

Unresolved disputes with sea carriers become statute barred unless suit is commenced within one year of delivery. This period can be extended by mutual agreement and most reputable carriers are prepared to grant time extensions provided application is made before the original 12 months expire.

Unless the contract of affreightment indicates otherwise, the Act operates only when goods are actually on board the carrying ship. Carriers' responsibility before shipment or after discharge is usually very limited and will be described in the bill of lading terms and conditions.

International convention and COGSA 1971 permit carriers to contract out of responsibility for loss or damage to cargo shipped on deck. In order to secure the benefit of any non-responsibility clause, the carrier is required to stipulate carriage on deck on the relevant bill of lading. 'Liberty to carry on deck' clauses do not usually automatically entitle a carrier to then invoke a non-responsibility provision (unless the bill is so claused) except in those trades where it is the normal practice to ship a substantial proportion of the cargo on deck.

The Hamburg Rules, the latest convention designed to deal with carriage by sea under modern transport conditions, remains moribund through lack of support by governments.

Carriage by rail

When railways first operated in the UK they were held to be common carriers (see p. 212) and this applied until the Transport Act 1962, which, inter alia, enabled the Railways Board to adopt contractual conditions setting out the terms under which goods are carried.

For domestic carriage, i.e. within the UK, the Railways Board operates at either owner's risk, or the Railways Board's risk, the applicable tariffs reflecting the difference between the terms.

Under owner's risk conditions the Railways Board remains liable for non-delivery except when caused by fire or an accident to a train or vehicle. Otherwise the Board's liability is limited to loss or damage caused only by wilful misconduct or default. In carriage at the Board's risk, the Board does accept liability for loss, damage and misdelivery where the fault is the Board's. The limit of liability is £2,000 per tonne and notification of loss, damage, etc., must be made to the Board within 3 days of the end of the rail transit and claims lodged within 7 days. These time limits for claims call for prompt action on the part of goods owners, if claims are to be considered by the Railways Board. Regular users of rail services who find it practically impossible to comply with these limits are recommended to approach the Board to obtain a relaxation of this contractual requirement.

International carriage of goods by rail is regulated by the CIM (Convention Internationale de Marchandises) Convention. Although the CIM Convention has never been enacted in the UK, it has been contractually incorporated by British Rail into its international rail consignment note. Thus, provided a CIM consignment note is issued, the Convention will apply throughout the international rail journey, even including the cross-Channel transit.

Under CIM Conditions, the railway authority is liable for loss, damage and delay in transit except where caused by the negligence of the trader, by inherent vice of the goods or through circumstances which the railway could not avoid, or by the absence or inadequacy of packaging.

Compensation is limited to 100 gold Germinal francs per kilo of gross weight for loss or damage. The UK and certain European states have adopted a fixed conversion of the gold franc into SDRs (Special Drawing Rights) at the rate of 1 SDR = 3 gold francs. Thus, the SDR limit amount is equivalent to a rate of about £21 per kilo or £21,100 per tonne (at an SDR value of £0.633960).

The amount of compensation payable for exceeding the transit period is on a sliding scale geared to the carriage charges. The maximum compensation is twice the amount of the carriage charges.

The CIM Convention provides a maximum of seven days for notification of claims for loss or damage (60 days for delay) and a limitation period of one year for actions.

Carriage by road

The domestic carriage of goods by road within the UK is not subject to legislative regulations. Hauliers can operate as common carriers, but most profess Conditions of Carriage, those of the Road Haulage Association (RHA) being the most commonly employed.

Under RHA Conditions, hauliers accept liability for loss, damage or misdelivery occasioned during transit up to a maximum of £800 per tonne. The latest (1982) version now incorporates a provision for compensation for consequential loss subject to a limit of the amount of the carriage charges. Acts of God, war, seizure under legal process, riots, strikes and civil commotions, insufficiency of packaging or labelling, inherent defect or vice and errors or omissions by the customer are the principal contractual defences open to the carrier. Total losses must be notified within 28 days and claims made within 42 days. Other losses carry a 3-day notification period with claims within 7 days.

On the European Continent, domestic road haulage tends to be regulated by national law, which lays down the circumstances under which compensation is payable and sets limits of liability, etc.

Within most of Western Europe, international movements by road are governed by the CMR Convention (*Convention relative au transport international de Marchandises par Route*). The UK enabling legislation is the Carriage of Goods by Road Act, 1965. Except for furniture removal, funeral consignments and carriage performed under the terms of any international postal convention, the CMR Convention applies to every contract for the carriage of goods by road for reward across a frontier, provided either the country of the place where the goods are taken over, or the country of the place designated for delivery, is a contracting party to the Convention. Traffic between the UK and Northern Ireland and Eire is specifically excluded under the UK Act. In the context of the Convention the nationality of the parties to the contract of carriage and where the contract is made are irrelevant. Because the UK is a contracting party, any international movement of goods by road beginning or ending in the UK will fall within the scope of the CMR Convention.

When goods move multi-modally, CMR can still apply so long as they remain loaded on a road vehicle for the entire journey. Thus, goods on a trailer shipped across the Channel remain subject to CMR, as do goods on a trailer carried 'piggy-back' on a rail transporter. The unloading of goods from one road vehicle to another, either from accident or as ordinary trans-shipment, does not break the continued application of CMR. However, when goods are unloaded from a vehicle and thereafter move by sea, rail, air or inland waterways, the CMR 'chain' is broken at that point and CMR will only apply up to that point if, in reaching it, the vehicle crossed an international frontier.

The CMR carrier operates under a strict, but not onerous, regime of liability. The Convention makes the carrier liable for total or partial loss, damage and delay in delivery occurring between the time it takes over the goods and the time of delivery.

As with all international conventions dealing with the carriage of goods, a monetary limit is placed on the amount the carrier pays, if liable. The CMR monetary limit is 25 gold Germinal francs per kilo of the gross weight of the goods. The Convention defines the gold franc, but even so, fluctuations in the price of gold have given rise to considerable variation in the determination of the CMR carriers' monetary limit in different jurisdictions. In an attempt to iron out the anomalies the Geneva Protocol of 1978 substituted 8.33 Special Drawing Rights (SDRs) for 25 francs. This amendment has been adopted by a handful of Western European States, including the UK. The sterling equivalent of the CMR monetary limit is now about £5.33 per kilo, or £5,330 per tonne. Additionally the carrier is liable without limit for carriage charges, Customs duties and other charges incurred in respect of the carriage of the goods lost or damaged.

Compensation for delay in delivery is limited to the amount of the carriage charges. All compensation payments attract interest at 5 per cent per annum accruing from either the date a claim is lodged or the date on which legal proceedings are commenced, if no previous claim has been made.

The CMR Convention provides the carrier with certain specific defences whereby he is relieved of liability for loss, damage or delay if caused by the wrongful act or neglect of the claimant; by the instructions of the claimant given otherwise than as a result of a wrongful act or neglect by the carrier; by the inherent vice of the goods, or by circumstances which the carrier could not avoid and the consequences of which he was unable to prevent. Subject to burden of proof the Convention also contains certain grounds whereby the carrier may be relieved of liability when loss or damage is the consequence of: the expressly agreed use of open, unsheeted vehicles; lack of or defective packing; handling, loading, stowage and unloading by the sender or consignee; the nature of certain kinds of goods which renders loss or damage likely or inevitable to some degree; insufficiency or inadequacy of marks and numbers and the carriage of livestock.

Claims for loss or damage have to be notified to the carrier within 7 days of delivery (Sundays and public holidays excepted), unless reservations as to the condition of the goods are noted on the consignment note at the time of delivery, and claims for delay within 23 days of delivery. Non-delivery of goods within 60 days is treated as conclusive evidence of loss. If such goods are subsequently recovered within the ensuing year, the claimant has the option to re-possess them and make a refund of compensation, but is not obliged to do so.

The normal period of limitation for an action arising out of CMR carriage is one year. This period begins to run from the date of delivery in the case of partial loss, damage or delay; or in the case of total loss (non-delivery) from 30 days after any agreed date of delivery; or, where there is no agreed date of delivery, from 60 days after collection by the carrier. A written claim lodged with the carrier (and a telex is generally construed as written advice) suspends the period of limitation until (if at all) the carrier rejects the claim, when the limitation period starts to run again. There is no overall time-limit in CMR which will eventually terminate a claim lodged with, but not prosecuted against, a carrier. The Convention expressly allows national law to determine this, so that in the UK the ultimate period of limitation is governed by the Limitation Act.

In many instances in the international carriage of goods by road, the carrier with whom the contract is made may utilise the services of one or more other independent carriers. Thus a laden trailer may be moved as an articulated unit by tractor vehicles owned or operated by a number of different hauliers. The CMR Convention places the responsibility for this chain of haulage operations upon the shoulders of the carrier who makes the contract with the sender. Legal decisions in the UK and in some European jurisdictions have established that a 'carrier' within the meaning of the Convention does not need to own or operate a road vehicle. It is sufficient to contract as a principal for the international carriage of goods for reward to attract the role and responsibilities of a carrier. The

Convention recognises the difficulties which a prospective claimant may encounter in pursuing a claim where more than one haulier was involved. It gives the person entitled to claim for loss, damage or delay the right to proceed against the first carrier, or the last carrier, or the carrier who was performing the carriage where and when the loss occurred, or all or some of the foregoing jointly. The forum for an action is, however, restricted to the territory where the defendant is ordinarily resident, or has his principal place of business, or the branch or agency through which the contract of carriage was made, or the place where the goods were taken over by the carrier or the place designated for delivery.

Carriage by air

The Warsaw Convention of 1929 saw the emergence of the first international rules relative to transport by air. With the passage of time most countries ratified the Convention, which then applied to all carriage by air of persons, baggage and cargo between two states, both of which were contracting parties to the Convention. In 1955 The Hague Protocol amending the Warsaw Convention came into existence. The Carriage by Air Act, 1961 enacted the amended Convention in the UK. It came into force in 1967 through The Carriage by Air (Application of Provisions) Order No. 480.

The result of the 1961 Act and its enforcing Order of 1967 is to divide carriage by air into 'international carriage' and 'non-international carriage'. The distinction of one form of carriage from another does not depend upon the flight crossing a frontier, but upon whether or not the states in which the place of departure and place of destination are situated are contracting parties to the Warsaw Convention, or the Amended Convention. On occasion it may be necessary to make full enquiries to ascertain the precise legal position relating to the law applicable to the carriage of goods by air over particular routes. However, the rules governing 'international' and 'non-international' air carriage from, or within, the UK can be taken as a convenient yardstick for all movements by air.

The carrier by air also operates under a strict regime of liability and is liable for the destruction or loss of or damage to goods or delay caused or occasioned during the carriage by air. The carriers' responsibilities extend to the entire period goods are in the carrier's charge at any aerodrome, as well as during the time they are on board any aircraft. Air carriers transporting and delivering goods to places outside an aerodrome are not bound by the Convention and their liability is that of a carrier by land (see p. 216). The conditions under which air carriers undertake land delivery are normally incorporated into the contractual terms set out in the air waybill.

The only defences available to the carrier by air are to prove that he and/or his agents took all necessary steps to avoid the damage, or that it was impossible for him to take such measures.

The carrier's financial limit of liability for loss, damage or delay is 250 gold Poincaré francs per kilo of the gross weight of the package, or packages, concerned. The sterling equivalent of the gold Poincaré franc is fixed by Statutory Instrument and currently 250 francs has a sterling value of £10.05. The limit for 1000 kilos (one tonne) is 250,000 francs, or £10,045.00. It is calculated by reference to the SDR value of a gold franc converted into sterling at an average SDR/Sterling exchange rate.

The failure of a carrier to issue an air waybill which contains the mandatory notice concerning the possible application of the Warsaw Convention disentitles him from limiting the liability as described in the last paragraph.

Claims for damage to or loss of goods should be made within 14 days of the receipt of cargo, or within 21 days in the case of delay. Any right to damages is extinguished after two years. Under UK legislation an action for damages can be brought against the contracting carrier, the actual carrier, or both, together or separately.

Multi-modal transport

Through transport by one contracting carrier offering 'door-to-door', or 'depot-to-depot', conveyance and using different modes of transport has given rise to numerous differing contracts of carriage. Despite their multiplicity, through transport contracts divide into two broad categories. There are those where the carrier undertakes to transport goods from a named place of collection to a named place of destination and assumes responsibility for them throughout the journey regardless of the modes of transport employed or actual carriers who may perform the carriage. Such contracts tend to be called combined transport contracts of carriage to distinguish them from through transport contracts where the carrier offers to transport goods from one named place to another with part carriage only by his own service(s) and for the balance he undertakes to procure carriage on behalf of and as agents for the goods-owner. Both types may be referred to as 'through transport' contracts—as indeed they are—and a careful scrutiny of the conditions of carriage will be necessary to determine into which category a particular contract falls.

Where the carrier accepts responsibility throughout for 'door-to-door' movements, it is usual to apply the network system of liability. Under such a system different levels of liability prevail, dependent upon the nature and mode of transport being used when the loss or damage occurred, e.g. Hague–Visby, CMR, RHA Conditions, etc. Where loss or damage occurs for which the carrier is responsible, but which cannot be specifically attributed to any particular leg of the journey, the carrier will apply the contractually stipulated level and monetary limit of liability, which can vary from carrier to carrier. A monetary limit of US$2.00 per kilo is an average amount.

With the other form of through transport contract, the principal or contracting carrier will accept liability for loss, damage, and where applicable delay, which occurs during the portion of the journey which he himself performs. Where loss, etc. is occasioned at some other stage of the through movement, the claimant must negotiate effectively with the actual carrier concerned, as the principal carrier is contractually entitled to maintain that any such carriage was arranged, or procured, on behalf of and as agents for the owner of the goods. Quite apart from the 'arm's length' relationship so engendered, the owner of goods damaged in transit faces the added burden of determining how and where damage occurred in order to proceed against the actual carrier concerned.

The United Nations Conference on Trade and Development (UNCTAD) has sponsored a Convention on International Multimodal Transport which, inter alia, caters for loss of or damage to goods while in the hands of a through transport operator or a multimodal carrier and introduces a single liability regime based on presumed fault. To date the Convention has received little support from any nation and is not operative anywhere.

River transport

Special conditions apply to goods transported on waterways/rivers, canals, etc. and the carrier's liability is usually very restricted.

Others in the transport chain

Goods in transit may pass through other hands apart from those of carriers by land, sea or air. Statutory regulation in the UK is confined to those forms of carriage indicated in the preceding paragraphs. Freedom of contract exists elsewhere, although many suppliers of services, e.g. warehousing, freight forwarding, removal contracts, etc., employ the contractual conditions recommended by the industry or business association to which they belong. Responsibility for loss of or damage to goods entrusted to such parties varies considerably, as do monetary limits of compensation where liability is accepted.

FURTHER READING

Robert H. Brown, 'The Principles', *Marine insurance,* vol. 1: 4th Edition, London: Witherby, 1978, 256 p.

Robert H. Brown, 'Cargo Practice', *Marine insurance,* vol. 2: 3rd Edition, London: Witherby 1979, 348 p.

Robert H. Brown, 'The Institute Cargo Clauses 1982', *Analysis of marine insurance clauses,* Book 1: London: Witherby, 1982.

David Lowe, *The transport manager's handbook,* London: Kogan Page. Annually. (Includes a chapter on goods in transit insurance.)

Jasper Ridley, *The law of the carriage of goods by land, sea and air,* 5th Edition, London: Shaw, 1978, 297 p.

11

Insurance of Liabilities

H. F. Dillon, Insurance Manager, The Nestlé Company Limited

Liability insurances may be described as contracts intended to indemnify the insured against the financial consequences of accidents of one kind or another for which, in law, he is responsible.

To be more precise, liability insurance is concerned with the legal liabilities of a person or body corporate, at common law, under statute and sometimes under contract, to pay damages in respect of personal injuries, or damage to property or for other financial loss, accidentally caused, arising out of the occupation or ownership of buildings, the operation of machinery and plant, other professional or business activities, products sold or supplied and the employment of labour. (Liabilities peculiar to the ownership or operation of ships, aircraft or oil rigs and platforms are outside the scope of this examination, and the liabilities in relation to motor vehicles are dealt with in Chapter 12.)

The range of these insurable liabilities is extensive and this chapter is necessarily restricted to the principal aspects of such liabilities and to the features of the main forms of insurance available.

There is no tariff for liability insurances in the UK and cover for most types of risk is widely available in both the company market and at Lloyd's. The market is, however, more restricted for the specialist types of liability cover such as professional indemnity, while the capacity of the market generally to absorb particularly heavy-risk high-indemnity limits is at times suspect. Capacity problems, however, tend to be more a question of lack of support within the insurance market to underwrite a particular policy at a particular premium rather than the inability of the market to fully accept such covers.

The underwriting practice of individual insurers does of course vary considerably, with the result that some insurers are recognised as specialists or 'leaders' in certain classes of liability business, while others may be known as not being in the market at all for such classes of business or be known to severely restrict their acceptances in these or other types of liability covers.

'The right contract at the right price' is a dictum applicable as much to the purchase of liability insurance as to any other type of insurance, but in the case of liability insurance in particular such a contract without the backing of a first-class service for the handling of claims is unsatisfactory. An efficient, realistic approach to the handling of claims, including close liaison with the insured, and the avoidance of unnecessary litigation are essential to keep down the cost of claims, which in turn affects the premium. In addition, such an approach provides the insured with a service in the field of public and/or labour relations. An ineffective claims service can easily be a disservice.

For the purposes of this chapter, liability insurances are examined under three main headings:

1 Public (or general third party) liability.
2 Products liability.
3 Employers' liability.

Depending on the practice of individual insurers, it is quite common to find the first two categories of risk covered by the same policy, and there is also a developing tendency among insurers to offer a 'package' deal combining all three liability risks under a single contract.

Whatever forms of policy are used, it is essential to ensure that the indemnity provided is complete: there should be no overlapping of the covers and, more importantly, no unintended gaps between them. Although this should be simpler to achieve when all the insurances are with a single insurer—and this may possibly also be of assistance should a borderline claim arise—considerations of premium cost and/or availability of cover may of course be paramount in determining the choice of insurers.

PUBLIC LIABILITY INSURANCE

The terms 'public liability' and 'third party liability' are synonymous, but to avoid possible confusion the former term is used throughout this chapter.

Need for insurance

All business concerns are exposed in a greater or lesser degree to liability to members of the public for personal injuries or damage to property, whether due to defects in their premises or plant, or to the negligence of their employees. As this liability can involve very substantial damages, public liability insurance is really essential to any firm and, subject of course to availability, generous limits of indemnity are to be recommended.

Thus, although there is no statutory obligation for a person or firm to effect this form of insurance, it is nonetheless commercially prudent to be covered. On occasion, the cover is made compulsory by contract as for example where an employer, under a construction contract, makes it obligatory for the contractor to arrange certain forms of insurance including, inter alia, cover for public liability risks (see Chapter 14).

The need for insurance protection is emphasised by the rise in both the frequency and cost of public liability claims over the years. This can be attributed largely to increasing public awareness of rights and remedies at law, inflation, the effect of the legal aid system, and the higher incidence of accidents due to the pace and complexity of modern life with its rapid technological changes. The development of legal expense insurance in recent years may be regarded as another factor. There is also the tendency for commercial contracts to require one party to give very wide indemnities to the other, although the position has been mitigated since the introduction of the Unfair Contract Terms Act, 1977.

Insurance not only provides an indemnity for claims that are substantiated against the insured, including claimants' costs, but, because the conduct of claims is taken over by the insurers, also relieves the insured of the worry and expense of resisting claims, including those of a spurious nature. Even the successful defence of an action will not necessarily mean the recovery of costs when the plaintiff is of no substance or is legally aided, and such costs may be considerable.

Proposal

The proposal is usually referred to in a policy as being the basis of the contract and this applies whether a formal proposal form has been completed or there has simply been an exchange of correspondence. It is, moreover, usually a condition of the contract that the insurers are advised of any changes which materially vary the facts contained in the original proposal. It is advisable, therefore, for the insured to keep a copy of the proposal on file for future reference together with a copy of all subsequent particulars that are supplied to the insurers. It should also serve as the basis for a review of the insurance at least once a year, at renewal.

Form of policy

The basic policy forms used by individual insurers are adaptable to meet the needs of the vast majority of public liability risks, but although they are fundamentally similar in style, many points of difference are found both in the choice of wording and in the extent of the indemnity provided; these differences will be referred to in this chapter.

The form of policy is examined below under five main sections (leaving aside the preamble or introductory part of the wording): operative clause (or statement of cover provided), exclusions, schedule (or particulars of the individual risk), premium, and conditions. All of these are intended to be read in conjunction with each other. For certain types of liability which require special treatment, as for example professional indemnities for architects and solicitors, hotel owners' liabilities, and the general field of contingency risks, insurers usually provide a special form of contract, and brief notes on these liabilities and the cover provided are given at the end of this section.

Cover provided (operative clause)

The wordings used and the extent of the indemnity provided by this clause vary considerably between different insurers. Essentially the clause should indemnify the insured against all sums which he shall become legally liable to pay to third parties consequent upon bodily injury to any person and/or loss of or damage to property that:

1 Is accidentally caused, and
2 Occurs during the period of insurance, and
3 Arises in connection with the business, and
4 Occurs at any premises or place specified in the schedule or within the geographical limits.

Loss

The words 'loss of' may be omitted, but although the degree of risk is limited by the exclusion of property in the insured's custody or control, liability for loss can arise even though the insured may not be in direct control of the property, and it should be covered.

Property

This term is sometimes defined in the policy as material property and without this definition or some other form of restriction elsewhere in the policy the word must be assumed to have its wider meaning in law to include immaterial property.

Consequential loss

The intention of the clause should be to provide an indemnity not only for the actual cost of repairs or reinstatement of damaged property but for all payments for which the insured is legally liable as a result of the negligent act or omission causing such damage—that is, consequential loss. A claim for loss of business can be extremely expensive and if the insurance is limited to the cost of the physical damage alone there is a serious gap in the indemnity. For this reason the use of a phrase such as 'compensation in respect of damage to property' is preferred to 'compensation for damage', etc. The use of such words as 'compensation (or damages) consequent upon (or arising out of) damage to property' avoids any ambiguity on this point. For personal injury claims the consequential loss element is usually included in the damages as loss of earnings or earning power.

Accidents

Some policies may refer to 'accidents causing injury or damage' or 'injury or damage caused by accident', others to 'accidental injury or damage'. The latter expression is generally regarded to be the less restrictive while the omission altogether of the words 'accident' and 'accidental' in the operative clause—as is increasingly found nowadays—would appear to provide the widest form of cover, although it is the normal practice in such cases to incorporate a policy exclusion with regard to injury, loss, or damage which can reasonably be foreseen to be inevitable or deliberately caused. Whatever words are used, however, they are capable of individual interpretation, and the different shades of meaning can sometimes seem very fine. It is therefore desirable to establish with the insurers the intention behind their particular choice of words in this context so that both parties are *ad idem.*

The word 'accident' is not usually defined in the policy and when used gives rise to doubt as to whether it refers to the negligent act of the insured or the actual happening of the injury or damage. This is of relevance where there is a considerable lapse of time between the two events so that only one occurred within the period of insurance. If the insurers at the time of the injury or damage were not the insurers at the time of the negligent act, problems may arise and it is therefore advisable to check the position, particularly if any change of insurers is contemplated at any time or a new company acquired. (It is in any case a prudent safeguard to retain cancelled policies—if not indefinitely, at least for a good many years.)

Exceptions and the extent to which they may be modified

The exceptions are usually grouped together in most policies but sometimes an exclusion will appear in the operative clause or an endorsement. The exceptions listed below are those most commonly used but they do not all necessarily appear on all policies. It should be remembered that 'exceptions' are often used by insurers, as a form of underwriting control, to elicit the existence of special risks for which cover is usually negotiable.

Injury to employees in the service of the insured

This exclusion should be the subject of an employers' liability policy but it is worth noting that it usually applies to injury or disease arising out of *and* in the course of the employment in line with the description of indemnity in an employers' liability policy. When the exclusion is so worded it means that if the injury should arise in the course of the employment but not out of the employment, as can happen, the claim is not excluded from the public liability policy.

Damage to property owned by the insured

As a public liability policy is concerned only with liabilities, property belonging to the insured should be covered under an appropriate form of material damage insurance. Apart from emphasising the point, the exclusion also serves to exclude the insured's legal liability for making good damage to his own property, which may arise, for example, under the terms of a lease he has granted to a tenant.

Damage to property in the custody or control of the insured

This exclusion applies for much the same reason as the previous one. It is basically intended to exclude damage to both movable property for which the insured is responsible as a bailee and immovable property, e.g. premises leased or hired to him. Insurers are, however, generally prepared to modify the exclusion so as to cover, for example, liability for cars left in an insured's car park, or for damage to a hall hired for a particular event.

A motor trader is accepted as a special class of bailee by insurers with regard to customers' vehicles, and a warehouseman may also be able to effect a legal liability cover for customers' goods when his conditions of storage or warehousing warrant it.

'Custody or control'. Unfortunately the words 'custody or control' lack clear legal definition and misunderstandings sometimes arise particularly when work is carried out on a third party's premises or when property is temporarily left on an insured's premises for no specific purpose. In an effort to clarify their intentions to some extent insurers quite commonly amend the exclusion so that it does not apply to premises, or the contents thereof, that are temporarily in the insured's charge for work therein or thereon.

Employees' effects including motor vehicles. In some policies property belonging to employees is specifically excluded but most insurers now cover this liability.

Leased premises. A tenant is liable in negligence for damage to the premises he occupies in the absence of any agreement in the lease to the contrary. In particular he is liable for fire and explosion damage to such premises caused by his proven negligence and, even though the landlord may effect insurance and charge the tenant premium, this may not fully protect the tenant if the landlord's insurance is inadequate. In many cases, too, the tenant may have no beneficial interest in or control over the landlord's fire insurance so that the potential liability to which he is exposed is accentuated unless he is able to contract out of all responsibility by the terms of the lease. Although some insurers provide cover for a tenant's liability in negligence for leased premises under a public liability policy there has been a reluctance among insurers to do so, particularly for fire and explosion risks, and other forms of cover may be offered which are usually more expensive. Where, of course, the tenant specifically accepts responsibility for fire and explosion damage to the premises he needs to effect suitable material damage insurance although the situation may be complicated by the terms of a covenant to insure contained in the lease.

Property being worked on. The exclusion is sometimes extended to apply to damage to that part of property on which the insured is or has been working if such damage directly results from the work.

This is designed to exclude claims for making good defective or faulty work, which is regarded as a trade risk, but difficulties and inconsistencies in interpretation have led some insurers to omit this exclusion except for certain types of risk such as contractors.

Fire and explosion

An occupier of premises may be liable for damage to neighbouring property or injury to persons caused by fire or explosion originating in his premises if negligence can be proved against him or if a dangerous substance kept by him on the premises should get out of control and, say, cause an explosion. An owner of property (as distinct from an occupier) or a contractor working on the premises would be under a similar liability.

There is therefore a real need to cover this liability, which can reach catastrophic proportions as, for example, with a chemical works or oil refinery in industrial or dock areas. Most public liability insurers will readily provide cover in the majority of cases but will normally continue to exclude liability arising out of the explosion of boilers and other steam pressure vessels. This is due to a peculiarity of British insurance practice whereby such liability is traditionally included in the standard indemnity of a boiler and pressure vessel policy (see Chapter 13). At present it is not uncommon to find the explosion exclusion limited to property, so that liability for third party personal injury is covered under both the public liability and the boiler policies, although the limits of indemnity may differ. A similar overlapping of cover may arise with pressure vessels not under steam. There is, however, no reason why liability for full explosion should not be covered by a public liability policy, and some insurers are prepared to do this, thus allowing the boiler policy to be restricted to damage to the insured's own property and the statutory inspection service. It is a development that should become more widespread in the future.

Vehicles, vessels or craft

Although the wording of this exclusion varies, it is intended to exclude liability arising out of any mechanically propelled vehicle, ship or aircraft, as these should be the subject of separate insurances.

The vehicles exclusion is, however, often amended so that it applies only to vehicles that are used on the public highway—that is, those subject to the Road Traffic Act—and vehicles such as forklift trucks that are used exclusively within private roads or grounds may be covered by the insurance. Moreover, the exclusion should be modified so as to complement the limitation in the motor insurance with regard to the loading and unloading risks, for example, to cover the liability arising out of loading and unloading beyond the limit of any carriageway by persons other than the driver or attendant of the vehicle. Should there be doubt about whether the two covers do in fact dovetail in this respect, confirmation should be sought from the insurers.

Lifts, hoists and cranes

Such plant is often excluded 'except when specified in the schedule', but it is in fact the common practice of insurers to cover such equipment by deletion of the exclusion, although some still prefer to treat passenger lifts separately.

Goods sold or supplied

Some insurers prefer to deal with this risk as a separate liability insurance (products liability) and it will be discussed more fully later on. The exclusion is, however, often modified so as to cover, for example, the food poisoning risk arising out of meals sold or supplied in a firm's canteen. Although primarily intended to protect the insured in respect of meals served to visitors such cover could, in certain circumstances, also apply to claims made by employees.

The exclusion must of course be cancelled if products liability is to be covered under the policy.

Subsidence

The extent of this exclusion is normally expressed as liability caused by 'the removal or weakening of support'—although subsidence may also be specifically mentioned—and may apply to injury as well as damage caused thereby. It is not a hazard of general concern but may have serious implications in some cases, notably when building work is being undertaken. Vibration is usually included in the exclusion for much the same reason and, although the risks are insurable, insurers wish to be able to consider each case on its merits, possibly limiting the amount of cover and imposing an excess.

War and kindred risks

Such risks are uninsurable.

Nuclear and radioactive risks

Special insurance arrangements are necessary for such risks, which are outside the scope of this examination.

Contractual liabilities

This exclusion is normally expressed as liability assumed under a contract or agreement unless such liability would have attached to the insured in the absence of such agreement. This means, in substance, that when the insured's position at common law (or statute law) is unaltered by the assumed liability, the policy is unaffected, but in all other cases it is necessary to obtain the insurer's consent to extend the indemnity appropriately. Many trade and professional institutes, government departments and nationalised industries have their own recommended forms of contract wording, all of which contain indemnity clauses of one kind or another, and it is vital that the insurers are aware of the conditions of contract accepted by the insured if the policy is to provide effective cover. It is not uncommon for a contract to impose liabilities on one party which are far more onerous than would be the normal legal position, although the situation has been improved by the Unfair Contract Terms Act, 1977. It may be, too, that the cover required is beyond the scope of the indemnity provided by the policy: for example, cover may be required for subsidence, which is normally an excluded risk, or for a risk which is uninsurable. Such liability clauses therefore also require careful scrutiny in relation to the policy indemnity, even where the policy omits this exclusion or restricts it to liability arising out of non-performance or non-completion of a contract and any penalties attaching thereto.

Responsibility for insurance under contract. Many of the standard forms of contract recommended by professional and other bodies impose a duty on one party, usually the contractor but sometimes the employer, to effect insurance, often in the joint names of himself and the other party or parties, for public liability risks and other liabilities or loss.

Of particular interest in this respect is the responsibility of a contractor, under clause 19(2)(a) of the Royal Institute of British Architects' form of contract, to effect insurance on behalf of the employer, in their joint names, for any expense, liability, loss or claim that the employer may incur by reason of damage to property—other than the contract works—due to collapse, subsidence, vibration, etc., *caused other than* by the negligence, omission or default of the contractor, his servants or agents. Not only is damage to property of third parties included but also property of the employer, except for such damage that may be at the employer's risk by other conditions of the contract. Damage due to defective design or of an inevitable nature is also excluded. The foregoing is in addition to the contractor's obligation to effect insurance for third party liability risks due to his negligence, etc., and for specified risks of damage to the contract works as required elsewhere in the contract. It is necessary, however, for an employer specifically to request cover in the terms of clause 19(2)(a), if required. (For special insurance considerations applying to contractors reference should be made to Chapter 14.)

Subcontractors

Where this exclusion appears it is to elicit the existence of subcontracting so that a suitable premium can be charged to cover the insured's liability in respect of subcontractors, if required. Such liability may be covered either by deletion of the exclusion or by having the insured's interest noted in the subcontractor's policy. However, as it is difficult to ensure that the arrangements made by the subcontractor are effectively maintained, the insured is well advised to cover his own contingent liability.

Liability arising outside geographical limit

The territorial limit is usually defined as Great Britain, Northern Ireland, the Channel Islands and the Isle of Man. However, it is fairly standard for insurers to extend cover, when requested, to overseas commercial visits of the insured or his employees normally resident in the insured territories, subject usually to the action being brought against the insured in this country. A firm engaged in trading abroad with its own establishments or working on contracts abroad will of course require wider geographical limits—if such overseas operations are not separately insured—and an extension to include actions brought against it in the courts of the country where the injury or damage occurs and preferably extending the jurisdiction worldwide.

Flood, fumes, pollution, effluents

Although this exclusion does not always appear, where such hazards arise insurers would normally exclude them unless due allowance was made in the premium. The flood risk is of concern where privately owned rivers, lakes or reservoirs, etc., are involved, while the other exclusions relate to the discharge of noxious effluents or gases, causing pollution of rivers or the atmosphere.

Particulars of the individual risk (or schedule)

Insured

If it is intended to include subsidiary or affiliated companies, these should be named or suitably described in the schedule, and should it be necessary to include the interest of any principal of the insured, this is normally dealt with by a specific clause. It is generally desirable, whenever there are joint insureds, to incorporate a cross-liabilities clause in the policy, which has the effect of treating each party as though separately insured in the event of a claim being made by one against the other, although subject to the insurers' liability not exceeding the stated policy limit. It may also be relevant to extend the policy to cover the individual liability of directors or employees where work of a private nature is undertaken on their behalf by other employees of the company.

Business

This should be described in the broadest terms to allow for normal business development but even so certain activities incidental to a particular business may need special mention by endorsement. Examples are first-aid treatment by a firm's own medical staff, the activities of its fire-fighting squad, special sales promotions on the insured's behalf or demonstrations on the premises of third parties. The interest of a firm's social or sports club may also need to be covered and the indemnity in this case should include member-to-member liability as well as the liability of members and officials of the club vis-à-vis third parties.

Limit of liability

The monetary limit is normally expressed as a limit on any one occurrence, or series of occurrences consequent upon or attributable to one source or original cause. The words 'accident' or 'event' may be used instead of 'occurrence'. Legal costs recoverable against the insured and those incurred by the insured with the insurers' consent are covered usually in addition to the limit of indemnity. The limit chosen should be revised periodically but today a limit of £500,000 would seem a necessary minimum for most ordinary policies, although the limit can run into many millions, particularly where there is a heavy fire or explosion hazard. It should be remembered that liability at common law is unlimited in amount. For the higher indemnity limits, the additional amounts of cover are usually arranged by separate policies on a 'layered' basis, i.e. if the primary policy has a limit of £500,000 the next layer of cover may run from that limit to, say, £2,000,000, and so on.

Premises (or places to which the insurance applies)

In addition to covering any premises owned, leased, or occupied by the insured, the indemnity should extend to apply wherever the insured's employees may be engaged in connection with the business. Special mention may also be necessary for such property as neon or other signs erected on the premises of third parties. (Some policies simply refer to the geographical limits so that there is no reference to premises).

Plant (or lifting equipment)

Unless the exclusions relating to vehicles and lifting equipment respectively have otherwise been modified—as indicated earlier— all plant intended to be covered, e.g. cranes, forklift trucks and lifts, should be specified in general terms under this heading: for example, as 'all lifting plant owned or used by the insured', even if the insurers should require a detailed list to be established for premium purposes.

Premium

There are several methods of premium calculation in use. Shops or small businesses, for example, may be rated on a per capita basis or on a flat premium. The principal method employed is to charge a rate per cent on either:

1 Total annual payroll (including or excluding clerical staff), or, less frequently,
2 Annual turnover.

The premium in these cases is adjustable each year, that is, the provisional premium charged at the beginning of the insurance period on estimated payroll or turnover is compared with the premium calculated on the actual payroll or turnover for the period and the difference is either refunded to or paid by the insured.

There may also be certain fixed additional premiums for extensions of cover. Where a rate per cent is charged this can differ considerably between businesses and even between firms engaged in the same business. Premium rates depend on many factors: location of the premises, type of manufacturing processes, extent to which employees have contact with the public, etc. The normal bases of rating mean that the premium increases (or decreases) keep in step with payroll or turnover and are justified by insurers as reflecting inflation and the general expansion (or contraction) of the business with a corresponding increase (decrease) in the public liability risks. It may be argued, however, that these methods of rating are somewhat arbitrary, and that in some cases neither method is wholly satisfactory. Higher turnover may be due to greater productivity without any increase in workforce or premises used. Higher prices, too, are reflected in turnover, but insurers also have their higher claims and service costs for much the same reason.

Similar shortcomings may be found in the payroll basis of rating, but it should be remembered that the rating of public liability insurances is far from being an exact science, and the premium—together with the other terms and conditions of any contract—should be revised from time to time in the light of experience and the development of the business.

Conditions

Many of the conditions are common to most insurance policies, but those calling for special mention are as follows.

Notification of claims. Written notice of any accident or claim must be given to the insurers as soon as possible and every letter or summons received forwarded immediately.

Conduct of the insured in the event of an accident. The insured must not enter into any negotiations in connection with any accident or claim without the insurers' consent, so as to avoid the risk of prejudicing his legal position. He must also assist the insurers as far as he can.

Payment to insured of limit of indemnity to discharge insurers' liability. The insurers have this option, which may be exercised when a particular claim looks likely to exceed the policy limit for any one accident, and thereafter they are under no further liability. The object is to avoid the insurers' involvement in costs out of proportion to their actual liability under the policy.

Alteration in risk. Any alteration materially varying the facts on which the insurance was arranged must be notified to the insurers as with other classes of insurance, and it should perhaps be mentioned that when a particular liability is not specifically excluded this does not necessarily mean it is covered if it has not been divulged to the insurer. It is a question of degree. A minor liability may be covered on the basis of facts disclosed at the inception of the contract, but should this liability increase significantly it is material and must be disclosed.

Premium adjustment clause (where applicable). This simply refers to the adjustable nature of the premium, and the information to be recorded by the insured and supplied to the insurers at the close of each period of insurance.

Precautions to be taken to prevent accidents. An insured is required to exercise reasonable care on the selection of competent employees and in seeing that his buildings and plant are sound and fit for the purposes for which they are used. Moreover, all reasonable precautions to prevent accidents must be taken, including com-pliance with any statutory enactments.

SOME TYPES OF SPECIAL LIABILITY INSURANCE

There are certain forms of legal liability which require an indemnity beyond that normally provided by a public liability policy. As these usually call for a special form of contract, examples of such liabilities are briefly commented on below.

Professional indemnity

Professional indemnity policies are designed to protect such individuals or firms as architects, accountants, solicitors and insurance brokers against claims for financial loss that may be made against them by reason of their failure to exercise that degree of care and skill that is expected of them in the conduct of their profession or business. The indemnity therefore usually applies to liability arising out of any negligent act, error or omission on the part of the insured or his employees. It is thus not dependent on the happening of bodily injury or damage to property as under an ordinary public liability policy. There are variations in the policy wordings and the exclusions and extensions according to the special features of each profession and market experience; for example, a solicitor's indemnity may be extended to include actions for libel and/or slander. An excess will often apply, either voluntarily to reduce the premium, or imposed as part of the terms of cover.

Directors' and officers' liability

A director or officer of a company owes duties and responsibilities to the company, its shareholders, employees and the public. These are individual responsibilities and arise at common law and under statute, principally the various Companies' Acts but also, for example, the Health and Safety at Work Act. If accused of a wrongful act the director cannot rely on company funds during the course of legal proceedings, nor hide behind the corporate veil. He is personally liable and indemnity provisions in the Articles of Association of the company cannot guarantee the degree of protection he might reasonably expect. Although the shareholders and employees are obvious potential claimants, other parties such as takeover-bidders may also seek redress if they have suffered a loss through reliance on the incorrect representations of a director.

Insurance cover has therefore developed to indemnify individual directors and officers in respect of their liability at law for breach of trust or duty, including error or omission, mis-statement or misleading statements committed in the course of their duties. Cover is subject to an excess for each and every loss and excludes certain actions including those brought against an individual director or officer as a result of his own dishonest, fraudulent or malicious conduct. Concurrent with such an insurance there is cover available for the company itself in so far as it may be required or permitted at law to indemnify the director or officer.

While this type of insurance is widely used in the USA it has so far only sparsely attracted UK companies but the increasing demand for greater individual accountability of those in positions of responsibility may well promote the growth of this type of insurance in the future.

Legal expenses insurance

This type of cover, which is of fairly recent origin in the UK, may be described as a form of liability insurance if only in a somewhat limited sense. It basically provides for the payment of legal costs and expenses in pursuing or defending the insured's legal rights in or out of the civil courts and in defending criminal proceedings against the insured and/or his employees arising out of their normal business operations or duties. The form of cover differs as between that offered to a commercial concern, or its employees, and that offered to an individual and both may be limited to certain types of legal proceedings to reduce the premium cost. A limit for any one incident applies, usually in the region of £25,000. This form of insurance is of rather more interest to individuals and the smaller firms, particularly with the plethora of employment-related legislation over the past decade, such as the Employment Protection Acts, Equal Pay Act, Sex Discrimination Act and the Health and Safety at Work Act.

It should also be mentioned that while general third party liability insurers are basically concerned with the insured's legal liability for bodily injury or damage to property, some are prepared to include within their policy cover the insured's liability and, where appropriate, that of its employees, to pay legal costs and expenses (including compensation that may be awarded but not fines or penalties) in defending prosecutions under the Health and Safety at Work Act and on occasions proceedings under other employment-related legislation.

Hotel owners

In addition to his liabilities in negligence, an innkeeper within the meaning of the Hotel Proprietors Act, 1956 has, subject to certain conditions and limitations, a strict liability: that is, it is not necessary to prove fault or negligence to recover damages for loss of or damage to the property of 'guests', as defined by the Act. It is therefore necessary for a hotel owner to ensure that his liability insurance provides an indemnity adequate to cover this statutory liability.

Contingency

Contingency is a generic term used by insurers to describe the type of insurance that may be effected to cover one of a variety of liabilities giving rise to financial loss in transactions of one kind or another, dependent on the happening of certain fortuitous possibilities. The insurance provides against the happening of a specific and foreseeable event described in exact terms rather than events of a general defined nature as is usual in most other classes of insurance. Special forms of policy are usually called for and each contract involves individual underwriting consideration.

For example, a purchaser of property may seek protection against claims that may be made against him by reason of some defect in the title he has acquired. Restrictive covenants, although long dormant, may preclude use of the property for the purpose intended by the purchaser, who may in consequence seek cover against the contingency of the covenant being enforced before further expense is incurred.

The indemnity may sometimes be required in favour of a person other than the proposer, as, for example, when a third party is requested to take a course of action in favour of the proposer which, although reasonable and right in equity, may be unsafe in law.

Thus, an executor or administrator of a will may agree to distribute the share in an estate of a beneficiary who has been missing for many years among the other beneficiaries if the latter provide him with an indemnity against the missing beneficiary reappearing to claim his inheritance. A counter-indemnity is usually required by the insurers in such cases.

Other forms of contingency insurance include issue and marriage risks, missing documents, and recovery of sanity.

Very careful enquiries are made by insurers before underwriting any contingency risk, and they must be satisfied that there is at least a reasonable doubt of the contingency arising and that the act for which the indemnity is required is not illegal.

PRODUCTS LIABILITY

Need for insurance

Liability for products sold or supplied may arise not only in negligence at common law but also under statute—of which the most important is the Sale of Goods Act, 1979, which, inter alia, provides that proof of negligence is unnecessary in certain circumstances—or by breach of any other condition of sale imposed by contract.

The duty owed by a manufacturer or supplier of goods to exercise care towards all those whom he might reasonably foresee suffering by reason of his failure to take such care is thus usually a very high one and the demand for insurance protection has led to a considerable development in this type of insurance over the years.

In the UK, however, the buyer of a product is in a far more favourable position vis-à-vis the seller than that of all others who may use the product because of his contractual relationship. If he can show that the product causing injury, damage or financial loss was defective at the time of purchase, he can claim damages for breach of contract against the seller. The seller would be liable regardless of fault.

Some manufacturers endeavour, by imposing stringent conditions of sale, to contract out of their more onerous responsibilities for the consequences of injury or damage caused by defective goods supplied. The validity of such disclaimers today must be highly questionable, particularly with the advent of the Unfair Contract Terms Act, 1977—which, inter alia, prohibits contracting out of liability in negligence for personal injuries—and it is perhaps even more relevant for an insurer to know whether the producer is accepting greater liability for his products than the law requires.

The potential liabilities for certain industries are, of course, enormous and from time to time there are problems of capacity in the insurance market to meet requirements.

The liabilities of manufacturers, especially for bodily injuries caused by their products, have been the subject of much serious debate during the past decade following the growth of consumerism, particularly in the aftermath of the thalidomide tragedy. It is generally accepted that there is need for an improvement in the present legal position in favour of the consumer (including the non-purchaser) to ensure a more satisfactory means of redress for injuries sustained as a result of a defective product.

Already in the USA, strict liability of varying degrees has been imposed on producers by the courts in many states although efforts are being made by the Federal Government to bring about a more uniform and sensible approach to this subject. Strict liability may be described as liability imposed by law, irrespective of fault on the part of the person made liable, subject to whatever defences are prescribed in a particular case.

In Europe, the Council of Europe's Convention on Product Liability—known as the Strasbourg Convention—in 1977 and the EEC Draft Directives on this subject, as well as our own Pearson Commission Report in 1978, have all come out strongly in favour of a system of strict liability on producers. The recommendations of these bodies differ in many respects and some of the important issues that have to be resolved include the development risk (whether the manufacturer should be permitted the 'state of the art' defence), limitation of liability as to amount, the defence of contributory negligence and whether or not insurance should be made compulsory. There can be little doubt that strict liability will be imposed on manufacturers in Europe, including the UK, and only the final form it will take and the date of its implementation remain in doubt. For the pharmaceutical industry in Germany it is already a fact.

It still remains highly debatable to what extent insurance premiums will be increased by a system of strict liability, bearing in mind that in the UK at least there is already a large measure of strict liability under existing law as between the buyer and seller of the product.

A product liability policy may be considered under five main headings, as with a general public liability policy, namely: the operative clause (or statement of cover provided), exclusions, schedule, premiums and conditions. As with a public liability policy, the proposal made by the insured is the basis of the contract.

Cover provided (or operative clause)

The wording of the operative clause varies in much the same way as with public liability policies according to the individual practice of insurers. It may, for example, be limited to the happening of an accident or it may cover legal liability for 'accidental bodily injury or accidental damage to property arising out of any product or its container'. Sometimes the reference to 'accident' or 'accidental' may be omitted altogether (although qualified by the usual form of exclusion of injury or damage of an inevitable nature) or the cover may be restricted to claims 'for' injury or damage due to any product rather than 'arising out of' (or 'in consequence of') such injury or damage and so may infer the exclusion of consequential loss (see the comments on 'consequential loss' and 'accidents' on pp.228–9).

The word 'defect' may also appear in the qualifying clause, as in 'caused by any defect in the products', but as defects in design are normally excluded the restriction in cover is minimal. Very exceptionally, a wording may be used which covers all claims caused by defects of manufacture so that consequential loss due to a failure or breakdown of the product is included without the need for there to be injury or damage.

It is important that the operative clause should include the containers of the products including their labelling, particularly where bottled or canned goods are involved or where the packaging forms an intrinsic part of the product.

The interpretation of the wordings used is by no means uniform and if doubts exist about the scope of a particular cover then clarification should be sought from the insurers, who are sometimes prepared to use broader terms in selected cases subject to possible adjustment of the premium rate. The operative clause must of course be read in conjunction with the exclusions, which again are not necessarily standard in all policies.

Exclusions and extent to which they may be modified

Liability for injury to insured's own employees (arising out of and in the course of their employment) and liability for damage to property owned by or in the custody or control of the insured

The first exclusion is normally covered by the employers' liability policy and the second exclusion by other forms of insurance, but the latter may be modified so as to exclude only the insured's own property.

Liability for injury or damage to property arising out of the products while in the insured's custody or control

The indemnity is only intended to apply once the products have left the insured's control as up to that point the risk should be covered by the public liability policy.

Liability for injury or damage caused by products sold outside the territorial limits

These limits are usually specified in the schedule (see below) and are especially important when products are exported all over the world.

War risks, nuclear and radioactive risks

War risks are uninsurable and special arrangements must be made for radioactivity due to nuclear fuels or explosive nuclear devices.

Liability assumed by agreement

This exclusion usually applies so that the insurers may be aware of any express warranty or contract condition which places on the insured a more onerous liability than they have undertaken to insure.

The insured's normal contract conditions should therefore be made known to the insurer and any variation of those conditions in a particular case which increases the insured's liability must be disclosed to the insurers. The exclusion may also apply to any rights or recourse against any party that may be waived by the insured in respect of products supplied to him.

Liability for the cost of repairing or replacing defective products

This is regarded as a normal trade risk and is not insured except in very rare cases as under products guarantee covers mentioned later.

It may, however, be possible to cover the cost involved in recovering or recalling defective products, as distinct from their replacement cost, although such cover (known as *products recall*) is not widely underwritten in the UK. It would nevertheless appear to be a natural development of products liability insurance in cases where heavy recovery expenses may be involved, bearing in mind that if the defect is of a kind liable to give rise to injury or damage then the manufacturer or supplier is obliged by the policy conditions to take all reasonable steps to remedy or make good such defects, quite apart from humanitarian considerations and the desire to safeguard his reputation.

Liability arising from faulty or inadequate design or specification

This exclusion concerns defects in the design or conception of a product as opposed to defects in the product itself: it excludes cases in which the product is made as intended but is defective because of some oversight or failure in its basic design. Such a restriction may sometimes be removed, but this very much depends on the nature of the products and on the insurer's knowledge of the manufacturer. When such cover is granted it is normally limited to liability for bodily injury or damage to property caused by the defective product. A demand has, however, developed from those engaged in design work, including some contractors, for specific *defective design* cover to provide for claims arising out of any negligent act, error or omission in respect of design or specification and this may apply to all sums that the insured shall become legally liable to pay irrespective of whether there has been any bodily injury or damage to property. Such cover is akin to professional indemnity insurance and is very selectively underwritten in the limited market for such contracts.

Products guarantee. Products guarantee cover represents about the widest extension of products liability coverage available, although the insurance market is understandably very wary of providing it and would normally only consider doing so if the product is well tried and reasonably non-hazardous. The cover extends the normal products liability policy to incorporate liability for failure of the product to correctly fulfil its intended purpose, including the consequential losses of the insured's customer arising therefrom. The usual exclusions of defective design and liability assumed by agreement cease to apply and the cover may include the cost of replacing the product. The market for such cover is restricted, and insurances of this kind are comparatively rare in the UK.

Particulars of the individual risk (or schedule)

Insured

In addition to any subsidiary or affiliated companies (or parent company) that it may be intended to cover, it may be necessary to include a reference in the schedule, or by a separate clause, to any subcontractor or distributor to whom an indemnity may be given in respect of the products.

Business

This should be adequately described, as the insurance is often limited to the carrying on of the business so defined 'and no other for the purpose of this insurance'.

Products

All products to be covered, whether manufactured and supplied or supplied but not manufactured by the insured, should be embodied in the description of the products.

Premium offer goods. The practice of manufacturers or suppliers promoting sales by offering customers free gifts or goods at a discounted price provided a certain quantity of the firm's own products are purchased gives rise to a products liability risk in respect of those gifts or goods even if this is only a contingent liability. The articles offered may not be those in which the particular firm usually trades or of which they have special knowledge, and the inherent hazards of such products may be quite different from those of the firm's own products. The risk is slight where well-known branded goods are involved or guarantees are obtained, but if the goods are purchased from an obscure foreign manufacturer or a supplier of little substance the potential liability could be much more onerous. Clearly the degree of risk depends on the nature of the goods on offer; an electrical appliance, for example, is more of a problem than, say, chinaware.

The type of goods offered in these promotions is necessarily varied, and firms engaged in this form of trading are well advised to make provision for such goods in their products liability coverage.

Limits of indemnity

Normally insurers limit the *amount* of indemnity in respect of 'any one person' or 'any one accident' and 'in total' for all claims during any one period of insurance. The total limit should, where possible, be at least twice that of the single accident limit. The amount of indemnity chosen by the insured will depend on the type of products, but except where the liability is fairly innocuous a single accident limit of at least £500,000 might be advisable. In many cases, of course, far higher indemnities will be required running into millions of pounds and this is particularly necessary if the cover extends to include claims brought against the insured in North America, where the level of awards is so much higher than elsewhere. Legal costs are usually covered in addition to the indemnity limits.

Sometimes the indemnity is subject to claims being brought in the British courts or settled in accordance with English (or Scottish) law. This may be sufficient when the insured holds no permanent assets abroad but it is infinitely preferable when the territorial limits extend overseas that foreign jurisdiction should also be covered and this is essential if the insured owns assets abroad, even though claim payments may well have to be made in sterling in the UK.

Territorial limits

These depend on the requirements of the insured firms and the nature of its organisation, but exporting firms usually require cover on a worldwide basis. However, if the insured firm has its own local establishments abroad, with possibly local subsidiary companies, the position is more complex and special consideration should be given to the form of coverage best suited to the insured's particular needs, taking into account the fiscal and insurance laws in the countries concerned as well as the practical aspects of claims servicing, premium cost and other relevant factors.

Premium

Premium is most commonly calculated by applying a rate per cent to annual turnover, a provisional premium being charged on estimated turnover which is 'adjusted' on the basis of the actual turnover for the year when known. Other bases of rating include production units and occasionally payroll instead of turnover or a flat premium may be applied. Premium rates depend, quite naturally, on the type of products supplied; a drug manufacturer represents a much higher risk than, say, a manufacturer of chinaware but other considerations also apply including the general competence of the insured, his record of claims over a period of years, conditions of sale and the extent of the indemnity provided.

Conditions

Typical policy conditions are very similar to those applicable to public liability policies (see p. 239) including the option open to the insurers to discharge their obligations under the contract on payment to the insured of the appropriate limit of indemnity (less any sums already paid as compensation).

Of special importance, however, is the condition governing the conduct of the insured to prevent accidents. This usually requires all reasonable steps to be taken to prevent unsound products being sold and to comply with all statutory obligations. In the event of any defect or damage being discovered the insured must remedy or make good such defects and take such additional precautions as may be required.

EMPLOYERS' LIABILITY

Need for insurance

An employer has a duty both at common law and under statute to prevent personal injury (including disease) to his employees arising out of and in the course of their employment. At common law, for example, the employer is liable in negligence if an employee is injured as a result of the employer's failure to use reasonable care and skill in any of the following:

1 The selection of competent staff.
2 The provision and maintenance of fit and proper premises or plant.
3 The provision and maintenance of a safe and proper system of working.

Statutory liability

Under various statutes an employer's responsibility has been increased so that he is also liable for personal injury:

1 Due to the negligence of fellow employees towards each other. (The Law Reform (Personal Injuries) Act 1948 completely abolished the defence of common employment.)
2 Due to defects in equipment provided by the employer that are attributable wholly or partly to the fault of a third party— Employer's Liability (Defective Equipment) Act, 1969—even though the employer is not precluded from attempting to obtain redress from the responsible party.
3 Due to a breach of a statutory duty to provide for the safety of employees—for example, under the Factories Act, 1961 or the regulations relating thereto which are concerned, inter alia, with the secure fencing of dangerous machinery in factories or under the Offices, Shops and Railway Premises Act, 1963, which is likewise concerned with the health, safety and welfare of persons employed on such premises and, more recently, the Health and Safety at Work, etc., Act, 1974. (Where the duties imposed by statute are absolute or strict ones, proof of negligence against the employer is unnecessary; there is sufficient cause of action if the breach results in injury to the employee and this may include breach due to a latent defect.)
4 By reason of the provisions of other statutes which, although not imposing a strict duty on an employer for occupational accidents, may give rise to liability that would not otherwise apply at common law.

(a) The Fatal Accidents Act, 1846 and the Law Reform (Miscellaneous Provisions) Act, 1934 both amended the law relating to liability for accidents in cases where a personal action for damages was terminated by the death of either party.

(b) The Law Reform (Contributory Negligence) Act, 1945 provides in effect that, where an injured party has himself contributed to the accident by his own negligence, damages are reduced according to the degree of blame attributable to him. Hitherto, contributory negligence on the part of the injured man would have prevented him from recovering any damages at all.

The defence of contributory negligence is usually the one most relied upon in contesting personal injury claims except perhaps where a denial of negligence is available.

Compulsory insurance

The Employers' Liability (Compulsory Insurance) Act, 1969, which came into operation on 1 January 1972, made it compulsory for every employer (with a few exceptions) carrying on business in Great Britain to insure against liability for bodily injury or disease sustained by his employees and arising out of and in the course of their employment in that business in Great Britain. The Act also now applies to Northern Ireland, the Channel Islands, the Isle of Man and offshore installations.

Employees to be covered

All individuals under a contract of service or apprenticeship with an employer—whether such contract is express or implied, oral or in writing—must be covered. The only exceptions are:

1   Certain categories of relatives of the employer.
2   Employees not ordinarily resident in Great Britain unless they are in Great Britain in the course of their employment for a continuous period of not less than 14 days.

Excepted employers

1 Local government bodies and any police authority.
2 Nationalised industries or undertakings.
3 Any employer who may be exempted by future regulations.
4 An employer who does not have a place of business in Great Britain.

Requirements of the insurance policy

1 It must be an 'approved policy' with an authorised insurer.
2 The limit of indemnity must be at least £2,000,000 in respect of claims relating to any one or more employees arising out of any one occurrence.
3 It must prohibit the application of certain conditions in the policy relieving the insurers of liability in the event of some failure or omission by the employer or policyholder, whether before or after the happening of an event giving rise to a claim, but without prejudice to any rights of recovery the insurers may subsequently have against the policyholder.

Certificate of insurance

1 A certificate in prescribed form must be issued by the insurer to the employer giving particulars of the insurance contract within 30 days of its commencement or renewal.
2 A copy or copies of the certificate must be conspicuously displayed during its currency by the employer at each place of business at which he employs any person whose claims may be the subject of indemnity under the policy.
3 The employer is also required to produce the certificate when requested to do so by an authorised person.
4 Failure to comply with these requirements may incur a fine of up to £50.

Other conditions

1 The policy of insurance must be available for inspection by any inspector authorised by the Secretary of State for Employment.

2   An employer who is uninsured for any day is guilty of an offence and liable to a fine not exceeding £200 per day and, if such an offence is committed by a corporation with the consent or connivance of any director, manager, secretary or other officer of the corporation, such person is similarly liable in addition to the corporation.

Implications of the legislation

Although it is necessary for policy conditions to comply with the requirements of the Act, the obligation that the employer (or policyholder) owes to the insurers under the insurance contract remains unchanged. Any breach of a 'prohibited' policy condition by the employer, which in the past would have enabled insurers to refute liability for a claim made by an employee against the employer, is now invalid but insurers are free to recover from the employer all sums that they have had to pay which they would not have been liable to pay but for the provisions of the Act. The contract is usually claused to this effect.

Cover provided (or operative clause)

There is little variation in the standard form of policy issued by insurers. This generally provides a full indemnity to the insured (or employer) for his legal liability in respect of injury or disease to any person:

1   Under a contract of service or apprenticeship with the insured.
2   Caused during the period of insurance.
3   Arising out of and in the course of his employment.
4   In the business described in the schedule.

Limit of liability

Normally no limit of amount to the insurers' liability is expressed in the contract, that is, liability is in effect unlimited in amount although the statutory limit is only £2,000,000. Legal costs incurred with the insurers' consent are also covered and the indemnity is extended to cover the insured's personal representatives in the event of the insured's death in respect of liability incurred by the latter before his death in order to provide for claims made under the Law Reform (Miscellaneous Provisions) Act, 1934. It should be noted that for a claim to be admissible the injury or disease must have been caused during the period of insurance. As such claims may be made some years after the injury actually occurred or the disease was contracted it is essential to retain old policies for a good many years after the period of insurance has expired. This applies particularly if there has been a change of insurers.

Exclusions and the extent to which they may be modified

There is very seldom a section of the policy headed 'exclusions' but those that appear relate to:

Geographical limits. Liability is normally restricted to injury or disease occurring within Great Britain, Northern Ireland, the Isle of Man or the Channel Islands, but in respect of employees temporarily engaged outside these countries insurers will generally provide the appropriate cover subject to any action for damages being brought in the British courts.

Contractual liability—indemnity to principals. At one time liability assumed under contract or agreement which would not otherwise have attached was a standard exclusion, but the demands of commercial practice have led to the removal or modification of this clause so that it is now fairly common to find the indemnity extended specifically:

1 To include the insured's liability assumed under contract and
2 To indemnify the principal in like manner to the insured in respect of the former's liability to the insured's employees under contract.

It is, however, a requirement of such cover that the insured has arranged with the principal for claims to be conducted and controlled by the insurers and that the principal is subject to the terms and conditions of the policy.

Special exclusions

In some cases insurers may impose special exclusions of certain forms of work of a hazardous nature, such as the use of woodworking machinery, power presses or excavation work below a certain depth, and usually require advance notice if such work is to be covered. If such a condition is breached and a claim arises, the insurers are free, on settlement of the claim, to seek reimbursement from the insured on the grounds of non-disclosure. It is therefore infinitely preferable, if excluded work may be undertaken in the future, for arrangements to be made with the insurers to hold cover in advance, subject to their being informed within a reasonable period of the start of such work, so as to avoid the risk of an accidental omission or delay in giving prior notice.

Special extensions of cover

Liability under contract for employees of third parties

Although such liability is normally the subject of a public liability policy, conditions may arise under contract when it may be necessary to arrange cover under an employers' liability policy. As an example, if plant is hired with a driver, the terms of the contract may require the hirer, for purposes of the indemnity, to treat the driver as his own employee for the hire period. Such cover normally requires the agreement of the insurers and an appropriate clause included in the policy, although many insurers now provide this cover automatically. (The contract conditions may also require the hirer to make similar arrangements with the public liability insurers for the actions of such 'employees' vis-à-vis third parties.)

Labour-only subcontractors and 'self-employed' persons

The development of labour-only subcontractors supplying gangs of men to do a specific job originally presented a problem in so far as the subcontractor or labour-master seldom effected an employers' liability insurance or had the wherewithal to meet his liability for accidents to his employees. It therefore became common practice for the employing contractor to specially arrange for his own employers' liability insurers to have such labour gangs treated as his own employees. (Similar arrangements are made with his public liability insurers to cover claims by third parties due to the negligence of such 'employees').

Even before the Employers' Liability (Compulsory Insurance) Act was promulgated the necessity for the contractor ensuring that suitable insurance is effected for employees of labour-only subcontractors was demonstrated in the case of Donaghey v Boulton & Paul (1967), when the contractor was held liable for breach of statutory duty to such an employee despite his entitlement to a full indemnity from the subcontractor.

The situation with regard to the employment of self-employed persons raises a similar problem and special arrangements are necessary if such persons are to be treated in the same way as ordinary employees.

It is however now fairly common to find provision for both such types of 'employee' automatically included in the policy cover, the premium being based on the payments made by the insured for such labour.

Schedule

Insured

Reference has already been made (see 'Exclusions' on p. 256) to the indemnity provided to any principal of the insured under contract or agreement. Arrangements can also be made to cover the personal liability of any director, manager or other officer of the company in respect of work carried out on their behalf by other employees of the company.

Business

A typical employers' liability policy applies to liability for accidents only to employees 'in the business (as stated in the policy) and no other for the purposes of this insurance'. Therefore, if the activities of the firm change the insurers must be advised.

Premium

For all trade and business risks the premium is calculated by applying a rate per cent to the total annual payroll. For smaller firms several rates may apply according to the different categories of employment and separate payroll figures would then need to be supplied for each category. Over a certain size, however, it is customary to apply a single rate to the payroll of all staff other than clerical, commercial travellers, managers, etc., for whom a standard rate of 0.025 per cent is customarily applied. A provisional premium is paid at the beginning of each insurance period based on estimated payroll and this is adjusted when the actual payroll figures are known, that is, a refund is allowed or additional premium charged to the insured according to whether the actual figures are below or above the estimates.

Premium rates are subject to revision periodically in the light of claims experience over a period of, say, 3 years, although where large numbers of employees are involved the final claims experience for a particular year is unlikely to be known for possibly several years and provision must therefore be made in the claims figures for the anticipated cost of unsettled or expected claims. These estimates for outstanding claims should be adjusted at each review of the premium rate according to the actual payments made so that the true claims experience is reflected.

When very substantial premiums are involved many insurers are prepared to offer alternative schemes of premium payment that are less dependent on the provision for outstanding claims and recognise the time taken to actually pay claims. Such schemes often take the form of premium payments by instalments over several years.

Conditions

The policy conditions have much in common with those applicable to public liability policies, particularly the requirements with regard to:

1 Notification of claims (including any accident likely to give rise to a claim).

2   Conduct of the insured in the event of a claim.
3   Premium adjustment.

The insured is also required to take reasonable precautions to prevent accidents or disease.

The failure of an employer to comply with the above requirements no longer enables insurers to refuse liability for an employee's claim (see 'Implications of the legislation' on p. 255).

ACCIDENT PREVENTION AND SURVEYS

Apart from the humanitarian aspect of accident prevention, it is very much in the interest of employers as well as insurers and, indeed, the national economy, that accidents, especially those at work, should be avoided or reduced as far as practicable.

Insurance may relieve the employer of the direct cost of claims caused by accidents—although such costs must ultimately affect the premiums he pays—but it does not protect him against the other costs in time and labour that may ensue, including:

1   Time lost by injured personnel and other workers who may be involved.
2   The need to find and train replacement staff.
3   The general disruption of production.
4   The bad feeling that a poor accident record may evoke in the workforce.
5   The prospect of proceedings by the factory inspector and all that this entails.

There are, therefore, direct incentives to the employer to minimise the incidence of accidents, and one measure firms are increasingly adopting to improve their accident record is the appointment of safety officers where the size of the factory warrants it. This trend is encouraged by insurers, as a safety officer, in addition to promoting safety generally within the factory, is usually responsible for ensuring that the insurers' own recommendations, once agreed, are implemented and maintained. Accident prevention, however, is very much an attitude of mind, and can only be effective if it emanates from the top down in any organisation. A safety officer, however competent, is ineffectual if he does not have the active support of those appointing him.

The introduction of the Health and Safety at Work, etc., Act, 1974, which greatly increased the employers' obligatory responsibilities to ensure safe working conditions and the powers of the state to enforce such conditions, has increased the need for and, indeed, the importance of the safety officer. The Act has had the effect of focusing attention on safety and accident prevention generally. The obligatory appointment of safety representatives from within the workforce and the formation of safety committees should ensure continuing improved performance in these areas.

Most insurers are also able to offer assistance on risk improvement. In addition to surveying the premises to be insured, particularly in the underwriting of employers' liability risks, and possibly imposing certain minimum safety measures as a condition of the insurance, many insurers also offer the services of their safety engineers in an advisory capacity. Even a safety-conscious firm with a reasonable accident record can benefit from the advice of an outside specialist, experienced in the field, provided he offers reasonable, practical ways of reducing the real danger spots at moderate cost and with due regard to the exigencies of the business.

CLAIMS PROCEDURE

There are certain aspects of liability claims—especially those relating to bodily injuries—which call for particular comment.

Reporting accidents

Prompt notice of any accident likely to give rise to a claim is necessary so as to give the insurers an opportunity of investigating the circumstances of the accident while the facts are still fresh in the minds of all concerned. The problem of deciding which accidents at work should be reported is sometimes avoided by reporting every one, but insurers are clearly not concerned with every minor incident and in order to save on administrative costs it is preferable if a practical system is agreed to avoid the unnecessary reporting of accidents, for example, by reporting only accidents which result in an employee's absence from work for three working days or more, i.e. on similar lines to the requirements for reporting notifiable accidents to the Department of Health & Social Security.

Moreover, relatively few of the accidents reported would normally result in claims and it should not be necessary to include in the initial accident report other than brief details of the accident, but sufficient to indicate the seriousness of the injury. More detailed information is of relevance only if and when a claim materialises and need therefore be supplied only in that event.

When a claim is made by a third party the insurers normally require a claim form to be completed to elicit the relevant facts of the incident, including any contractual obligations that may exist between the parties involved.

It is most important when an accident of any seriousness occurs that the statement of witnesses should be taken as soon as possible while the facts are still fresh in their minds so that these statements do not become subjective.

Any communication from or on behalf of a claimant, whether third party or employee, must be passed unanswered to the insurers for them to make the appropriate response.

Settlement of claims

It is very much in the interest of the insured that his insurers should contest unreasonable claims and not act over-generously, whether the claimant is his own employee or a third party.

For his employees he will expect a fair and sympathetic settlement of their just claims within a reasonable period and without unnecessary litigation, particularly if they should not be legally represented by their union or own solicitors. Although not directly involved in the claim negotiations, an employer may nevertheless be called upon to assist the insurers and he may on occasion wish to intervene on an employee's behalf if he feels the circumstances warrant it.

The settlement of third party property damage claims is usually a straightforward matter of assessing what is the measure of loss sustained by the third party by reason of the insured's negligence.

Where customers of the insured are involved the question of goodwill may arise, although normally this is not a matter for the insurers to take into consideration.

Bodily injury claims by third parties can present a special problem when consumer products are involved and the claim on a strict legal liability basis is dubious or exaggerated, as it may be expedient to consider a compromise payment. It is a question of weighing all the costs of litigation and the adverse publicity to the insured that even the successful defence of the action may entail against the undesirable practice of encouraging spurious or inflated claims, and of course the amount at stake. Differences of opinion can arise in such cases and it is therefore highly desirable that there should be close consultation between insured and insurers and a realistic approach adopted by both parties.

FURTHER READING

John Munkman, *Employers' Liability at Common Law,* 9th Edition, London: Butterworths, 1979, 653 p.

P. Madge, *Liability Insurance in the United Kingdom,* London: Palace Publishing, 1975, 64 leaves.

Greville Janner, *Janner's Product Liability*, London: Business Books, 1979, 405 p.

12

Motor Insurance

P. D. Whiley,* Insurance Manager, UK, Fisons plc

LEGISLATION

The motor vehicle is perhaps one of the most potentially lethal items of equipment in general use in civilised society. Add to this the fact that by comparison with the rest of the world the United Kingdom has one of the highest concentrations of motor vehicles per mile of road and it is no surprise that in its short history the motor vehicle has attracted a very substantial amount of legislative control.

The current legislation regarding the insurance and use of motor vehicles is:

1 Road Traffic Act 1972/Road Traffic Act 1974.
2 Road Traffic Act (Northern Ireland) 1970.
3 Road Traffic Act 1963 (Isle of Man).
4 Road Traffic (Compulsory Third Party Insurance) (Guernsey) Law 1936.
5 Motor Traffic (Third Party Insurance) (Jersey) Law 1948.
6 Road Traffic (Compulsory Third Party Insurance) (Alderney) Law 1950.

Since the 'Regional' Acts are very similar to the Road Traffic Acts 1972/1974, in the following comments reference is made only to those Acts (the specific references relating to the 1972 Act).

The principal requirements of this legislation are that:

*The author is indebted to Mr G. V. Hoon for material retained from the previous edition.

1 A motor vehicle must not be used on a road within the meaning of the RTA unless a valid insurance is in force covering liability (unlimited in amount) in respect of the death of or bodily injury to any person arising out of the use of that vehicle on the road (Part VI Sections 143(1) and 145(3)).

'Any person' includes passengers but does not include an employee killed or injured in circumstances which arise out of and in the course of his employment (Part VI, Section 145(4)). This latter aspect is covered by the Employers' Liability (Compulsory Insurance) Act 1969, which requires an employer to insure his legal liability for personal injury to employees.

2 Liability for 'emergency treatment' (defined in the Act) must also be insured (Part VI Section 155).

3 A certificate of motor insurance in the form prescribed in the Act must be delivered to the insured (Part VI Section 147).

4 In the event of an accident involving personal injury or damage to another person or his property, the driver must stop and give his name and address, the registration number and the name and address of the owner of the vehicle to any person reasonably requiring the information. If the driver does not supply the information at the time he must report the accident to the police within 24 hours of the occurrence (Part I Section 25).

5 In the case of an accident involving personal injury to another person the driver is also required to produce his certificate of insurance to the police either at the time or within 24 hours. If he cannot produce the certificate of insurance at that time he must produce it within 5 days at a police station specified by him at the time the accident is reported (Part VII Section 166(1) and (2)).

6 Details regarding insurance must also be given to any person reasonably requiring the information when a claim is made for personal injuries (Part VI Section 151(1)).

It should be noted that insurance covering legal liability for damage to property is not required by law.

FORMS OF COVER AVAILABLE

Financial loss arising out of an accident can fall upon the owner or driver of a motor vehicle for many reasons other than injury caused to third parties and, therefore, it is seldom that a motor insurance policy covers only legal liability as required under the Road Traffic Act. Cover provided by different companies varies widely but policies issued fall mainly into the following broad categories:

1 Road Traffic Act only.
2 Full third party insurance.
3 Comprehensive cover.

As there are some basic differences between the policies issued for different types of vehicle, the various policies will be dealt with separately under the broad headings of Private Cars, Commercial Vehicles and Motor Cycles.

PRIVATE CARS

Road Traffic Act only

This type of policy provides only the minimum cover which the user of a motor vehicle is compelled to obtain by law. The policy, therefore, covers only legal liability to third parties including passengers in the vehicle, for accidental death or personal injuries caused by the insured vehicle, the cover being restricted to accidents happening in places to which the Acts apply.

Full third party insurance

The normal third party policy covers, for unlimited indemnity, the insurance of legal liability for accidental death or personal injury to any person including passengers and damage to the property of third parties. Third party policies can be extended to include loss or damage to the vehicle by fire and/or theft.

Comprehensive cover

The comprehensive policy insures all the risks which would be covered under the third party policy but in addition provides indemnity to the insured against loss of or damage to the motor car or motor cars described in the schedule of the policy. Accessories and spare parts while on the car or in the insured's private garage are also normally insured.

The value of the car is declared to the insurers when the insurance is effected and this represents the maximum sum insured but payment in the event of total loss is normally the market value at the time of loss, which may be less than the declared value. However, some insurers agree to pay for replacement by a new car of the same make and model if the insured car is less than (say) twelve months old when stolen or destroyed. More rarely, a value for settlement in the event of a total loss can be agreed at each renewal.

When a car is repairable the insurer normally pays the cost of repairs. In addition, the cost of necessary protection and removal of the car, if disabled, to the nearest competent repairer is borne by the insurers and so is the cost of redelivery to the insured after repairs.

The comprehensive policy also provides a lump sum benefit in the event of death of the insured (and sometimes of his/her spouse or even other members of the family residing with the insured) by accident in direct connection with the motor car or in the event of such injury as loss of sight, loss of limbs etc. Medical benefits are provided (usually of at least £50 per person) for the insured or an occupant of the car if it is involved in an accident. The policy also provides cover for loss of or damage to rugs, clothing and personal effects while in or on any insured motor car (usually at least £50).

Young and inexperienced drivers

The usual comprehensive policy issued by most companies excludes, in respect of damage to the insured vehicle, the first (say) £40 or £75 of any claim while the vehicle is being driven by a person under (say) 25 or 21 years of age respectively. Such excess is in addition to any voluntary one which is taken for the purpose of premium reduction. An excess of (say) £40 also applies to inexperienced drivers even if over 25 years of age.

Premium

The premium charged for private cars under the various classes of insurance varies according to a number of factors. Those taken into consideration include:

1   The use to which the vehicle is put.
2   The area in which it is garaged and/or used.
3   The type of vehicle and in some cases its age.
4   The driver and/or drivers.
5   Other factors.

The insured value of the car, unless it is at the top end of the range, has no significant effect upon the premium.

Use

This falls into three main classifications as follows:

Class 1. Use for social, domestic and pleasure purposes, and use by the insured *in person* in connection with his business and that of his employer.

Excluding use for hiring or for commercial travelling, or racing, competitions, rallies or trials or use for any purpose in connection with the motor trade.

Class 2. Use for social, domestic and pleasure purposes, and use for the business of the insured and that of his employer.

Excluding use for hiring, or for commercial travelling, or racing, competitions, rallies or trials or use for any purpose in connection with the motor trade.

Class 3. Use for social, domestic and pleasure purposes, and use for the business of the insured and that of his employer.

Excluding use for racing, competitions, rallies or trials or the carriage of passengers for hire or reward.

The majority of family cars fall into Class 1, which normally permits the insured to use his car on his employer's business provided he does so in person. This business use does not extend to any other driver and he may not give authority, for example, to his workmate to drive the car on his employer's business. Most other business use falls in Class 2, which usually attracts a premium which is approximately 25 to 33 per cent higher than that in Class 1, but a commercial traveller, for example, would need to have a Class 3 policy and this would attract a premium approximately 50 to 66 per cent higher than Class 1.

Occasionally, the Class 1 policy does not permit any business use at all and the cover should be carefully checked before any car insured on a Class 1 basis is used for business purposes.

With many insurers the exclusion relating to competitions does not apply to road safety rallies and treasure hunts but this point should be checked with the insurer concerned.

Area

It is assumed that the car will be predominantly used in and around the area where it is garaged overnight and, therefore, the location of its normal garage plays a major part in the premium calculation. Accordingly, a car garaged in Central London would attract a very much higher premium than the same car garaged in, say, Devon or Cornwall. However, a car garaged in Manchester or Glasgow might attract a premium which is similar to that for the same car garaged in Central London.

Vehicle

The wide variation in the performance of cars of similar cubic capacity and the considerable variation in the cost of repairs particularly for some foreign cars, together with the attraction of different cars to different types of driver, have led to the practice by insurers of grouping different types of cars together for rating purposes in a manner which does not necessarily relate to the capacity of the engine. We can find, therefore, that an Alfa Romeo Alfasud 1.3 has the same rating classification as, for example, a Ford Capri 2000S or a Jaguar XJ6.

Driver

It is clear that the driver is a very important factor in the rating of a motor car insurance. Experience has shown that in general the young man or woman is not as careful as the older person and, while the normal rates apply for drivers of mature years, special consideration is given to youth. 'The age of discretion' in driving is commonly looked upon as 25, although insurers vary in opinion and any age up to 30 may be considered specially. At the other end of the scale, some insurers allow a discount off their normal rates if the insured is over a certain age (60 or even lower in some cases).

Special consideration is also given to drivers with little experience, bad experience, prosecutions etc., irrespective of age.

Other factors

Other matters taken into consideration when rating the premium for a car include the previous accident record of the insured and any other regular drivers, whether driving is restricted to the insured or the insured and spouse, whether there is more than one car insured, and whether the insured will voluntarily carry the first amount (£25, £50, £75 etc.) of damage to the car (known as an 'excess').

Territorial limits

Comprehensive and third party policies are normally operative in the United Kingdom (including Northern Ireland, the Channel Islands, the Isle of Man) and sometimes the Republic of Ireland, and while the insured vehicle is in transit by sea between any ports therein, including loading and unloading incidental to such transit. Temporary use outside the aforementioned limits can usually be covered at additional cost. (See also Foreign use p. 282)

Legal liability of passengers for their own negligence

A passenger may become personally liable for his own negligence, for example by opening a door carelessly and causing an accident. In most cases this risk is included in private car policies, but where it is not the policy can usually be extended for a small additional premium.

Additional benefits

Unless specially restricted, the full third party and comprehensive policies usually permit, without additional charge, the driving of the car by any licensed driver with the permission of the insured and the policy indemnifies him against his liability as though he were the insured. However, if it is known that the car may be driven by a person who is young or inexperienced or has a bad claims record, this is a 'material fact' which must be disclosed to the insurers and, in some cases, an additional premium may be required.

Cover also includes payment of solicitor's fees for defence in a court of summary jurisdiction or representation at a coroner's court or fatal accident enquiry arising out of a third party claim, or payment of legal costs incurred in defending a charge for manslaughter or a charge of causing death by reckless or dangerous driving (although the latter may be subject to a fairly low limit).

The insured is also normally covered for third party risks while driving any car or motor cycle not belonging to him (unless the insured is a company).

If a policy covers business use, it is also usual for the insurance to indemnify the insured's employer but not whilst the insured is using a vehicle belonging to or hired by the employer.

COMMERCIAL VEHICLES

Although there are many different kinds of commercial vehicle, the majority are insured under one basic policy form. A description of this cover is given and special types are listed separately.

Road Traffic Act only

The legal requirements are basically the same as for private cars and therefore the policy cover is similar.

Full third party insurance

This covers the insured's legal liability for the accidental death of or personal injury to any person, including passengers, and damage to the property of third parties arising out of the use of the insured vehicle. 'Use' includes loading and unloading within the limits of any carriageway or thoroughfare. Liability arising out of bringing a load to the insured vehicle or taking away a load from the vehicle beyond the limits of a carriageway or thoroughfare is also insured provided this is done by the driver or attendant of the vehicle. To the extent that loading and unloading liability is not covered by the motor policy, this should be insured under a general third party liability policy (see Chapter 11).

Although the cover for liability in respect of personal injury is unlimited, liability for damage to property under a commercial vehicle policy is normally restricted. Depending upon the insurers, the limit is usually £250,000. Some commercial vehicle policies still exclude liability for damage to any bridge, weighbridge, viaduct, road or anything beneath caused by vibration or by the weight of the vehicle or its load although this exclusion is now less common than it used to be.

Third party policies can be extended to include loss of or damage to the vehicle by fire and/or theft.

Comprehensive cover

The comprehensive policy insures all the risks which would be covered under the third party policy as described above but it also indemnifies the insured for damage to the insured vehicle and accessories and spare parts while thereon. In the event of accident, the cost of necessary protection and removal of the vehicle, if disabled, to the nearest competent repairers is borne by the insurers as is the cost of redelivery to the insured after repairs.

There is no cover for personal accident risks, medical expenses, or personal effects as described under the private car policy and there is no cover for goods carried on the insured vehicle.

Trailers

The policy normally permits the gratuitous towing of any one disabled mechanically propelled vehicle, although damage to the towed vehicle is excluded. The towing of other trailers may require extension to the policy and may be the subject of additional premium, although it is now common practice to include third party risks while towing trailers. (See also Trailers, p. 286).

Additional benefits

Driving by any licensed driver with the permission of the insured is covered as with private cars. Solicitor's fees for defence in a court of summary jurisdiction or representation at coroner's court or fatal accident enquiry are covered on a similar basis to the private car policy.

Premium rating

Much the same considerations are given to the assessment of premium for a commercial vehicle as for a private car. However, the following differences apply:

1   Carrying capacity or gross vehicle weight, as the case may be, is an important factor because clearly a very large haulage vehicle is an entirely different piece of equipment from a 5 cwt van.
2   Trade is important. The policy, therefore, normally has a stipulation that the vehicle will not be used for any business other than that which has been declared and stated in the policy.
3   Value is of much greater importance than with a private car for the value of a vehicle may vary from little more than £1,000 for a 5 cwt van to £100,000 or more for a complex special-purpose vehicle.

Private use by or with the permission of the insured is covered without additional charge.

Young and inexperienced drivers

As with private cars, comprehensive policies are usually subject to an excess.

Territorial limits

Although the territorial limits of the commercial vehicle policy normally extend to, at least, Great Britain, Northern Ireland, Isle of Man, and Channel Islands the sea transit is not automatically covered. Cover outside these limits can usually be provided at additional cost.

Legal liability of passengers for their own negligence

This is now commonly covered as described under the private car policy.

Excess property damage liability insurance

As mentioned the third party property damage cover under a commercial vehicle policy is usually limited in amount. This limit can be increased by payment of an additional premium and limits of £500,000 or £1,000,000 are not uncommon. In some cases insurers will give unlimited indemnity in respect of third party property damage caused by commercial vehicles as they do with private cars. However, where a large fleet of vehicles is insured and a high indemnity limit is required alternative quotations should be sought. It may be cheaper to insure this excess liability cover under a separate policy with insurers who specialise in risks of this nature.

Special types of vehicle

Commercial vehicles come in a wide variety of forms, for example, vans, trucks, refrigerated transport, tankers, etc. Most of these types would be insured under the normal commercial vehicle policy. Those which would normally be insured under a special type of policy are:

1 Hire cars.
2 Coaches and buses.
3 Vehicles of special design used as mechanical tools such as rollers, excavators, diggers, cranes, bulldozers, agricultural tractors, etc.

Special policies are also issued for motor traders' risks.

Hire cars

Self-drive hire has become very popular in recent years and this is usually dealt with by a master policy effected by the hire car operator under which individual arrangements are made for each hirer. These may vary but it is usual to require an excess in respect of damage to the hired vehicle.

Coaches and buses

Premiums vary considerably according to seating capacity and the nature of use, for example, whether the vehicle is used for private or public hire.

Vehicles of special design

Special considerations are taken into account depending upon the type of vehicle and the premium charged may be affected accordingly. Examples are:

1   In connection with a crane, the toppling risk.
2   Whether liability is insured for goods being lifted.
3   Whether licensed for the road, etc.

Use of the vehicle as a 'tool of trade' is normally excluded from the commercial vehicle policy. Consideration should therefore be given to covering this risk under the general third party liability policy.

Very low premiums are usually charged for, say, agricultural tractors, which operate almost entirely on farmland and only go on to the highway to get from field to field.

Motor trade

Special considerations arise in connection with motor trade garages, where an employee frequently needs to take vehicles on the road which do not belong to him or his employer. Sometimes the vehicles are not licensed, are taken on the road under trade plates and may not be specifically insured elsewhere.

Motor traders risks fall into two main categories:

1   Road risks.
2   Internal risks.

Road risks

Under a policy issued for road risks only, there is no cover for vehicles on the insured's own premises. The policy is only intended to apply to the risk incurred when vehicles are driven on the road in connection with the business or are on premises not owned or occupied by the insured in the course of a journey, whether such vehicles belong to the trader or are in his custody or control. Use for pleasure purposes is only covered for named persons and in some cases the policy may include private hire (not self-drive hire) for vehicles up to a seating capacity of eight.

In addition to the normal factors which affect the premium, additional premium is charged for private hire where the seating capacity exceeds eight and also where driving by customers is allowed.

Cover can be comprehensive or for third party risks only. Premium is usually computed on what is known as the points basis, that is, a number of points is allocated for each trade plate, vehicle owned and driver and a calculation made on the total number of points.

Internal risks

There are two principal types of internal risks policy:

1 Third party only
2 Damage and third party

Third party only. This policy covers:

1 Third party liability in respect of personal injuries—unlimited in amount.
2 Third party liability, usually up to a limit of £250,000, in respect of property damage but excluding property held in trust or in the insured's custody or control. In effect this means that liability for damage to customers' vehicles is not covered.

However, the policy usually extends to cover the full third party liability risk (other than road risks) in respect of the premises and the trade carried on therefrom.

Damage and third party. In addition to the above, this policy includes liability for damage to customers' vehicles within the limit of £250,000 for any one accident and damage to the insured's own vehicles up to, say, £10,000 per vehicle subject to an excess of £50. Fire, explosion and other risks normally insured under a fire policy are excluded.

In both cases premiums are usually based upon the total wage bill or vehicle capacity of the premises. An important aspect of both policies is that products liability is not insured—in other words, if the motor trader, through bad workmanship, incurs liability for an accident involving the vehicle on which he has worked after it has left his possession, he is uninsured under any of these policies. This risk can be covered by special extension at an additional premium.

MOTOR CYCLES

Motor cycle policies are usually issued for motor cycles (whether with or without sidecars), motor scooters, mechanically assisted pedal cycles and invalid carriages. It is not usual to issue a motor cycle policy on three-wheeled cars, which are normally insured under a private car policy.

As with cars and commercial vehicles, policies can be effected for Road Traffic Act risks only, full third party (with or without fire and theft) or comprehensive insurance. The policy cover is something of a mixture of that provided for private cars and commercial vehicles.

Until 1972 it was unusual for an insurer to agree to cover liability to pillion passengers. However, the legal position changed when passenger liability became compulsory under the Motor Vehicles (Passenger Insurance) Act 1971, which was subsequently consolidated into the Road Traffic Act 1972.

Motor cycle insurance is normally restricted to one named driver although additional drivers can be added at additional premium.

Third party liability arising from driving other motor cycles by the insured may be covered (unless the policy is in respect of a specified machine).

CARAVANS

Although caravans are towed by a vehicle their main purpose is normally the use which they have before each journey starts or after each journey finishes and therefore they are worthy of special consideration.

Special caravan insurance policies are available covering the structure of the caravan, its equipment, including fixtures and fittings, and personal effects which may be carried in it but which are not normally part of it. Such policies also cover legal liability arising from use of the caravan.

The caravan itself

The cover for the caravan and equipment is normally on an 'all risks' basis subject to such exclusions as depreciation, wear and tear, mechanical and electrical breakdown, loss of use etc.

Baggage and personal effects

This cover is also on an 'all risks' basis but may exclude loss of money and have some restriction on jewellery or valuables.

Third party liability

This cover is usually in respect of legal liability arising from an accident by or in connection with the caravan whilst detached from a vehicle. The third party towing risk is normally covered under the motor policy. (See Trailers, page 286.)

Territorial limits

Since the caravan is insured under a separate policy, it is necessary to watch the territorial limits if the caravan is taken abroad. A 'green card' is necessary for the towing vehicle and so insurance arrangements on it are not usually forgotten but the caravan can easily be overlooked. The policy should be checked and the territorial limits extended, if necessary.

Additionally, the motor insurer should be advised if a caravan is being towed abroad so that it can be shown on the 'green card'.

CONTINGENT THIRD PARTY LIABILITY

Although those who are prudent and insurance-minded take out various policies against their liability to the public, liability to employees and liability from the use of motor vehicles, there is an area of risk which often escapes notice. This falls into two main categories.

Use by employees of their cars (or other vehicles) on company business

Although, as stated under the section dealing with private cars, most private car policies indemnify the insured's employer if the employee's car is used on company business, the policies issued by some insurers do not automatically provide for this. Further, the employee's cover may be inadequate for the use of the car. The position can arise therefore that a car used by an employee on his employer's business can be involved in an accident in circumstances where the employer may be held vicariously liable and where the employee has no insurance to provide indemnity. Such events are rare and therefore the premium for a contingent liability policy issued to the employer to cover this liability is very modest. It is usually based upon a declaration of the number of employees authorised to use their cars on company business.

Hired vehicles

A contingent risk can exist when, for example, a vehicle is hired from a contractor with driver for the purpose of doing a specific job and the driver is given very specific instructions by the hirer resulting from which an accident occurs. Such events are also rare but they are not covered by a motor or any other policy unless special provision is made. A special contingent policy can be effected by the hirer and the premium is usually based on annual hiring charges.

These policies only cover the third party liability of the hirer. The contractor must ensure that he has adequate cover himself for the specific purpose for which the vehicle is being used.

SOME GENERAL POINTS

Car sharing

Since the introduction of the Transport Act 1978, private car policies are normally extended to include car sharing arrangements. The policy will not be invalidated by the receipt of contributions as part of a car sharing arrangement in respect of the carriage of passengers for social or other similar purposes including travelling to and from work and such use will not be regarded as constituting the carriage of passengers for hire or reward providing that:

1   The vehicle is not constructed or adapted to carry more than seven passengers (excluding the driver).
2   The passengers are not being carried in the course of a business of carrying passengers.
3   The total contributions received for the journey concerned do not involve an element of profit.

Certificates

For the purpose of complying with the Road Traffic Acts, the insurance certificate is the all-important document. It does not matter what the policy says or whether the insurer agrees to meet a claim, if there is no certificate covering the use of the vehicle, an offence has been committed. It is important, therefore, to check the certificate carefully to see that the effective dates, persons entitled to drive, use and vehicle are stated correctly. However, many insurers now issue 'blanket' certificates of insurance which do not quote the registration number of the vehicle but merely refer to any vehicle owned by the policyholder. This does not, however, remove from the insured the obligation to advise the insurers of any change of vehicle, except in the case of large fleets where the insurer may have agreed otherwise.

Exclusions

Whilst it is not practicable to list all conditions and restrictions, the following are some of the more usual exclusions found in motor policies:

1   Liability for death of or injury to any employee arising out of or in the course of employment.
2   Loss of use, depreciation, wear and tear, mechanical or electrical breakdowns or failures.
3   Damage to tyres by braking, road punctures, cuts or bursts.
4   Damage caused by pressure waves from aircraft and other aerial devices travelling at sonic or supersonic speeds.
5   Any accident, injury, loss or damage which is caused by or is the result of:
    (a)   earthquake
    (b)   riot or civil commotion outside England, Scotland, Wales, the Isle of Man and the Channel Islands. (Note: riot or civil commotion in Ireland is not covered)
    (c)   war risks
    (d)   ionising radiations, radioactivity from nuclear fuel or waste or any explosive nuclear assembly.
6   Any liability accepted by agreement or contract unless such liability would have existed otherwise.
7   Any liability, injury, loss or damage while any motor vehicle is being driven by any person who is disqualified from driving or has not held a licence.

It is important for each policyholder to check the policy and understand how far he is or is not insured, as these restrictions may vary from one policy to another.

Fleet rating

Although insurers have a standard schedule of rates designed to produce overall a reasonable income for the claims which are likely to be met, a fleet of vehicles can be rated in a way which reflects its own claims experience. In these circumstances a no claims bonus is not applicable and instead either a fleet discount is allowed or a fleet surcharge is levied, depending on the claims experience of the individual fleet. This has the advantage of reducing administrative work for both the insurer and the insured.

Where very large fleets of vehicles are involved standard rates may be dispensed with altogether and unit charges agreed which provide a reasonable premium based upon overall claims experience. Insurance for major fleets is a very specialised subject and may involve split covers (the practice of arranging the various sections of a 'comprehensive' cover through different insurers), self-funding arrangements on accidental damage, self-insurance of compulsory third party cover utilising Certificates of Deposit and even the use of captive insurance companies.

Administrative savings can result from fleet policies in that it is usual to issue only one policy for each class of vehicle or, where large fleets are involved, one combined policy covering all the vehicles. In such cases the vehicles are not listed and no details are shown, reference being made to the vehicles by a general description only. At the beginning of each renewal period, the insurers require some information about the fleet; this may be a detailed list or cumulative statistics under various classes. In the case of small fleets, additions and deletions may be recorded by endorsement but this is usually dispensed with if the fleet is large. In these latter circumstances a premium adjustment is made at the end of an agreed period, usually on the basis of charging fifty per cent of the difference between the opening and closing positions.

Foreign use

The majority of motor insurance policies are written basically to cover the vehicles while being used in the United Kingdom and in some cases the Republic of Ireland. Most insurers are prepared to provide cover for the vehicle while temporarily used in the Irish Republic (unless, of course, already included in the territorial limits) free of charge or on the Continent of Europe at an additional charge. A 'green card' is required if the vehicle is taken to the Irish Republic (unless an Irish Certificate has been issued) or to most Continental countries and this will exempt the user from taking an insurance policy locally. The 'green card' system is recognised in most European countries.

Although it is now a legal requirement that a UK motor policy must, in these circumstances, provide the minimum third party insurance required in other EEC countries, it is still necessary to advise insurers of proposed journeys to ensure that the full cover provided by the policy continues to operate.

Extension normally includes transit by recognised sea passage of a duration not exceeding 65 hours.

Special considerations arise in Spain, where there is a risk that if a road accident takes place the police might use their powers and impound the vehicle (or imprison the driver) unless a deposit is made in money for the disbursement of potential claims for damage or injury. Such deposit, impounding of the vehicle, or imprisonment can usually be avoided by the production of a 'bail bond'. Although it is issued by insurance companies usually at additional charge, a bail bond is not an insurance as such. It is a guarantee that damages, if awarded against the driver of the vehicle, will be paid. The person to whom the bail bond is issued is himself liable to reimburse the insurer who issues the bail bond. In many cases, however, his liability would be covered by his motor insurance so that no money would actually change hands. The insurer who issues the bail bond is normally the insurer of the vehicle which issues the 'green card'. The limit of the guarantee under the bond is £500 or £1,000 depending on the insurers concerned.

'Knock for knock'

Most insurers are parties to some form of 'knock for knock' or sharing agreement, the object of which is to minimise the cost of handling claims and counterclaims on the 'swings and roundabouts' principle.

The main provision under the 'knock for knock' agreement is that, in the event of an accident between two vehicles, the insurer of any comprehensive policy involved pays for the damage to their insured vehicle, irrespective of blame, without endeavouring to recover from the third party's insurers. Thus, if A and B are both insured comprehensively, then insurer A pays for A's damage and insurer B pays for B's damage.

Where only one of the vehicles is insured comprehensively the situation is more complicated and to overcome any inequality most insurers now include a 'partial indemnity' clause in the agreement in relation to 'fleet' risks. This states that when a motor fleet is insured for (a) third party (with or without fire and theft) risks or (b) comprehensive risks with a large excess, the insurer of the fleet will pay half the cost of the damage caused to the other (comprehensively) insured vehicle.

Agreements exist in connection with other aspects of claims, all having the same or a similar objective.

Payment under a 'knock for knock' agreement does not cause loss of no-claims bonus if the insured can establish that but for the operation of the 'knock for knock' agreement he could have recovered 100 per cent of his loss from the third party's insurers and consequently there would have been no claim on his own insurers. Another system, known as third party sharing agreements, usually provides that, irrespective of legal liability, the total cost of settlement of any claims will be borne in equal shares between the insurers who are party to the agreement.

Laid up vehicles

Subject to prior notice and surrender of the certificate, most insurers of private cars and commercial vehicles will allow a rebate of premium if the vehicle is laid up for, say, a minimum period of six weeks. It is unusual, however, to allow rebates for motor cycles or 'special' vehicles, such as tractors etc., or where the policy is 'fleet rated'.

Loss of use

If a vehicle is badly damaged in an accident or is stolen, it is frequently some time before either the vehicle is back on the road or, in the event of complete loss, money is available from insurers for its replacement. In such circumstances, the insured may be put to a good deal of expense in fares or hiring alternative transport which is not covered under the normal motor policy. There will be occasions, of course, when it is possible to recover this from a third party who was responsible for the accident. However, it is seldom certain that this can be done and it may take a long time. It is possible to insure such loss-of-use expenses under either a motor policy or with other insurers who specialise in this class of risk. The cost depends upon the class of use and type of vehicle.

At least one major insurer now offers, in the comprehensive private car insurance, a hire car for a limited period without additional charge.

No-claim bonus

Except where a schedule of vehicles is fleet rated it is the usual practice to allow a no-claims bonus on the premiums for private cars, commercial vehicles and motor cycles, where no claim has been made for the insured vehicle for one year or more. The amount of bonus can vary from company to company (some do not allow a bonus on commercial vehicles or motor cycles) and according to the number of claim-free years that there have been. However, it is fairly common under a private car policy to allow a bonus something on the following lines:

Number of claim-free years	Bonus
1	33%
2	40%
3	50%
4	60%

In most cases the bonus is not fully lost if the policy has run for more than two or three years without claim and, for example, the 60 per cent bonus may drop to 40 per cent in the event of a claim in the fifth or succeeding years following a claim-free period.

In the event of an insurance being transferred from one insurer to another, it is the practice to allow a transfer of bonus subject to evidence being produced of the appropriate claim-free period.

Some insurers also offer 'protected no-claims discount' under which the policyholder who has already earned a specified no-claims bonus (usually 60 per cent) can insure, sometimes for a small additional premium, against loss of no-claims discount provided no more than (say) two claims occur in (say) any five consecutive years.

Safeguarding the vehicle

In all motor policies there is a condition in some form or other which states that the insured must take all reasonable steps to protect the insured vehicle from loss or damage and to maintain it in good and efficient condition. This condition should be carefully considered because from time to time it is invoked by insurers. Some examples of circumstances under which it has been invoked are:

1 Frost damage (where not excluded)—insurers may consider that they should not pay for damage by frost if antifreeze has not been used during the normal winter season.
2 Vehicle left in the open—damage to a vehicle permanently kept in the street might be looked upon as uninsured unless the circumstances have been made known to the insurers.
3 Faulty tyres, brakes and steering, etc.—insurers expect the vehicle to be kept in a roadworthy condition and a number of cases have gone to court on this point.

The 'small print' on a motor insurance policy often goes unread. It is, however, important. Although insurers do not usually apply such restrictions harshly, they are there for the protection of the insurer where it is considered that the insured has not taken due care.

Servicing and repair

Most insurers continue to give the full protection of the policy when a vehicle is in the hands of the motor trade for service or repair. In these circumstances any policy restrictions on driving or use are normally waived.

Trailers

The private car policy usually permits the towing of a trailer and includes without charge the third party risks of the trailer while attached to the car (see page 278). Comprehensive insurance for trailers used for carrying luggage or personal effects, goods or livestock and third party risks while detached can also be included in the policy at an additional charge. Under a commercial vehicle policy, however, an additional premium may be required for a trailer even while attached, whether this is insured for third party risks or comprehensively. Care should be taken to ensure that the trailer and equipment on or forming part of it is adequately insured, both attached to and detached from the vehicle and while the equipment is being used.

Transfer of interest

A motor insurance policy is a contract between the insurer and the insured and cannot be 'sold' with a vehicle.

Windscreens

Although accidental damage to the windscreen and windows of the insured vehicle has always been covered under a comprehensive policy, to avoid a claim prejudicing the no-claims bonus it is now the practice of most insurers to include this cover under private car and commercial vehicle policies without loss of bonus and irrespective of the policy excess.

CONCLUSION

Within the highly competitive insurance market there are no standard motor policies and it has only been possible to describe very briefly what is 'usually' covered. A number of insurers have special schemes and have their own particular form of 'offer' in order to sell their policies to the most desirable section of the market.

It will be appreciated that it has not been possible to give more than a broad outline on motor insurance in the space available but it is hoped that the information provided will be sufficient to help the reader to understand what is available and assist him in directing his attention towards further fruitful enquiry.

FURTHER READING

The Road Traffic Acts 1972/1974, HMSO
Motor Insurance, The Chartered Insurance Institute, Tuition Service

13

Engineering Insurance

D. A. Curd, Director, NEI Furness (Insurance Services) Ltd

As its name implies, this class of insurance is concerned with plant and machinery in its many and varied forms. It is considered to be a specialised form of insurance as it is not transacted directly by all the companies operating in the United Kingdom. The market consists of three or four specialised engineering insurance companies, who are in the main subsidiaries of larger groups, although retaining their own identities and having worldwide reputations, and some composite companies who transact the business in their own engineering departments.

In addition, other insurance companies who neither own an engineering subsidiary company nor have set up a comprehensive specialised engineering department, accept engineering insurance using the inspection and other services of one of the specialised engineering insurance companies. Lloyd's underwriters also transact engineering insurance.

Engineering insurance can be split into two groups *Inspected Classes* and *Contingency Risks*. The fundamental difference between these two categories is that the former, as its name implies, incorporates or solely provides an inspection service with every item of plant covered, whereas the latter is more akin to insurance as transacted in other departments and the inspection service is not common in this group.

INSPECTED CLASSES

Inspection requirements

Inspected classes are the foundations of engineering insurance as we know it today and were born out of the Industrial Revolution in the mid 19th Century. With the expansion of the cotton mills in Lancashire came simultaneously a dramatic increase in the number of boiler explosions with serious consequences to life and property. Arising from this in 1854, the Manchester Steam Users Association was formed. This Association struck at the root of the problem in acknowledging that the way to minimise such accidents was by regular inspection of steam raising plant by competent persons.

Initially, insurance was not contemplated by the Association but in 1858 a company which now forms part of the National Vulcan Engineering Insurance Group commenced underwriting boiler insurance coupled with an inspection service.

Legislation was to follow and the Boiler Explosion Act 1882 required notification to be made of all 'boiler explosions' except of boilers used for domestic purposes only, under a penalty of a fine. Between 1882 and the passing of the Health and Safety at Work Act 1974, numerous Acts of Parliament have been passed, one of the principal ones being the Factories Act 1937. This Act laid down a new definition of boilers which can be summarised as 'any closed vessel in which steam is generated under pressure greater than atmospheric including an economiser and superheater'.

In addition, the Act provided for the compulsory periodical inspection of all steam and air pressure vessels; water sealed gas holders; lifting machinery, including chains, ropes, blocks etc. The Act also laid down the following maximum period between inspections:

Steam boilers	14 months
Steam and air receivers	26 months
Water sealed gas holders	24 months
Lifts and hoists	6 months
Chains, ropes and miscellaneous lifting tackle	6 months
Cranes and other lifting machinery	14 months

Such inspections have to be carried out by a competent person. The competency of a person to carry out particular inspections or tests is a matter of fact on which the owner must be satisfied. In the event of legal proceedings, it will require to be demonstrated in court that the person chosen is indeed competent for the job in question. There is no statutory definition of the term but the following extract from *A Comprehensive Guide to Factory Law* by Robert McKown (4th Edition) is often quoted:

> The person chosen should have such practical and theoretical knowledge and actual experience of the type of machinery or plant which he has to examine as will enable him to detect defects or weaknesses which it is the purpose of the examination to discover and to assess their importance in relation to the strength and functions of the machinery and plant.

It is not sufficient for the person making examinations to be able to detect faults, he must also, from his knowledge and experience, be able to assess their seriousness. It must however be emphasised that it is not against the law to have one's own employees carrying out the statutory inspection but this is not generally recommended as in the event of an accident involving plant and machinery subject to statutory inspections, in any proceedings the employer who uses an independent person to inspect such plant would be in a stronger position in defending the action.

It must also be pointed out that there are companies other than insurers offering an inspection service of plant and machinery to comply with the Acts, but offering no insurance protection. Such insurance may be obtainable from insurers separately under non-engineering policies.

It is emphasised that under the Factories Acts there is no compulsory insurance requirement. Insurance is only mandatory under the Road Traffic Act in respect of any boilers and pressure vessels on motor vehicles.

Health and Safety at Work Act 1974

It is pertinent in this chapter to mention the above Act in its relation to engineering insurance. This is an enabling Act under which the

Health and Safety at Work Executive can issue regulations and guidance notes as it thinks fit. Briefly, the Act requires employers to provide a safe system of work and maintain safe plant and machinery in addition to having a written policy on safety. Therefore, it will be readily appreciated that the Executive has wide powers to change the existing periods for statutory inspections of plant if considered necessary or even to introduce statutory inspections for new types of plant or other equipment, e.g. wiring installations.

The Appendix to this chapter summarises the types of plant and current statutory requirements governing their inspection and permission to reprint this information is acknowledged with grateful thanks to British Engine Insurance Limited.

Insurance covers

The principal classes of insurance within this group are Boiler and Pressure Plant, Electrical and Mechanical Plant, Lifting and Handling Plant. With engineering insurance, as with other classes of business, the current economic and competitive climate has had considerable impact on the way these risks are marketed. Insurers now seek to obtain all a client's business in this group and as a result often one policy to cover all items of the above plant is available. Such a contract may well result in premium economy as there is now no premium tariff for engineering insurance business. However, as the risks covered differ, specific comment will now be made regarding each class.

BOILER AND PRESSURE PLANT

The reader will notice from the chapter on Fire Insurance that the Standard fire policy, even with the explosion extension, excludes the explosion of all steam pressure plant unless used for domestic purposes. Therefore in respect of a steam boiler used in a works there is no cover and the need for separate insurance must be considered. In respect of such plant whilst boiler explosions are rare they do occur and can cause considerable damage. It is generally recommended that insurance on all pressure plant be effected.

Types of plant insurable

Some of the types of plant which are insurable under a boiler and pressure vessel policy (although this is not necessarily an exhaustive list) are:

steam boilers, economisers, superheaters, steam and feed piping, hot water heating and domestic supply boilers; hot water heating pipes and radiators and other hot water heating equipment such as calorifiers, storage tanks etc., steam-jacketed pans, air heating and drying batteries; ironing machines and presses, hot plates; bakers steam tube ovens, air and gas receivers.

From the above, it will be seen that the boiler policy can cover any items which are under pressure or vacuum.

The basic cover of a boiler policy is explosion or collapse of the pressure plant. Explosion is defined as 'the sudden and violent rending of the plant by force of internal steam or other fluid pressure (other than pressure of ignited flue gases), causing bodily displacement of any part of the plant, together with forcible ejection of the contents'. Collapse is defined as 'the sudden and dangerous distortion (whether or not attended by rupture) of any part of the plant caused by crushing stress by force of steam or other fluid pressure (other than pressure of ignited flue gases)'.

The reader should note the exclusion in both cases of flue gas explosion. This would be covered by the explosion extension of the standard fire policy.

The basic boiler policy is capable of being extended to include the risks of flue gas explosion (if not already covered by the fire policy) cracking, fracturing, weld failure, nipple leakage and overheating of boilers. However, if such extensions are considered desirable it would be wiser to consider not the basic cover of explosion or collapse with extensions but a wider form of cover which is now freely available. This covers the plant against sudden and unforeseen damage and can be defined as 'sudden and unforeseen damage (including damage caused by explosion due to force of internal steam or fluid pressure) which necessitates immediate repair or replacement of the plant before it can resume normal working'.

Whilst the wording of the wider form of cover varies very little between insurers, to determine the extent of the cover consideration must be given to the exclusions in every case.

ELECTRICAL AND MECHANICAL PLANT

The basic cover is 'breakdown' which is defined 'the actual breaking or burning out of any part of the plant whilst in use arising from either mechanical or electrical defect in the plant causing its sudden stoppage and necessitating immediate repair or replacement of the plant before it can resume normal working'. Alternatively, a wider form of cover is available for sudden and unforeseen damage. The definition of this is 'sudden and unforeseen damage which necessitates immediate repair or replacement of the plant before it can resume normal working'.

The company must now consider the need for insurance of this type of plant. Unlike boilers which can cause considerable damage, electrical/mechanical plant is not so hazardous and if a breakdown occurs any damage may be confined to the plant itself. Therefore whilst a breakdown will inevitably cause a loss to the company insofar as it will incur cost in carrying out the repairs, the question to be answered is the impact this will have on the company's financial situation. As a result of this it may be considered only necessary to insure the larger items of plant, e.g. ignoring fractional horse power motors. Consideration should also be given to effecting cover on any specialised items of test equipment. Before deciding to proceed with cover for electrical/mechanical breakdown the company will have also considered the various accident prevention precautions which could be taken, such as any improvements in the maintenance of plant or the provision of spare motors. The main impact of breakdown to installed plant may be not in the cost of repairs to such equipment but in the consequential losses that arise due to diminished production in the works during the outage of the plant. This aspect of the risk is considered in Chapter 6.

It must be pointed out that if insurance protection is not required then any statutory inspections which are required under the Factories Acts are separately available from insurers or specialised engineering companies.

LIFTING AND HANDLING PLANT

The standard form of cover available is loss or damage caused by breakdown as already defined for electrical/mechanical plant to which is added where applicable, toppling over, derailment or damage by other extraneous cause. Alternatively the wider cover of sudden and unforeseen damage is also available.

Here again the company must always question the need for such insurance, as in any factory, no matter how small, there is likely to be a variety of lifting equipment ranging from the smallest chain blocks to the largest overhead crane, including all forms of passenger lifts and hoists, mobile cranes, forklift trucks etc. It is generally accepted that with this type of plant a company will usually insure only the more hazardous plant, such as mobile cranes and forklift trucks being content to bear the risk of extraneous damage to overhead cranes and the smaller items of lifting tackle, but of course, arranging for statutory inspections to be carried out on such items of plant as required by the Acts.

Extensions to cover damage to insured's surrounding property and third party injury and damage

Having outlined the various forms of cover available on the three principal types of plant, if engineering insurance on any of these classes is effected, it is necessary to consider extending that insurance to cover damage to the insured's own surrounding property arising from insured damage to the plant, and legal liability for death of or injury to persons (other than employees who are already covered by Employer's Liability Insurance) and damage to third party property. Such extensions may already be automatically included in the standard policy cover or may be optional.

Clearly however, the financial effect of an explosion or breakdown may go beyond the cost of direct damage to the plant concerned in the accident and in many cases, the resulting cost in damage to other property (own and third party) and injury far exceeds the value of the plant involved. It may be however that such damage to other property and injury to third parties are already covered by either a general third party or fire policy and it is necessary to check to what extent that is so, in order to avoid either a gap or an overlap in cover between engineering policies and those other insurances.

Sums insured

With modern insurance practice the insured is normally relieved from the problem of arriving at an individual valuation for each item of plant as it is now the practice of insurers to offer a limit of indemnity of say £100,000 in respect of each and every item of plant insured. The company must however satisfy themselves that such a limit is adequate and can elect for higher limits of indemnity for say the largest boilers there may be in the works, which may have values well in excess of such a figure. Furthermore, if damage to the insured's surrounding property is to be included in the scope of the cover higher limits of indemnity are necessary, sufficient to cover damage to the plant itself and the estimated maximum damage to surrounding property. Careful consideration should particularly be given to the extent of damage which could be caused in the event of an explosion of the largest boiler in the works and a limit of indemnity of at least two or three times the value of the largest item of plant may be found desirable. Similar consideration should be given to the limit of indemnity under the third party extension if this is to be insured, and still higher limits may be required.

Premium rating

Each item of plant is rated by the insurer depending on its type, size and the indemnity limit selected. It will however be readily apparent that these rates are built up basically of two elements, one part for inspection and the other for insurance, of which the inspection element will usually form the largest proportion as unlike other forms of insurance cover this is normally a labour intensive contract. It naturally follows from this that insurance rates for the inspected classes of engineering business will increase with the rate of inflation to which the economy is subject. It is possible to obtain discounts if large schedules of plant are offered for inspection/insurance, particularly as the inspecting engineers employed by the insurers can then operate much more efficiently by carrying out more than one inspection at the same location with a resultant saving in time and overheads which the insurer passes on to the insured.

General exclusions and conditions

Apart from the usual exclusions of war risks, riot, nuclear risks, sonic bangs, certain other risks peculiar to the type of plant insured will be excluded. These generally relate to the cost of rectifying wear and tear, gradual deterioration, rust or corrosion etc., gradually developing flaws or defects or partial fractures and loose parts or defective joints or seams, unless these are the result of overheating caused by the general deficiency of water in boiler plant. The costs of maintenance work are of course also excluded.

Other conditions applicable to such contracts include the usual ones found in most insurances, i.e. those relating to control of claims, contribution, cancellation, arbitration. In addition to these, conditions will be found relating to the carrying out of special tests, alteration of working conditions and repairs which may be carried out by the insured. Finally, there is usually a condition relating to claims procedure and requirements.

Excesses

In respect of all items of plant a discount from the premium can be obtained if an insured is prepared to meet the first part of any claim himself. Obviously in relation to boilers and pressure plant the deductible would have to be of significant proportions say £10,000 to merit any worthwhile reduction in the premium. Conversely in respect of electrical/mechanical plant, if this is to be insured to any great extent then a worthwhile saving could be obtained in the premium if a deductible of £100 or £200 per claim is effected as this would rule out the more frequent minor claims.

Future trends

Inspected classes of engineering insurance are undergoing radical changes as a result of a development in the other classes of insurance business, namely 'assets all risks packages'. These are referred to in Chapter 5 in more detail but the insurance market is now offering an all risks cover on buildings and contents which effectively eliminates the need to specifically insure selected items of plant. The cover offered by such contracts varies considerably from insurer to insurer and the extent of the cover must be fully understood before any move is made to cancel, say, boiler insurance. Even if insurance cover is no longer necessary under engineering insurance the need to arrange for the provision of inspection services will of course remain.

SPECIAL SERVICES

It will be readily appreciated that with over a century of inspection work the engineering departments of insurers have built up considerable expertise in this field and they are able to offer specialised services of which the following are some examples.

1   A comprehensive service of approval on new plant construction at all stages of design, works manufacture, site erection and testing comprising:
    (a)   Design assessment using appropriate computer programmes from checking new or existing designs or proposed modifications to ensure compliance with a special construction code, be it British, Continental or International.
    (b)   Examination and tests of material to identify them with the specification and code requirements.
    (c)   Examination of work at key stages of production to ensure that quality is maintained.
    (d)   Final tests at the manufacturer's works on site.
2   Pipe stress analysis to determine:
    (a)   Reactions produced at pressure vessels, pumps, turbines, compressors.
    (b)   The stresses likely to arise in piping through changes in operating temperature, pressure or external loading.

3 Welding procedure approval and welder approval certification.
4 Chemical laboratories services; these include:
   (a) Metallurgical analysis.
   (b) Water analysis.
   (c) Scale analysis.
   (d) Debris analysis.
   (e) Analysis of oils and fuels.
5 Loss prevention services, e.g. accident prevention services which may be required under the Health and Safety at Work Act.
6 Plant valuations.

CONTINGENCY RISKS

Within this group are all the types of insurances transacted by the engineering department of a composite insurance office or a specialised insurance company which do not involve Statutory Inspections. The following is a summary of the principal insurance covers available.

WORKS DAMAGE INSURANCE

This insurance concerns itself with damage to:

1 Installed plant.
2 New products during the course of manufacture.
3 Products of the company returned for repair.

When this insurance was first introduced it was possible to insure installed plant only against the risk of impact. The market has broadened and it is now possible to insure installed plant and products against the wider risk of accidental damage.

It is a misconception that this class of insurance is only available to the engineering industry. In any manufacturing process if there is a risk of accidental damage to installed plant and products then that risk is capable of being insured.

Installed plant

In respect of this section of the insurance no cover is provided for explosion of boiler and/or pressure plant; or electrical/mechanical breakdown of lifts, cranes and other items of plant. Such cover is available only under the more specific insurances discussed previously. Additionally under this type of policy insurers will not cover accidental damage during the initial installation of machine tools or other items of plant, or major resiting operations within the factory. This is the subject of a separate cover which is discussed further on p. 309.

New and repaired products

When considering the need or otherwise to effect a works damage insurance, consideration must be given to the nature of the product and the processes through which it passes, including any final works testing, to evaluate the risks to which it is exposed and hence the need to carry insurance. Works damage insurances which include products, are usually tailor-made to an individual company's requirements but in general terms they offer accidental damage to the product from the time of allocation of material during manufacture, assembly and testing until the time of commencement of loading for despatch at the works.

If it is the custom in the industry concerned for a company to repair or overhaul its products, then such products returned for repair or overhaul are covered from the time they are unloaded at the works. The risks covered are usually accidental damage from any cause. However, the cover is subject to certain exclusions, the principal one being fire and other perils capable of being insured as extensions of a fire policy and depending on the nature of the product, the risk of theft is sometimes excluded.

Most products when they reach an advanced stage of manufacture are subjected to various forms of works testing and insurers generally try to exclude these risks from the scope of their covers but if a real exposure exists then it is possible to negotiate a cover for mechanical/electrical breakdown of the product whilst undergoing works test. In relation to this testing cover, it is usual for insurers to exclude the risks of faulty design, material or workmanship but not the damage which results from such faults. The wording of any such exclusion must be carefully read and discussed with insurers to find out the exact interpretation of the clause in relation to the product being manufactured. Taken literally it means that the insurer is not responsible for the costs incurred in rectification of the defect and in many cases this could mean the costs of access to the fault and the consequent re-assembly after rectification of the fault and repair of the damage. In a complicated engineering product these 'access' costs can form a major percentage of the total costs involved. In some cases, however, it is possible to reach agreement with insurers that those costs which are common to both the rectification of the fault and the repairing of the damage can be shared pro-rata which would result in a greatly improved form of cover.

Extensions

Depending on the nature of the products and the manufacturing facilities of the company the following extensions to a works damage policy can be arranged if required.

Subcontractors' premises. Given a product of a complex nature it is quite common for a certain amount of subcontracted items to be incorporated in it. Generally speaking such components are introduced into the product at the point of assembly but in some cases it is necessary for partially completed products to be sent to specialised manufacturers for some further work to be carried out upon them prior to return to the works for completion of the process. In such cases, it is certainly possible to insure the product whilst at subcontractors' premises but of course discussions must take place with insurers and the identity of such specialised subcontractors be revealed in order that insurers may assess the risk.

Inter-works transit. Whilst goods in transit insurance is freely available as a separate policy it is often found convenient to add a section relating to inter-works transit to a works damage policy to cover the transit risks to and from subcontractors' premises, any movement of the product between the various shops in one factory and between the company's factories. The need for such cover will be dependent on the production flow line techniques in operation in any given works situation.

Sums insured and premium rating

It is usual to arrange insurance contracts of this nature with one sum insured which would be sufficient to cover the maximum loss an insured might sustain arising out of any one accident. Premium calculations are usually related to throughput with a deposit premium payable at the outset and adjusted at the end of each period of insurance depending on the declarations furnished. The premium charged by this method will also include the premium for installed plant. The reader must not confuse works throughput with turnover. An insured's turnover figure as stated in the published accounts will reflect the sales values of finished articles, whereas the throughput values of the works will only reflect the output from the works which could relate only to partially finished products, especially if extensive erection periods on site are involved, together with other bought-in systems being added on site, and included in the final selling price.

If the policy contains the additional extension of mechanical/electrical breakdown of the product during test, then insurers will in all probability require details and values of the various items being tested and here again the same remarks as to value apply, as it quite frequently occurs that some of the items which comprise the finished product on site, e.g. exhaust systems, cooling systems etc. are not incorporated into the product at the point of works testing (such items being part of the test facility) and therefore should not be included in the declaration figures of products which have undergone works test.

Excesses

Insurers will always seek to impose a deductible. The size of this will be heavily dependent on the nature of the product but a deductible of £250 for accidental damage could be considered normal. If testing cover is included then the deductible covering this section would be much higher, probably starting at £2,500 but again dependent on the product.

Exclusions

The principal exclusions which relate to faulty workmanship design or material and mechanical/electrical breakdown of installed plant have already been dealt with. Fire and associated perils are also excluded, as these are covered by the fire insurance policy. If products are included in the cover, there will be an exclusion relating to prototypes and experimental products. The remaining exclusions are standard to engineering policies.

CONTRACT WORKS INSURANCE

A whole chapter in this book deals with 'contractors all risks insurance' but mainly as applied to the building and civil engineering industry. It is interesting to note however that in respect of a modern power station project, costing say approximately £1,000M, 30 to 40 per cent will be represented by civil works, the balance of the project being comprised of plant and machinery and it is the latter which is the subject of this section.

Before considering the insurance cover available for plant and machinery, consideration should be given to the contract conditions relating to the supply of such equipment. Standard conditions of contract for the supply and erection of plant in the UK do not vary greatly and for the purpose of this chapter reference is made to EB/BEAMA conditions 1979(A).

Clause 21 in broad terms imposes on the contractor liability for loss of or damage to the subject matter of the contract until a taking-over certificate is issued. In addition, liability for injury to third parties and damage to third party property is also imposed.

Clause 23 deals with insurance. Sub-clause (i) requires the contractor to cover the plant against specified risks during manufacture in the works. Sub-clause (ii) requires the contractor to insure in the joint names of himself and the employer the plant on site against certain specified risks.

In respect of export contracts, reference is made to Institute of Mechanical Engineers/Institute of Electrical Engineers (I MECH E/IEE) Model form B3 1980. In these conditions, Clause 22 again imposes a liability on the contractor for loss of or damage to the works until a taking-over certificate is issued and Clause 24 requires insurance in the joint names against certain risks including marine risks from at least the date of shipment.

Irrespective of the Conditions of Contract, it is generally accepted practice to insure the liabilities imposed under Clause 21 (EB/BEAMA) and Clause 22 (I MECH E/IEE) rather than insure for only the specified risks stipulated in the Contract but there are exceptions.

Marine and transit

It is interesting to note that in respect of Clause 24 of the I MECH E/IEE Conditions, insurance of the marine risk is clearly mentioned, which highlights the need to consider the transit and the erection risk as interlocking. It will be appreciated that with high technology products being transferred to site by road and/or sea, latent damage can occur during transit which may not manifest itself until an advanced stage of erection or testing on site has been reached. Therefore if the transit insurance is a separately negotiated contract with a different insurer, in a case of latent damage occurring during transit considerable difficulty could be encountered in recovering the cost from either insurer as each will require some proof that the damage occurred during the currency of the particular policy. If the carrier or shipper is holding a 'clean receipt' the chances of a transit insurer paying such a loss would be remote. Similarly, it is the practice in some industries for packing cases not to be opened until the contents are required for erection which could lead to a delay of some weeks or months after arrival on site. If again, a 'clean receipt' is given considerable difficulty would be incurred. Therefore, it is important that the transit risk be covered, ideally under the same policy as the erection risk. This is not so easily achieved in respect of export contracts, but there are ways of making these interlocking and the transit/marine risk should of course link back to the expiry of the works damage insurance.

Erection risks

Having mentioned the transit risk, which will usually be arranged on an 'all risks' basis, the cover during erection is normally against loss of or damage to the subject matter from any cause. Insurance commences from the time of completion of unloading on site (here again interlocking with the expiry of the transit risk) and continuing during erection and testing until a taking-over certificate is issued. It must be noted that the cover under this section of the policy must remain in force until the date upon which a taking-over certificate is issued and not the actual take-over date as mentioned on the certificate.

Maintenance period

Under Clause 30 of EB/BEAMA and Clause 31 of the I MECH E/IEE Conditions the contractor is responsible for making good defects in the plant which arise as the result of his faulty design workmanship or materials and for any damage which may subsequently arise as the result of the operation of such defects. Cover afforded by the maintenance section of a contract works policy varies considerably. The narrowest form only covers the plant whilst the contractor is on site for the purpose of making good any defects in the works or otherwise fulfilling his obligations under the contract. This is termed the 'visits risk'.

The widest form of cover will indemnify the contractor for damage to the plant which is his responsibility to rectify under the terms of the contract. It seeks to cover only his liability under the maintenance clause of the contract, consequently the insurance of the plant in its maintenance period under a contract works policy will not respond for damage to the plant caused by other external risks, e.g. fire damage or mal-operation by the purchaser.

Constructional plant

Under all contract works policies it is possible to insure constructional plant as a separate item. This would include all plant and equipment including temporary buildings and their contents as well as any mobile cranes etc. The cover is for all risks of loss or damage to the equipment, excluding mechanical/electrical breakdown of the plant.

Sum insured

The sum insured is usually fixed at the contract value, or the estimated final contract price if the contract is subject to contract price adjustment.

In respect of some of the larger contract works insurances which are effected on a blanket basis for the whole project and the sum insured is say, in excess of £1,000M insurers would be prepared to issue a first-loss policy, but the discounts offered for first-loss in this case can be relatively small, and it is dependent on the estimated maximum possible loss arising from any one cause. A separate sum insured is stated for constructional plant.

Excesses

Insurers always seek to impose a deductible in respect of all claims. This will vary between £25 and £250 depending on the nature of the products offered for insurance and the sum insured. If mechanical/electrical breakdown is covered for the testing/maintenance period, then the deductible can be expected to be considerably higher for that particular risk.

Exclusions and conditions

The principal exclusion in an insurance of this nature is the one that relates to mechanical/electrical breakdown arising either during commissioning or during the maintenance period and caused by a defect of workmanship, materials or design. The same remarks apply to contract works insurances as mentioned for works damage insurance in respect of the access costs (see p. 300) and it must be borne in mind that in the case of an export contract where substantial damage to part of the product has occurred necessitating return to the UK for repair, then the costs of ocean freight both ways can be construed as forming part of the access costs. Therefore great care must be exercised when discussing with insurers the extent of the exclusion of faulty workmanship materials or design.

The other principal exclusions found in this type of policy are the costs of rectification or making good fair wear and tear or gradual deterioration, rust, corrosion etc, and whilst insurers will pay for theft of plant or any part of it from site providing there has been a specific occurrence, the policy will not pay for inventory losses. In addition, the policy does not pay for liquidated damages arising from delay or in connection with guarantees of the performance or efficiency of the plant or any other form of consequential loss.

In respect of the commissioning risk prior to take over, insurers will usually seek to limit the cover to a specified period of months and would normally exclude all losses for mechanical/electrical breakdown in respect of testing which has overrun this period. The period of testing cover offered by insurers is negotiable and great care must be exercised when considering its adequacy. The remaining conditions and exclusions are standard to engineering policies.

Types of cover

The most common form of contract works policy is an annual blanket arrangement, whereby the insurer agrees to accept all contracts undertaken by the insured up to a predetermined limit. The annual premium is based on the annual total value of such contracts and at the end of each period, the insured declares the actual contracts covered by the policy and the premium is accordingly adjusted on the basis of the declaration. Blanket policies have the merit of relieving the insured from the need to make specific arrangements in respect of each individual contract, leaving him to arrange separate policies for contracts in excess of the blanket cover limits. Care must be exercised, however, in respect of contracts which are subject to contract price adjustment and commence at a value which is within the blanket limits but due to such adjustment escalate over and above the limits of the policy. In such cases, a separate declaration should be made to insurers who, in most cases, will agree that such contracts remain under the blanket cover.

In respect of the larger projects, it has become the practice of the purchaser to effect a single site contract works policy, covering himself, all contractors, subcontractors and suppliers for the erection and maintenance period of the project. Whilst this policy does have its advantages, there can be considerable disadvantages in it for both sides. From the purchaser's point of view, he is relieved from the burden of checking each individual contractor's arrangement as he knows exactly the extent of the cover operating on the plant he is purchasing during the erection commissioning period. He does however have to institute a focal point on the site to deal with the claims handling arrangements which may incur him in some cost. In addition to this, if he decides to proceed with such arrangements after the tenders have been received, he will require the contractors who will have included in their tender prices an allowance for contract works insurance to take out this insurance element from their tender prices. However, the sum total of the take out prices of all contractors on the project never seems to equate to the premium required for the single site policy and considerable negotiation sometimes takes place.

From the contractors' point of view, the main disadvantage with such an arrangement is that they have no part in the negotiations of these insurance contracts and may be penalised by a narrow wording, i.e. faulty parts exclusions and higher deductibles than they would normally be prepared to carry under their own arrangements. Sometimes further negotiations may be necessary with the purchaser to overcome any deficiencies which may be apparent in the single site arrangements. One of the main advantages to the contractor is that he has no claims experience record to preserve in order to maintain his own standing with his own insurers and there is a tendency to press all claims under such contracts to their limits.

In respect of some export contracts, it is the custom of the purchaser to require that contract works insurance be effected in the country where the work is being executed and in some tenders a preferred list of local insurers is given. The best way of tackling this problem is for the contractor to contact his own contract works insurer as it is quite possible the latter may have some reinsurance contact with one of the listed companies; or alternatively an insurance broker, if employed, may be able to make contact through the reinsurance market, failing which, there is no alternative but to contact the insurance company direct to obtain details of the rates and extent of cover offered. If the extent of the cover offered is somewhat less than that arranged with normal insurers in the UK it is possible to arrange a 'difference in conditions' cover with one's own insurers to bridge the gap between the two arrangements.

One of the problems which can arise in respect of policies issued abroad is that not only are premiums payable in the local currency, but also claims' payments, which can lead to serious problems if exchange control regulations apply and extensive costs are incurred in the UK in carrying out repairs etc.

Premium rating

The premium is arrived at by applying a rate to the sum insured. This rate is inter alia dependent on the total erection period including the maintenance period and acknowledges the fact that there is a gradual build-up of value on site. Insurers usually seek to charge the total estimated premium payable at the outset with an adjustment payable at the end of the maintenance period depending on the actual erection period and the final contract price, but in some cases where the erection period is to be spread over say 3 or 4 years, it is possible to negotiate that the initial premium is paid in annual instalments.

INSURANCE OF PLANT DURING INSTALLATION

As will be remembered from the section dealing with works damage insurance, the cover given on installed plant is only accidental damage, and no cover is provided under a works damage policy to protect new plant being installed or major resiting operations of existing plant.

In respect of new plant and equipment, if it is the buyers responsibility, and in respect of resiting of existing plant, insurance is available to cover the installation and commissioning.

The cover offered is on an all risks basis including the test running of such plant after installation or reinstallation. The sum insured must equate to the value of the property at risk and the insurance will be subject to a deductible, depending on the size of the plant. Premiums are based on the value of plant to be insured and the period for which cover is required.

HIRED-IN PLANT

Under standard hiring conditions from the time that delivery is taken of the hired-in plant the risk of loss or damage to the plant lies with the hirer and hire charges continue even though the plant may have suffered damage and the liability continues until the plant is returned and/or the hiring agreement is terminated. Insurance against these risks is possible and is usually effected on a blanket basis, insurers being normally willing to cover all types of hired-in plant with the exception of tower cranes, which would have to be declared specifically. Cover can be arranged against loss of or damage to the equipment so hired, together with an insured's liability to pay the hiring charges during the period that the plant is out of commission. The cover is accidental damage to the equipment from any cause, including mechanical/electrical breakdown and the sums insured are fixed on a blanket basis.

The premium is based on the annual hiring charges. A deposit premium being paid at the commencement of the risk and adjusted at the end of each period of insurance in accordance with the declaration of actual hiring charges for the period submitted.

COMPUTER INSURANCE

Computers play an increasing role in the efficient running of a business and insurance of such equipment has now been available for some years. Originally the insurance policies were designed to protect the main frame installations, but with the advent of the mini and micro-computer, the insurances have been redesigned and in general terms a complete package is offered by insurers comprising three main sections as follows.

Section 1 covers loss of or damage to the installation including any peripheral and ancillary equipment which would include any air conditioning plant. Such equipment to be located at specified premises in the UK, but terminal equipment will be covered at any other location within the UK. The cover is on an all risks basis including mechanical/electrical breakdown and/or derangement.

Section 2 covers loss of or damage to data carrying materials (tapes, cards, discs etc). Also included in the cover by *Section 2* is not only the cost of replacing such damaged software with new, but also including the costs of recompiling the data contained on the original material following loss or damage etc.

Section 3 covers the increased cost of working following damage or failure of the electricity supply etc.

Sums insured

The sum insured under section 1 would be the replacement value of the installation. The sum insured under section 2 must not only be sufficient to cover the cost of replacing the software but also be increased to allow for the cost of recreating the data on the tapes etc. and this latter figure could be considerably in excess of the cost of the material itself. Under section 3 the sum insured is calculated by taking the hiring time per hour of a similar installation and multiplying this by the number of hours used per day and the number of days and/or weeks that it is anticipated it would take to repair or replace the damaged installation. To the figure should be added an amount to cover overtime payments, travelling expenses etc. as for example, in the event of damage to a main frame computer the nearest installation which is comparable with the one insured may be miles away and any facilities offered may be available only during the night etc.

The premium is calculated on the sums insured under section 1 and 2 and on the sum insured and period of cover under section 3.

Exclusions and conditions

The principal exclusions under such policies are wear and tear and loss or damage provided for under the terms of a maintenance agreement. In respect of large main frame installations, insurers usually require a maintenance agreement to be in force during the currency of any insurance. The other exclusions and conditions would be standard for the majority of insurance contracts.

APPENDIX 13:1
STATUTORY REQUIREMENTS GOVERNING THE INSPECTION OF PLANT

Permission to reprint this information is acknowledged with grateful thanks to BRITISH ENGINE INSURANCE LTD

Premises at which plant is located	Factories (as defined in the Factories Act)	Docks Wharves & Quays	Warehouses at Docks, Wharves and Quays & Warehouses using mechanical power	Building Operations and Works of Engineering Construction	Shipyards Dry-docks & Shipbreaking yards	Coal Ironstone Shale and Fireclay Mines	Other Mines	Petrol Filling Stations	Quarries	Cinemas	Offices, Banks, Shops, Public Restaurants, etc.	Tank Vehicles carrying dangerous goods in Europe	Countries where CSC Agreement is recognised
Aerial Cable & Ropeways	A			C					T				
Air Receivers	A			A	D		F		H				
Bakers' Steam Tube Ovens	A												
Cranes & Lifting Machinery	A	B	C	C	A, D		F		H				
Dust Extraction & Ventilation Plant	J,K,L,M,N,S												
Economisers	A	A	A	A			F		H				
Electrical Installations & Earthing Systems							G	U	I	O			
Electrical Storage Batteries										O			
Excavators				C									
Fork Lift Trucks	A	B	A	C	A, D		F		H				
Freight Containers													R, V
Gasholders	A												
Lifts & Hoists	A		A	C						Q	Q		
Lifting Gear	A	B	A	C	A, D					Q			
Piling Frames				C									
Power Presses including Press Brakes	P												
Road Tank Vehicles												R	
Steam Boilers	A	A	A	A		E	F		H				
Superheaters	A	A	A	A			F		H				
Steam Pressure Vessels	A												
Vehicle Lifts	A												

KEY TO LEGISLATION

A Factories Act, 1961
B Docks Regulations, 1934
C Construction (Lifting Operations) Regulations, 1961 NO. 1581
D Ship Building & Ship-repairing Regulations, 1960

E Coal and Other Mines (Steam Boilers) Regulations, 1956
F Miscellaneous Mines (General) Regulations, 1956
G Miscellaneous Mines (Electricity) Regulations, 1956
H Quarries (General) Regulations 1956 No. 1778
I Quarries (Electricity) Regulations, 1956
J Blasting (Castings and Other Articles) Special Regulations, 1949
K Grinding of Cutlery and Edge Tools Regulations, 1925 and 1950
L Grinding of Metals (Miscellaneous Industries) Regulations, 1925 and 1950

M Pottery (Health and Welfare) Regulations, 1950
N Non-Ferrous Metals (Melting and Founding) Regulations, 1962
O Cinematograph (Safety) Regulations, 1955
P Power Presses Regulations, 1965 No. 1441

Q Offices, Shops, and Railway Premises (Hoists and Lifts) Regulations, 1968
R European Agreement concerning the International Carriage of Dangerous Goods by Road (ADR)
S Asbestos Regulations, 1969
T Quarries (Ropeways and Vehicles) Regulations, 1958
U 1969 Model Code Regulations (adopted by most LA) Main Act – Petroleum (Consolidiation) Act 1928
V International Convention for Safe Containers (CSC)

FURTHER READING

Munchener Ruckversicherungs-Gesellschaft, *Machinery Loss Prevention: a Handbook for Engineering Insurers.* Munich, 1978.

John Clark, *Engineering Insurance,* vol. 1. London: Chartered Insurance Institute Tuition Service, 1981.

A. Mukherjee, *Engineering Insurance,* vol 11. London: Chartered Insurance Institute Tuition Service, 1981.

D. Chare, Engineering Insurance in *Handbook of Insurance,* edited by R. L. Carter. Kluwer-Harrap, updated regularly, Section 6.

14

Contractors' All Risks Insurance

J. T. Deprez, Insurance Manager, The Wiltshier Group

FUNCTION OF CONTRACTORS' ALL RISKS INSURANCE

The main function of contractors' all risks (CAR) insurance is to provide, as far as practicable, to the principal who requires works constructed (variously referred to in contracts as the employer, developer, authority or purchaser) and to those who contract to construct them, protection by insurance against the potentially serious costs which they might otherwise incur in making good any physical loss or damage from a cause occurring before completion and handover of the works.

The policy benefits the contractor because it sets out to cover the contractual liabilities for material damage or loss that are imposed upon him by the employer.

It benefits the employer because the existence of an adequate policy ensures that funds will be available for the rebuilding of works destroyed, for example, by fire, which, even though the contractor may be contractually liable, could involve remedial costs beyond the financial capacity of the contractor.

DEVELOPMENT OF CONTRACTORS' ALL RISKS INSURANCE

A contractors' all risks policy was issued for the construction of Lambeth Bridge over the Thames as long ago as 1929, but such policies were rare until the boom in contracting following the 1939/45 war.

A building contractor normally confined his insurance to the fire risk on the works and covered other perils only in specific cases when he was required to do so or when he himself deemed it prudent to extend the scope of cover. Indeed the widely used RIBA form of contract (1939 edition) required the contractor to insure the works and unfixed materials against loss or damage by fire only.

The facility for wider site insurance coincided with a rapid expansion in the construction industry. New contractors entered the erection and construction industries and many traditional firms undertook several times their prewar volume of work.

The demand for wide cover on the works also greatly increased with the arrival of the second edition (January 1950) of the Institution of Civil Engineers general conditions of contract. This required the contractor to insure the works in the joint names of the employer and the contractor on an all risks basis excluding certain risks that were neither entirely of an extraneous or fortuitous nature nor directly associated with the manner of execution of the works. The employer retained responsibility for these risks which were, in the main, uninsurable by the contractor.

'All risks' cover became the practice rather than the rule and insurance companies and Lloyd's competed freely, conceding more cover at lower premium rates. Wide policy wordings were available extending even to include, for example, the cost of making good defective work (later withdrawn but latterly creeping back into policies in limited degree) and numerous other extras.

Employers' and public liability sections were included where required under the CAR policy, and this is still done occasionally.

Such competition reduced rates to an uneconomical level and insurers suffered heavy losses. Many underwriters and insurance companies then withdrew altogether from this form of insurance. The market then achieved more stability, rates increased substantially and heavy excesses were imposed and the cover, although called 'all risks', became comparatively restricted in scope.

Contractors generally reacted by pressing the market to provide the protection they needed in the face of high risk exposures and onerous contractual impositions. CAR policies now afford wider cover in several areas which were excluded even from the original widely worded policies. Several new insurers have entered the CAR market and currently there is much competition for contractors all risks' business with consequent financial disadvantage to insurers.

Basic wordings of CAR policies have been extended to include where not otherwise insured such extras as continuing hire charges on damaged plant; plant materials and employees' tools at any location within the territorial limits of the policy including materials at suppliers' premises; 'all risks' cover on existing retained structures; property of the employer for which the contractor is responsible.

There have been cases also where insurers have accepted under CAR policies an indemnity to the employer for advance rent and profits and/or additional cost of working (see Chapter 6 on Business Interruption Insurance). Some contractors have negotiated modifications to such policy exclusions as the design exclusion (see p. 327) and to the exclusion (unless specially agreed otherwise) of cover on uncompleted buildings taken into use or occupancy for their ultimate purpose prior to formal handover, as well as other standard conditions.

ANNUAL AND INDIVIDUAL POLICIES

Contractors' all risks policies can be issued either for an individual construction contract or on an annual basis whereby all contracts of a value individually below an agreed monetary limit are covered automatically without prior notification to insurers. There may, nevertheless, be features or developments such as use and occupancy by tenants and others on a particular contract which call for disclosure to insurers, and special agreement, under the annual form as well as the individual policy.

Under both individual and annual policies an initial deposit premium is paid. In the case of individual policies, this is based on the estimated contract price and under annual policies it is normally based on an estimate of turnover on the annual work to be undertaken. The premiums on both types of policy are retro-spectively adjusted, the individual policy on the actual value of the contract when known and the annual policy on the value of work undertaken during the period of insurance. It is nowadays rare for

CAR policies to be rated only on wages expenditure, but policies which include public and employers' liability sections will usually call for declarations of turnover and wages and salaries for premium adjustment and even subdivisions of the declarations against separate rates for different categories of work.

The annual policy has obvious administrative advantages and the interest can be noted of 'any principal' thus automatically including all employers as joint insureds to the extent required by the construction contract.

Under both annual and individual policies, CAR cover applies not only to the contract works—that is, the permanent works in progress—but also to all materials, temporary works (works that are removed as the permanent works are completed, like shuttering, timbering, formwork, etc.) temporary buildings and contents, constructional plant, tools, equipment and other things for use in connection with any site. The insured property can and should also be covered during transits to and from the site. Some policies extend to cover the foregoing items while at any premises within the geographical limits of the policy, that is, while held elsewhere than on site for use in connection with site works.

The typical policy provides for the payment of architects' and/or surveyors' and/or engineers' fees necessarily incurred in reinstatement following loss or damage, the costs of removal of debris and/or provision of temporary support where insured damage has occurred as well as the actual reinstatement of the damage.

Allowance is made in any claims settlement for escalation in costs and inflation normally expressed in the policy as a percentage of the contract sum. This may be related not only to the costs in making good the works damaged but also applied to the enhanced costs of completing delayed unbuilt works.

Contracts where the individual value is above the monetary limits of an annual policy or of a type stipulated by underwriters as warranting separate cover require special negotiation outside the annual policy and premium rates and excesses on such contracts vary considerably.

Differences have arisen as to what comprises the contract works and what must be regarded as third party property or the property of the employer other than the works. Briefly stated the rule of thumb test is whether the construction cost of the item is within the contract price and as such its construction forms part of the permanent or temporary works.

A definition of the works is given in some contract documents and in certain cases this may influence the interpretation as to whether the indemnity under the contractors all risks policy is to be invoked.

EMPLOYER-ARRANGED CAR POLICIES

On very large projects involving several contractors in consortium and with each contractor having numerous subcontractors there is much to be said for an 'umbrella' contractors all risks policy covering all the parties involved. The employer can best arrange this and thereby satisfy himself as to the similarity of cover for all contracting parties, the proper annotation of his own interest and the adequacy of the overall protection and control settlement of claims.

Contracts are generally placed with one main contractor who engages all subcontractors and in these cases also it is possible to effect a 'developer's all risks' policy broadly covering risks similar to the basis CAR policy effected by contractors. For such orthodox contracts there are disadvantages in this arrangement. In practice a contractor tendering for such a contract will not have foreknowledge as to the scope of the employer's policy on the works and will have added to his tender price at least the premium for a 'differences' or 'security' policy to provide contingent cover in the light of the unseen employer arranged policy, which may have exclusions or restrictions which the contractor is unwilling to leave unprotected. The effective cost to the employer may thus be greater than he thinks. Such employer's policies may exclude constructional plant, temporary works, temporary buildings and contents etc. and may exclude transits to and from the site or goods held away from site which would be included under a CAR policy arranged by the contractor. The dovetailing of one policy with another in the contractor's total insurance portfolio is frequently disturbed, e.g. for economy or other reasons he may have negotiated a special CAR policy wording which enables him to reduce the scope of or eliminate other covers. Moreover, where the employer insures the works the contractor remains responsible for loss of or damage to them and any inadequacies in the employer's policy will most often operate to the detriment of the contractor.

Because the contractor is more frequently involved in arranging CAR insurance than the employer there is likely to be more expertise in the insurance administration of the established contractor and possibly so with his brokers handling the insurance and the ultimate cost to the employer is likely to be less if the arrangement is left to the contractor.

Often it is the broker representing the employer who may suggest the employer arranged contract works insurance mainly to acquire a greater volume of business. Commissions are comparatively high on this class of insurance and reasons advanced by some brokers for transferring to the employer the obligation to insure new works are not always valid. For such policies the term 'construction all risks' may be used.

OVERSEAS CONSIDERATIONS

Contract wordings vary considerably and it is not uncommon for British contractors to qualify their tenders for works overseas so that they are based on the FIDIC forms of contract, issued by Federation Internationale Des Ingenieurs-Conseils (also known as the International Federation of Consulting Engineers) and associated bodies for building works as well as civil engineering projects. These conditions follow the United Kingdom ICE form of contract issued by the Institution of Civil Engineers jointly with other bodies fairly closely as regards the liability, responsibility and insurance clauses.

There is a good deal of concern about the shortage of capacity in the world insurance market for very large projects in overseas areas where there are frequent natural disasters such as earthquakes or hurricanes and before tendering the contractor and his brokers must make exhaustive enquiries to check the availability of cover.

Normally CAR insurances can be placed through the UK insurance market and UK wordings are adapted to the requirements of the overseas contract but in territories where it is mandatory for cover to be placed with local or nationalised insurers this can be achieved best with the help of a specialist broker who may be able to arrange suitable reinsurance for the major percentage with the UK/European market. Here again a 'security' or 'difference in conditions' policy should be considered to provide contingent cover for any gaps in the local policy wording. An investigation of local law is advisable where, as is often the case, policies are subject to local jurisdiction.

DECENNIAL INSURANCE FOR STRUCTURAL DEFECTS

In France it has long been a stipulation of the French Civil Code that building contractors, architects and engineers under contract with a developer are responsible for errors during construction and thereafter for 10 years from completion and handover. Only architects are legally bound to be insured, but contractors and engineers have been obliged in their own interests to take out policies to cover their liabilities for faults in construction which become apparent during the period. The law also imposes on property developers selling new buildings a 10 year liability to the purchaser for defects which occur after sale.

This liability is also often imposed in Middle Eastern countries and in some developing countries in Africa, in particular where the law is based on the Napoleonic legal system.

The property developer's standard cover is for the cost of repairing material damage to the building due to defect rather than liability for other costs arising out of defects and, unless specially agreed, there is no waiver of subrogation rights against the architect, engineer or contractor. These latter participants arrange liability insurance covering their respective responsibilities and liabilities arising out of a presumed fault in the structure. There is a system of pre-contract checks, technical control and periodic inspections by an approved independent organisation.

The contractors' all risks policy may be extended to include damage to the works in the terms of the decennial responsibility but only for the period of maintenance, normally up to 12 months. The CAR policy is thus of little value in this context and the contractor must arrange for specially related liability insurance unless he can obtain a waiver of subrogation against him under the Developer's Decennial policy for the full period.

For several years the NHBC scheme in the United Kingdom has provided cover to purchasers of private dwelling houses and their successors in title. A decennial type of policy is now available on a selective basis to developers for all types of properties constructed in the United Kingdom and the interest of the architect and in isolated cases of the contractor can be included but most contractors appear willing to bear the risk rather than attempt to obtain indemnity under this type of insurance.

EXCESSES

An excess of £250 for each and every claim is quite normal but the trend is for higher excesses to be applied by insurers especially in civil engineering projects such as tunnels, 'wet risks' and other works involving potentially high exposures. Some large contractors voluntarily accept substantial excesses of say £10,000 any one occurrence, and may well accept even higher excesses. Obviously the higher the excess the lower the premium for a particular policy.

CONTRACTUAL CONSIDERATIONS

Many different forms of contract are currently in use for construction, erection and maintenance works in the United Kingdom and abroad. A basic feature common to all agreements is that the contractor whose tender has been accepted by the employer shall be bound to complete the works for which he has contracted and do so in conformity with the contract documents.

This primary obligation of the contractor is expressed, for example, in Article 1 of the Joint Contracts Tribunal's 1980 standard forms of buildings contract (formerly known as the RIBA forms of contract) as follows:

> For the consideration hereinafter mentioned the contractor will upon and subject to the contract documents carry out and complete the works shown upon, described by or referred to in those documents.

In the form of agreement annexed to the current ICE conditions of contract for works of civil engineering construction, the undertaking is stated in clause 3:

In consideration of the payments to be made by the employer to the contractor as hereinafter mentioned the contractor hereby covenants with the employer to construct, complete and maintain the works in conformity in all respects with the provisions of the contract.

Such clauses impose wider responsibilities upon the contractor than are contemplated in the obligations to insure specified in the same forms of contract. A contractor, when arranging CAR insurance on works, temporary works and constructional equipment, will have to secure protection for himself against certain risks of physical loss or damage for which the employer does not specify he shall be insured but to which the contractor is nevertheless exposed.

It is important to note the responsibilities that a contractor has under a contract and in particular how his liability is limited for specific unforeseeable events and for interruptions to progress which are beyond his control—in other words, how far the principals retain responsibility.

In form GC/Works/1 (Edition 2) (as amended September 1982) and used for all but minor contracts for the Department of the Environment and other government bodies, clause 1(2) defines the risks accepted by the DoE in relation to loss of or damage to the works as follows:

The accepted risks means the risks of:
Pressure waves caused by aircraft or aerial devices whether travelling at sonic or supersonic speeds.
Ionising radiations or contamination by radioactivity from any nuclear fuel or from any nuclear waste from the combustion of nuclear fuel.
The radioactive, toxic, explosive or other hazardous properties of any explosive nuclear assembly or nuclear component thereof.
Civil war, rebellion, revolution, insurrection, military or usurped power or King's enemy risks (within the definition of that expression contained in section 15(1)(a) of the War Risks Insurance Act 1939 as for the time being in force).

In this form of contract and the minor works form GC/Works/2 there is not always a requirement that the contractor shall insure. For many years it had been the practice to make the contractor responsible as defined leaving him to seek such available insurance protection as he deemed advisable. However, the form of tender now makes reference to the requirement of appropriate insurance and may also require that the CAR and public liability insurances for a project shall be placed on a prescribed wording through a broker specified by the Department of the Environment.

The ICE conditions stipulate, in clause 20(2), the risks in relation to the works that are 'excepted' or excluded from the contractors' responsibility.

The 'excepted risks' are war, hostilities (whether war be declared or not), invasion, act of foreign enemies, rebellion, revolution, insurrection or military or usurped power, civil war, or (unless solely restricted to employees of the contractor or of his subcontractors and arising from the conduct of the works) riot, civil commotion or disorder, or use or occupation by the employer of any part of the permanent works, or a cause solely due to the engineer's design of the works, or ionising radiations or contamination by radioactivity from any nuclear fuel or from any nuclear waste from the combustion of nuclear fuel, radioactive toxic explosives, or other hazardous properties of any explosive, nuclear assembly or nuclear component thereof, pressure waves caused by aircraft or other aerial devices travelling at sonic or supersonic speeds, or any such operation of the forces of nature as an experienced contractor could not foresee, or reasonably make provision for or insure against all of which are herein collectively referred to as 'the excepted risks'.

By clause 21 of the ICE conditions, the contractor is required to maintain insurance against all loss or damage from whatsoever cause arising (other than the excepted risks) to works, temporary works, material, plant and other things brought on to the site.

Under the current standard JCT forms of building contract there is no 'care of works' clause specifically detailing the responsibilities of the contractor in relation to the contract works. The employer relies upon the contractor's undertaking to complete and the obligations to insure against fire and the specified perils listed in clause 22 (JCT 1980 edition) for the full reinstatement value of the works. The standard risks that are listed in clause 22 do not so far include subsidence/collapse, frost, accidental damage, impact damage, malicious damage, theft and certain more remote categories of loss or damage.

For some years many employers under JCT building contracts have amended clause 22A being the clause obligating the contractor to insure the works (clauses 22B & C require the employer to insure) so that instead of insuring merely the fire risks and the perils specified in clause 22A the contractor must insure against all risks of loss or damage or as sometimes expressed 'all insurable risks of loss or damage' to the works and materials and goods intended therefor. Contractors and insurers have accepted this amendment in JCT forms; the ICE form has long required such a wider scope of cover.

It is suggested that the JCT Standard Forms of Building Contract may be modified at some future date to require an all risks indemnity to the employer in substitution for the present clause 22A obligations. Similar 'excepted risks' ought also to be introduced in that event.

THE JCT STANDARD FORM OF CONTRACT WITH CONTRACTORS' DESIGN (1981)

In this contract the insurance clauses closely conform to the orthodox JCT contract obligations and although disclosure to insurers of such contracts is required the contractors' all risks policy (on the works) is not normally modified solely by reason of the design having been made by the contractor even though the risk exposure is increased. The contractors' public liability and professional indemnity policies may require reviewing if such contracts are entered into though these policies will normally have been arranged with design and build work in contemplation.

INSURERS' REACTION TO WIDER INDEMNITIES

In general underwriters link their policy wordings to the indemnities required by contracts and consequently it is the insurers who are asked to absorb extensions to the contractors' responsibilities and obligations. Not infrequently the amendments are of such a nature as to be an uninsurable proposition. At such times CAR insurers having a long and satisfactory relationship with a contractor will go further in assisting their client than they might otherwise.

In an age where new companies are offering cheap terms and in a climate of increased exposure of insurers, the buyer of insurance should be wary of very low premium levels which may serve his interests in the short term but may well produce adverse loss ratios resulting in a restrictive attitude on the part of insurers to claims settlements and perhaps a refusal to renew or the requirement of increased premiums at renewal.

Continuity of a stable relationship with long standing CAR insurers is of great value. A sympathetic approach on both sides is the best basis and the insurers are likely to adopt a more generous view when controversial cases arise.

AMENDED FORMS

Problems can arise when the negotiated standard forms of contract are amended. The amended contracts may contravene the Unfair Contract Terms Act 1977 Section 3 and any ambiguities would be construed contra preferentem i.e. to the disadvantage of those who seek to rely upon them.

ALTERNATIVE FORMS OF BUILDING CONTRACT

Possibly as a reaction to the alleged complexities of the 1980 JCT Forms there is an increasing tendency for employers representatives to base building contracts on the previously little used contract conditions issued by the Faculty of Architects and Surveyors or on a newer form of main contract issued by the Association of Consultant Architects.

The first of these, the FAS form, requires under clause 25 that the contractor shall insure new works against fire and specified perils, much as the 1977 revision to the JCT 1963 form and allows in similar fashion an alternative for the employer to insure the existing structure and his contents and new works and materials for similar risks when the contract is for alterations or additions to existing buildings.

The ACA form under clause 6 also has alternative options requiring the contractor to insure new works and the employer to cover, where it applies, the existing building, contents and new works. In the first alternative requiring the contractor to insure new works the insurance is to be in the joint names of employer and contractor 'against all those contingencies against which the contractor can reasonably obtain insurance' for the full reinstatement value plus fees. There is a requirement that insurance monies shall be paid to the employer. This method would not seem to create any undue problems so far as concerns damage to the works, though the contractor may find a slight complication in this method of payment where some element of the insurance claim settlement relates to his plant, temporary works etc. As the employer is a joint insured it is an admissible practice from insurer's viewpoint whilst possibly impeding the freedom of a contractor in the negotiation of a compromise settlement.

It is hoped that the reader gaining experience in the field of construction insurances will appreciate the need to refer to specific contract documents to check for any deviations from standard wordings which may affect liability, responsibility and/or insurance obligations.

POLICY WORDINGS

The contractors' all risks policy is also known as a 'contractors' combined' or 'contract works' or 'contractors' indemnity' policy and although nominally covering 'all risks' it does incorporate exceptions.

The form of cover is designed not only for building and civil engineering but also for mechanical, electrical and chemical contractors and in consequence the exceptions will vary to deal with aspects peculiar to a form of construction, for example, abandonment of tunnels and mechanical or electrical breakdown of plant.

As previously indicated, the extension of the policy to provide public liability protection is optional. Readers are referred to Chapter 11 on Liabilities and to p. 330 et seq. in this chapter.

Section 1: all risks

The operative clause of the policy will normally state the following or similar:

> The insurers will indemnify the insured against loss of or physical (or material) damage to the insured property howsoever caused and occurring during the period of insurance.

Exclusions

Because of the wide scope of the operative clause, the risks against which insurers will not grant an indemnity are specified. The more common exclusions are:

1   An excess or retained liability.
2   Loss or destruction of or damage to:
    (a)   Deeds, bonds, bills of exchange, promissory notes, cash, bank notes, cheques, securities for money or stamps.
    (b)   Any item of machinery or plant (not being a boiler used for domestic purposes only), tools or equipment caused by its own explosion, breakdown or derangement. This exclusion does not apply to damage arising as a consequence of such an explosion, breakdown or derangement.
    (c)   Any vessel or craft or thing made or intended to be waterborne or airborne.
    (b)   Any vehicle for which a licence and/or certificate of insurance is required other than mobile cranes, mechanical navvies, shovels, grabs, excavators and site-clearing and levelling plant and vehicles with plant permanently attached.
3   The cost of replacement or rectification rendered necessary by a defect in design, materials or workmanship or by wear, tear or other gradually operating cause. This exclusion does not apply to loss of or damage to other insured property (that is free from such a defect) that results from such defect, wear, tear or gradually operating cause.
4   Penalties under contract for delay or non-completion or consequential loss of any nature whatsoever.
5   Any loss of property either by disappearance or by shortage if

such disappearance or shortage is only revealed when a routine inventory is made.

6   Any property of the employer existing at the time of the commencement of the contract other than materials supplied by the employer for incorporation in the constructional works.

7   The permanent works or any part thereof in respect of which a Certificate of Completion has been issued. This exclusion shall not however apply to any loss or damage occurring for which the contractor is responsible under the ICE form of contract during the first 14 days following the issue of the Certificate of Completion provided always that the insurers shall not be responsible for loss or damage due to use or occupation by the employer his agents servants or other contractors (not being employed by the contractor).

This exception shall not however apply to loss or damage (not otherwise excluded by this policy) occasioned:

(a)   Within the period of maintenance or the defects liability period and arising from a cause occurring prior to commencement of the maintenance or defects liability period or

(b)   By the contractor during the maintenance or defects liability period in the course of any operations carried out by him for the purpose of complying with his obligations under the general conditions of contract relative thereto.

8   Loss or damage:

(a)   Of or to any private dwelling house after dwelling has been completed pending sale, for any period in excess of 90 days.

(b)   Caused by or arising out of the occupancy with the permission of the contractor of the permanent works or any part thereof for which the contractor remains responsible under the terms of the contract other than when occupied for the performance of the contract unless such occupancy has been agreed to by the company

This exclusion shall not however apply to:

(a)   Loss or damage caused otherwise than by fire or explosion.

(b)   Any contract solely for the construction of office or apartment blocks, shops or similar projects (but always excluding warehouses and factories and excluding

absolutely loss or damage arising from any process of manufacture).
9   Loss, destruction or damage directly occasioned by pressure waves caused by aircraft and other aerial devices travelling at sonic or supersonic speeds.
10   Loss or damage arising in consequence of riot or civil commotion in the Republic of Ireland or Northern Ireland.

Schedule

It is normal in a policy to define such terms as 'insured', 'insured property', 'period of insurance' in a schedule which is incorporated in and forms part of the policy. Typical definitions to be found in a schedule are as follows.

The insured. This will define the parties who are indemnified— normally the main contractor and his employer although it can be extended to include, for example, any party having a financial interest in the works, the contractor's subsidiary companies and all subcontractors.

Period of insurance. This will be the same as the period of construction and maintenance and should make provision for extension of cover to provide for circumstances where the contract is not completed on time. There will also be references to the defects liability or maintenance period, and where testing and commissioning of the completed works is required cover will extend to cover loss or damage to the works during the testing and commissioning period. Although not defined in the policy the term 'completion' or 'practical completion' means the stage of the works at which they are reasonably capable of use and occupation by the employer and so certified under the contract.

The contract. The general nature of the works and the location and address will be stated.

Estimated contract price. The figure is quoted.

Sum insured. This will be based on the estimated contract price, plus any professional fees, and the value, over and above the contract value, of temporary works, temporary buildings and contents, plant, equipment etc. to be insured.

Whether or not expressly included in the sum insured due allowance should be made for debris removal and temporary supports, to convert the estimated contract price to a figure representing full reinstatement value.

Premium. A rate (quoted as a percentage of the sum insured) subject to adjustment on final contract price and/or in accordance with the policy formula.

Insured's retained liability. The excess or excesses are stated here. There may be a requirement by insurers that the first, say £500 of each and every occurrence of loss by certain risks such as subsidence, collapse or landslip shall be borne by the insured. The excess applied to all other risks may be lower. In practice the excess falls to be met by the contractor. On some sites the compulsory excess on frost, storm, tempest, flood and all water damage may be higher than for other risks. In some areas it is the risks of theft and/or malicious damage that attract the highest excesses.

Indemnity. The wording here will be as follows or similar '100 per cent of the amount which the insured is entitled to recover under the terms of the specification which is declared to be incorporated in and to form part of this schedule.'

Property insured. This will be defined in the specification typically as follows:

1 Constructional works and temporary works executed in performance of the contract and materials for use in connection therewith.
2 Constructional plant, tools, equipment, temporary building and other things for use in connection with the contract.

... all not otherwise insured by or on behalf of the insured, the property of the insured or for which they are responsible, while on or adjacent to the contract or in transit thereto and therefrom anywhere in (the territorial limits).

Public liability

There is no standard wording but, where this section is included, insurers will set out to indemnify the contractor up to a limit for any one occurrence but unlimited in all during the period of insurance for his legal liability for injury to persons other than persons under contract of service with the insured and/or loss of or damage to property (other than property being directly worked upon) arising out of or in connection with the work undertaken. Products liability cover is normally included and unless specially arranged otherwise it may be confined to an indemnity up to a stated limit in the period of insurance.

It is important to give consideration to the following points.

Insured. The definition must be sufficiently wide to protect all parties needing an indemnity under the policy. The insured's trade or business must also be stated fully.

Territorial limits. These must conform to the insured's area of activity or business interests.

Period of insurance. In addition to the construction period the insured must be protected while undertaking maintenance and where necessary cover should be extended to include the contractor's liability for injury or damage arising from defects in the construction after he has vacated the site.

Exclusions. Contractors will need to have certain of the common exclusions to basic policies deleted. Damage to property in their custody or control should be covered and also liability arising out of any contract or agreement.

Latent defects. No adequate insurance is available for the cost of remedying physical damage to the structure caused by latent defects in material, workmanship or design but legal liability cover for injury to persons and/or accidental damage to third party property due to the latent defect is available under the contractor's public liability policy. The contractor should have additionally a professional indemnity policy to indemnify in respect of his liability for the cost of replacing or making good defective design but not defective materials or workmanship. The latter risk would have to be insured under a 'products guarantee' policy and this is currently available only with very restricted terms and period and renewable only at the discretion of insurers.

TYPICAL 'CAR' POLICY CONDITIONS

1 If any change shall occur materially varying any of the facts existing at the date of the policy the insured shall immediately give notice in writing to the first named of the insurers and the premiums shall if necessary be adjusted by agreement.
2 The policy does not cover:
   (a) Any consequence of war, invasion, act of foreign enemy, hostilities (whether war be declared or not), civil war, rebellion, revolution, insurrection, military or usurped power, confiscation, commandeering, nationalisation or requisition or destruction of or damage to property by or under the order of any government, de jure or de facto, or public, municipal or local authority.
   (b) Loss or destruction of or damage to any property whatsoever or any expense whatsoever resulting or arising therefrom or any consequential loss directly or indirectly caused by or contributed to by or arising from:
      (i) Ionising radiations or contaminations by radioactivity from any nuclear fuel or from any nuclear waste from combustion of nuclear fuel.
      (ii) The radioactive, toxic, explosive or other hazardous properties of any explosive nuclear assembly or nuclear component thereof.
3 The insured shall:
   (a) Upon receiving notice of any accident or claim give immediate notice in writing thereof to the first named of the insurers and, at the insured's own expense as soon as practicable, supply full particulars as may be required by the insurers. In no case shall the insurers be liable for any loss or damage not notified to them within three calendar months (NB sometimes less) after the event.

(b)   Send to the first named of the insurers immediately on receipt any writ, summons or other proceedings which may be commenced against the insured.

(c)   Give to the insurers all information and assistance to enable the insurers to settle or resist any claim or institute proceedings.

4   The insured shall take all practical steps—including in the case of goods lost or stolen or of wilful damage to goods the giving of immediate notice to the police—to recover any property lost and in the case of theft or wilful damage, to discover the guilty person or persons and to have such person or persons prosecuted at the expense of the insurers. The insured shall not negotiate, pay, settle, admit or repudiate any claim under the policy without the written consent of the insurers. The insured shall not in any case be entitled to abandon any property to the insurers whether taken possession of by the insurers or not.

5   The insured shall, if required by the insurers, produce or give access to any property alleged to be damaged and the insured shall be bound to satisfy the insurers by such reasonable evidence as the insurers may require that the loss or damage in respect of which a claim is made has actually arisen from one of the risks insured against.

6   If a claim be made by or on behalf of the insured which shall be in any respect fraudulent or if any false statutory declaration be made or used in support thereof, all benefit under the policy is forfeited.

7   In the event of a claim or claims arising for which the insurers shall be liable under the policy, the insurers shall be entitled:

(a)   To undertake, in the name and on behalf of the insured, the absolute conduct, control and settlement of any proceedings.

(b)   To take proceedings, at their own expense and for their own benefit, but in the name of the insured, to recover compensation or secure an indemnity from any third party in respect of anything covered by the policy.

(c)   To pay to the insured in respect of any claim or claims the maximum liability of the insurers as stated in the specification and thereafter the insurers shall be under no further liability in respect of such claim or claims.

8   The insured shall take all reasonable precautions in the selection of labour and to maintain in an efficient condition all plant and appliances used in connection with the contract and to ensure that all such plant and appliances requiring inspection under any statute or order shall be so inspected. The insurers shall at all reasonable times have, by their representatives, access to all such plant and appliances. The insured shall also take and cause to be taken all reasonable precautions to prevent accidents and in the event of an occurrence covered by the policy shall take such immediate action as is necessary to minimise the loss.

9   The insurance does not cover any loss, damage or liability which, at the time such loss damage or liability arises, is insured by (or would but for the existence of this policy be insured by) any other policy or policies except in respect of any excess beyond the amount which would have been payable under such other policy or policies had this insurance not been effected.

10   The insurers may, by notice in writing to the insured under registered cover to the last known address of the insured, cancel this policy at any time paying on demand a proportion of the premium corresponding to the unexpired period of the policy.

11   If any difference shall arise as to the amount to be paid under this policy (liability being otherwise admitted) such difference shall be referred to an arbitrator to be appointed by the parties in accordance with the statutory provisions in that behalf for the time being in force. Where any difference is by this condition to be referred to arbitration the making of an award shall be a condition precedent to any right of action against the insurers.

PREMIUMS

It is impracticable to specify rates applied by insurers as much will depend on a particular contractor's claims experience, his policy wording, the excess he bears, the type of work, and so on. Rates can vary from as low as 0.075 per cent for very simple forms of construction on land to 5 per cent or more for difficult forms of construction off-shore.

It is a condition of the majority of policies that the deposit premium shall be adjusted within a given period following the expiration of the period of insurance.

Adjustment may be subject to a minimum retained premium.

POSITION OF A SUBCONTRACTOR

It is perhaps obvious but essential to say that this depends upon the conditions imposed by the main contractor. In practice the responsibilities of the subcontractor are likely to differ considerably between contractors. In some cases the main contractor may require the subcontractor, by his subcontract conditions, to assume responsibility for all risks of loss or damage to the subcontract works material, plant, equipment etc., even though the standard forms of subcontract do not go anything like so far. It is vital that the subcontractor should check his responsibilities under each different subcontract order and not rely on his terms of quotation alone. Often subcontractors have wrongly assumed that because the main contractor may be made responsible by the employer for insurance of the contract works and subcontract works, then, because they are subcontractors, they can have no responsibility for loss or damage to the contract or subcontract works.

Just as main contractors object to amendments made by employers so subcontractors through their associations are continually endeavouring to persuade contractors to adhere to standard contracts.

JCT forms of subcontract

This is a subject which can be dealt with in depth but here we can do little more than summarise the usual position under the standard forms of building contract and subcontract in common use. The 1980 Editions introduced the forms of subcontract with reference numbers NSC4 for subcontractors nominated by the Architect/ Supervising Officer and DOM/1 for domestic subcontractors being firms engaged by the contractor's own selection. If the conditions of subcontract are those of the Joint Contracts Tribunal, clauses 8 and 10 supported by clause 5.1 will govern the position which is generally interpreted as follows:

Subcontract works. Either the employer (under clause 22B or 22C of the main contract where either applies) or the main contractor is responsible for loss under 22A where applicable, for damage caused by the risks which are specified in clause 22. So far as the subcontractor is concerned in practice he would anyway look to the main contractor to be responsible for the loss or damage whether 22A or 22B or 22C applies.

Permanent materials. The main contractor is responsible only for the risks stated in clause 22 in relation to such materials and goods whether fixed or unfixed until such time as they have been 'fully finally and properly incorporated into the main contract works' other than where loss or damage is caused by the negligence, omission or default of the main contractor or any other subcontractor or of the employer.

The phrase 'fully finally and properly incorporated' gives rise to doubt and difficulty. It attempts to allocate risk but is open to interpretation in different ways not least because of the differing nature of the various trades. Many contractors seek in arguing the interpretation of the subcontract on this point with subcontractors to apply the logic that it means more than that the materials shall have been fixed in the ordinary sense of the word. They contend that the residual risks pass to the main contractor when the subcontract works are in a collective state of readiness for handover.

Temporary materials, plant, equipment, etc. on site. These are at the risk of each subcontractor as stated in clause 10. A subcontractor will nevertheless retain certain rights in tort against a main contractor for loss of or damage to the subcontract works or materials.

Thus, in the JCT forms the main contractor assumes, under clause 8, responsibility for loss of or damage to incomplete subcontract works and also materials and goods properly on the site for incorporation into the subcontract works, but only for the perils stated in that clause. The main contractor does not therefore automatically assume responsibility for loss of or damage to incomplete subcontract works in progress or materials by such other risks as, for example, subsidence, collapse, frost, impact, accidental damage, malicious damage or theft.

However, in relation to completed subcontract works—that is, where materials or goods have been fully, finally and properly incorporated into the main works before completion of the sub-contract works—the main contractor will be responsible for all loss of or damage to such materials and goods except for any loss or damage caused to them by the subcontractor, his servants or agents. Note that in relation to such fixed materials or goods the burden is shifted to the main contractor to prove that the subcontractor whose works were affected caused the damage to them and if the main contractor cannot do so then he is presumed to be responsible to that subcontractor for the cost of making good any such loss or damage to such completed parts of the works. As already stated there are many disputes under these subcontract conditions over what is or is not fully, finally and properly incorporated into the main works.

Turning now to the insurance aspects, the prudent subcontractor must assume that the main contractor's insurers will maintain all their rights of subrogation. Even though the sum insured on the contractor's policy covers the cost of the subcontractor's works and materials, main contractors often prefer to have in their policies a condition that the only property insured shall be the 'insured's own or that for which he is responsible'. The net effect of such a condition is to confine cover under the contractor's all risks policy to property that is owned by the main contractor or property for which the main contractor is responsible whether under the main or the subcontract conditions.

Proposals have been advanced by subcontractors' associations from time to time that main contractors and their CAR insurers should provide an all risks indemnity to all subcontractors to obviate disputes. This would clearly increase the main contractors' claims experience and premium costs in the long term and might create difficulties as regards proof of loss. Nevertheless the trends are towards adoption of that alternative. In spite of the consensus view of main contractors that subcontractors should retain responsibility for theft of or accidental damage to their own materials.

PROTECTIONS TO THE EMPLOYER

When a construction contract is arranged, the employer's representative should utilise any right he has to call for evidence of the contractor's insurances, in particular to check them against the responsibilities imposed upon the contractor by the contract conditions.

The contractor will, or should, allow for adequate insurance premiums in his tender price. In the long run, therefore, the employer is paying for insurance as necessary in the light of the site conditions, the project value and the insurance obligations in the contract.

When checking the contractor's insurances, the employer and/or his professional advisers should see that:

1   The insurers are well-known and afford an adequate security.
2   The policy provides the requisite indemnity to the employers.
3   The sum or sums insured conform to the requirements of the contract.
4   The period of insurance is satisfactory. The contractor may be asked to provide evidence, if the policies are renewable, that they have been renewed on the same or closely similar terms.

Any exclusions or exceptions on the policies must be carefully noted and if these conflict with any of the operations envisaged, objections must be raised.

The employer must bear in mind the need to transfer the new structures to his own insurance or to alternative arrangements at the stages of sectional or practical completion.

CLAUSE 21.2.1 OF THE STANDARD JCT (1980) FORM OF BUILDING CONTRACT

(Corresponding to clause 19(2)(a) of JCT 1963 Editions)
This subclause is invoked only when required by the bills of quantities where a provisional sum (that is, a sum to be expended if approved by the architects under clause 13.3 of the contract conditions) is inserted in the bills. The requirement may appear therein by reference to the clause number with merely the pro-

visional sum alongside, or otherwise included in the section listing the provisional sums in the summary, or even elsewhere in the bills on occasion. Strictly, if there is no provisional sum there is no insurance requirement, but there may be cases of ambiguity where the contractor would be wise to seek clarification from the architect.

Subject to its provisions, clause 21.2.1 is designed to protect the employer against claims for damage to property by subsidence, collapse, vibration, weakening or removal of support or lowering of ground water arising out of, or in the course of, or by reason of, the operations and due otherwise than to the negligence of the contractor or subcontractors, or their respective servants or agents.

Clause 20.2 provides that, in effect, the contractor cannot be liable to indemnify the employer for damage to property if the contractor's negligence or that of his subcontractors is not involved. However, a neighbour whose property has been damaged may have legal rights against the employer, if, for example, pre-existing support has been removed.

The usual clause 21.2.1 insurance indemnifies the employer in respect of claims for damage to property from the causes defined in the clause for which he cannot look to the contractor under clause 20.2 and which are outside the scope of the insurance prescribed by clause 21.1. It is always subject to the exclusions in clause 21.2.1 which do effectively limit the indemnity.

The need for this subclause became apparent following Gold v Patman & Fotheringham Ltd (1958) 2 AER 497. Since it first appeared in the 1963 edition of the RIBA form of contract it has been modified and the intentions of the clause are more clearly expressed in the current edition. This type of cover is called for occasionally in connection with contracts under Institution of Civil Engineers conditions, and in such circumstances requires careful attention in view of the existing indemnity in clause 22.

Much has been written elsewhere about clause 21.2.1 but although its meaning and legal connotations are generally understood, determining when a particular event falls to be dealt with by insurers under clause 21.1 or clause 21.2 still gives rise to difficulty. Thus it is advisable that clause 21.1 and 21.2 insurances should be placed with the same insurers.

It is most often assumed, when damage to neighbouring property occurs, that it could have been avoided if the contractor had taken greater care. There may be inherent factors, however, of which neither the employer nor any of his professional team could have had foreknowledge when specifying the work to be done. In examining a case of damage one may ask whether the instruction to the contractor was in all respects capable of compliance without damage resulting, if reasonable care were exercised. Were there contributory causes which, even with maximum prudence, the contractor could not have contemplated in carrying out architects' instructions? Where movement occurs due, for example, to underground voids or water courses or other features which were unexpected even after proper pre-contract checks on ground conditions, insurers will be persuaded more readily that resultant claims are within the category of 'non-negligent damage' and therefore fall to be dealt with under the clause 21.2.1 insurance. The counter-considerations in determining whether this insurance should meet a particular claim are:

1   As to whether alternatively the damage was not fortuitous or accidental but in the excluded category of damage being the inevitable result of the nature of the work or the manner of its execution (e.g. if by causing support to be removed and/or removing it in the only possible manner the adverse consequences were foreseeable).
2   It occurred for want of reasonable care on the part of the contractor in the execution of a quite reasonable instruction given to him.

Whereas in example 1 neither the policy arranged under clause 21.1.1 or clause 21.2.1 of the JCT 1980 contract would provide cover, in example 2 the clause 21.2.1 insurers could rightly refer the claim for consideration under the clause 21.1.1 'negligent damage' policy.

The clause as it appears in the standard JCT Forms of Building Contract excludes not only damage that is inevitable but also that which is due to faulty design. The deliberate omission of normal and reasonable precautionary measures perhaps for reasons of economy is unlikely to be construed as negligence and may mean that there is no cover either under clause 21.1 or 21.2 policies.

The insurance effected under clause 21.2.1 is for the benefit of the employer. Primarily it is a 'physical damage' and 'consequential loss' insurance rather than a liability cover though it is most often best insured by extension of or in conjunction with the contractors public liability policy. Employers may choose to effect this category of insurance through their own arrangements and the contractor need take no action if this is made clear in the contract bills. However, in such cases when claims arise there could be protracted contention between two or more groups of insurers as to whether there had been negligence in connection with the damage.

There are proponents for the abolition of this clause from building contracts on the grounds that the public liability policy of the employers under the contract can absorb the risk of damage to property where no negligence can be established against the contractor or subcontractor. This proposition merits careful checks with insurers. Whereas the public liability policy of the employers sets out to deal with his legal liability for damage to third party property only, i.e. not damage to the employers own property, the normal clause 21.2.1 insurance also covers damage as defined in that clause to the employers own property other than the works and the employers own consequential loss arising therefrom and therefore goes beyond the normal scope of the employers' public liability policy.

On this analysis the employer should not assume his existing policy obviates the need for clause 21.2.1 insurance without special extension. Nor indeed does it justify the associated contention that the clause can be abolished as serving no useful purpose.

All things considered the better and safer course is to continue with the current clause 21.2.1 obligation upon the contractor in its present form, if the employer opts for the insurance at all. Whether or not he invokes the clause (by inserting a provisional sum in the contract bills) will be governed by the nature of each risk exposure.

Certain other forms of contract used in the industry have clauses similar to JCT clause 21.2. In the Agreement and General Conditions of Building Contract issued by The Faculty of Architects and Surveyors clause 26.3 conforms fairly closely to the wording of the original 1963 version of RIBA clause 19(2). In omitting the exclusions those drafting FAS clause 26.3 may not have widened the scope of the insurance obligation as it seems likely that, in the event, the insurers providing cover could establish that the JCT 21.2 exclusions merely express what was implicit in the 1963 version and that even with FAS 26.3 wording it is not the intention to cover inevitable damage nor damage due to error or omission in design nor, of course, due to contractor's negligence.

Another form which is adopted as an alternative to the JCT form is the ACA form of Building Agreement 1982 issued by the Association of Consultant Architects. This contract includes under clause 6.5 an obligation to insure in terms broadly similar to clause 21.2.1 and incorporates the exclusions of clause 21.2.1 plus another particular to the ACA form.

Occasionally clause 47 of GC/Works/1 is amended to require the contractor to allow for insurance in wording similar to JCT clause 21.2.1.

Placing clause 21.2 cover

It is impracticable in most cases, though desirable, to arrange this insurance before a contract commences and there are many unsatisfactory features about the application of this clause. Delays may be encountered in obtaining information for disclosure to insurers or the arrangement of an insurance survey and ensuing report to the insurers, receiving a quotation and obtaining the approval of the employer's representative.

It is often in the early stages that the highest risk occurs and if a delay is expected, the contractor, with the employer's approval, should obtain temporary cover from inception of the works for a reasonable limit of indemnity. A contractor, if required, can arrange an annual policy covering any principal jointly with the contractor to which each new 21.2.1 case agreed is added and a certificate summarising the terms and conditions could be issued by insurers or brokers where called for.

Special arrangements should be made with insurers who appoint independent professional surveyors, if the surveyor's report is to be passed to other insurers for the purposes of alternative quotations. A time-on-risk charge from the insurers providing temporary cover must be anticipated if their quotation is not accepted.

Although now a decreasing practice, certain insurers will extend the wording of their policies so as to include personal injury not necessarily resulting from damage to property. Other extensions or variations may be requested including utilisation of the original

1963 19(2)(a) wording. Some of these variations can be more fully and properly insured outside the clause 21.2.1 policy. Often these variations seem to arise because insurers have taken the expedient of acceding to the particular wishes of an employer or his representatives, possibly not always expert in insurance matters, under a direct arrangement between employer and insurers.

Once this is achieved the same variations are repeated by amendment to the wording of subsequent contracts. Thus unjustifiable concessions to 'whims and fancies' by one insurer can create difficulty for the general insurance market and for the insurance manager.

FURTHER READING

L. J. Piper, *Contractors All Risks & Public Liability Insurance,* Buckley Press Limited.

Construction & Erection Insurance, Report by Advanced Study Group No. 208 of The Insurance Institute of London 20 Aldermanbury, London EC2.

John Uff, *Construction Law,* Concise College Texts, 3rd edition, Sweet & Maxwell, London: 1981.

15

Insurance of Personnel

T. E. W. Slatter, Director of Risk Management, Blue Bell, Inc.

To any company, its personnel are an important asset. To protect their liability to its personnel, as required by law, a company will effect Employer's Liability or Workmens' Compensation coverage, as described in Chapter 11, Insurance of Liabilities. In addition to these basic forms of legally required cover, supplementary insurances are available.

These supplementary policies now form part of the employee benefit package. To attract the right employees, many companies provide additional personal benefits by this means. These policies take the form of either individual or group contracts for personal accident, permanent health (long-term disability), and private medical coverage.

Any form of such additional cover is an extra overhead cost which has eventually to be reflected in the price of the product or service supplied by the company. Careful consideration is therefore necessary as any benefit given may not be so easily removed in the future. This especially applies to pension benefits as many employee benefit plans now include final retirement benefit, death in service lump sum benefit, and widows and orphans pensions. However, as the latter form a major area on their own and would justify a separate book, the subject is not dealt with here. Expert advice should in any case always be sought in arranging such schemes.

It is a legal requirement in many European countries that any additional employee benefit be applied to the majority (normally over 75 per cent) of the employees in the level being considered.

Employee benefit schemes certainly serve to improve relations between employers and employees by giving the latter an increased sense of security.

Undoubtedly, the higher an employee progresses in his company, so the greater the benefits become. This perhaps reflects the value of that employee to the company as his responsibility and importance increase. As companies expand and their markets become more international with perhaps the use of company-owned aircraft, employers tend to acknowledge the additional risks to employees required to travel on business and arrange personal accident and medical expense insurance. This coverage may be restricted by the employer only to the period when the employee is travelling on business, rather than provide full 24-hour cover.

A company should be aware that, within its organisation, many other groups of employees may consider themselves equally to be at risk. Aside from the employee who travels internationally, there are the sales representatives and others who travel nationally, and the manual workers themselves. It may be necessary for the company to draw a well-defined line with sound reasons as to why they do or do not afford additional personal coverage to particular groups of employees. A common complaint from employees travelling extensively on company business by car is that personal accident coverage is not provided under the company's vehicle coverage; this coverage normally only being provided 'free' under motor policies issued to individuals, and then only for a nominal insured sum. A counter argument by the company may well be that manual employees working for the company are perhaps working in occupations where a higher exposure to personal injury exists, yet no additional cover has been arranged.

However, the use of cars by sales personnel, whether company-owned or not, is generally accepted to increase the personal risk of the employee to injury or death, in view of the substantial mileages that may be travelled. In many cases, companies arrange personal accident coverage, with the benefit being payable to the employee or his dependants, with the cost borne by the company.

There may be occasions when coverage is required for the benefit of the company. For example, a senior employee or director may be vital for a particular function; he may have expert knowledge of a new development or be engaged in important negotiations. In such a case, the death or prolonged disability of the individual could have serious repercussions on the business and, in these circumstances, a life and/or personal accident and/or permanent health insurance policy would be a prudent safeguard, with the benefit payable to the company. At the company's discretion, the benefits may be used to offset the cost of replacing the employee, the continued payment of full or partial salary by the company, or any benefit which may have been paid to the insured employees' dependants.

PERSONAL ACCIDENT AND SICKNESS INSURANCE AND INDEMNITY

Most insurance policies are contracts of indemnity which means that, in the event of a claim, the insurer's job is to put the insured in the same position after a loss as the insured enjoyed immediately before the loss or, at least as far as is possible in monetary terms. The insured should never receive more than an indemnity as this would mean that he would profit out of a loss, but equally, assuming an adequate sum insured, the insured would not receive less than a full indemnity. Personal accident and sickness policies are normally exceptions to this rule in that they usually provide a stated fixed benefit, and this is payable without any regard to the question of indemnity at the time of the claim. However, insurers do not ignore the principle of indemnity. When an insurance is effected for the benefit of an employee, insurers always try to ensure that the benefits are reasonable, bearing in mind the insured person's station in life. On proposal forms, there is usually a question asking for details of any other personal accident or sickness insurance in force with that or any other insurer and they sometimes state that the total amount of benefit for temporary total disablement from all insurances should not exceed a certain percentage of average earnings—this varies from 50 to 75 per cent according to insurers. The intention is that the total benefit including social security benefits should not exceed normal net earnings. Thus, the higher salary earner can normally have a higher percentage of salary as benefit because the social security benefit does not increase in proportion to earnings over a certain level.

For capital benefits, it is not so easy to adopt such a yardstick but, in any case, who can measure the value of a human life or limb? In life assurance, the benefit is normally governed by the assured's ability to pay the premium but, this does not apply to accident insurance where premium rates are much lower. In practice, few problems arise and commonsense prevails. Obviously, an insurer is likely to ask questions if he receives an application from a low paid worker for insurance against death by accident for a benefit of £100,000.

As a personal accident and sickness policy is not a policy of indemnity, the principles of subrogation and contribution cannot apply. As subrogation does not apply this means that if a third party caused the death or injury, even if a successful claim is made directly against the third party for damages, the benefit under the personal accident policy will not be affected. It is an established point of law that the benefit under a personal accident policy should not be taken into account in any assessment of damages. In these circumstances, the insured can recover in full from both parties, thus deriving benefit from his prudence in effecting a personal accident policy.

Similarly, as contribution does not apply, the insured can have several policies with different insurers and can recover the full benefit from each, always assuming he has not been guilty of misrepresentation on the proposal form to the extent of other insurance covers, and subject to any overall percentage of earnings limit imposed by insurers.

Many times, when policies are arranged by companies on behalf of their employees, insurers will not require a completion of a proposal form or, if one is needed, details of individual policies held by employees are normally not given; such disclosure being left to the discretion of the company.

STANDARD PERSONAL ACCIDENTS ONLY POLICY

As this type of policy forms the basis of all personal accident policies, whether individual or group, and to set the general scene, it will be convenient to consider briefly its benefits, terms, etc. Insurers' policy wordings are, of course, more detailed and should be studied closely to examine the individual coverages granted, together with exclusions and conditions applicable.

Definition of an accident

The obvious differences between life and personal accident policies is sometimes forgotten. A personal accident policy will only pay the insured benefit as the result of an accident to the insured. The normal accident definition may read as follows:

> Bodily injury caused solely by violent accidental external and visible means which injury shall directly and independently of any other cause result in death or disablement.

The wording of this definition will vary a little with different insurers, but the meaning and intent are similar. Thus, the cause of the injury must be violent (although the smallest degree of violence will suffice), visible and external (although the result need not be visible or external), as well as unexpected.

Proximate cause

Sometimes, problems can arise out of establishing the chain of cause and effect because accident as defined in the policy must be the proximate cause of the injury. Proximate cause has been defined as:

> The active efficient cause which sets in motion a train of events which brings about a result without the intervention of any force started and working actively from a new and independent source.

Thus, proximate in this context means proximate in efficacy rather than in time. Two examples of the working of proximate cause in relation to personal accident policies will help to explain it. A man was thrown from his horse while hunting and landed in a ditch. His injuries were such that the could not climb out of the ditch and he lay in the wet for some time before being found. As a result of his wetting, he contracted pneumonia and died. It was held that the cause of his death was an accident, since there was no break in the chain of cause and effect. (Re: Etherington v Lancashire and Yorkshire Accident Insurance Co. Ltd. [1909].)

A man is in hospital as a result of a broken leg. While in hospital, he contracts an infectious disease from which he dies. In these circumstances, the cause of death is disease, and insurers would not be liable under an accidents only policy as a new force intervened to bring about death which was not the natural and probable result of the original injury. On the other hand, if the broken leg had necessitated an operation, and the patient died while under the anaesthetic, the accident would be considered the proximate cause of death.

Benefits

The description of benefits varies between companies but, they are normally provided under the following headings:

1 *Death—by accident.*
2 *Loss of one limb or one eye.* Normally this means the loss by physical severance of a hand or foot at or above the wrist or ankle respectively or the total and irrecoverable loss of sight. Some insurers include total *loss of use* of an entire hand, arm, foot or leg and this is a very useful extension of the benefit.
3 *Loss of two or more limbs or eyes.* Definition of 'loss' would be the same as for loss of one limb or eye and would include any combination of limbs and eyes, for example, one arm and one leg or one leg and one eye, if lost together, would come within this benefit.
4 *Permanent total disablement from following any occupation.* Some insurers may be prepared to offer permanent total disablement from *usual* occupation. This is a very much wider benefit.
5 *Temporary total disablement from engaging in usual occupation.* This is a benefit payable on the basis of so much per week or month during disablement. Payment of benefit is normally restricted to a maximum of 104 weeks in respect of any one accident.
6 *Temporary partial disablement from engaging in usual occupation.* This benefit is designed to cover the person who, probably during a period of convalescence, can give some, but not total, attention to his usual occupation. It cannot be insured without the previous benefit and there is normally an overall limit on the

benefits of 104 weeks; in other words benefits *(5)* and *(6)* together have a combined total limit of 104 weeks in respect of any one accident. This benefit is usually restricted to 40 per cent of benefit *(5)*.

Benefits *1 to 4* inclusive are usually referred to as capital benefits. The death or disablement for which benefit is provided must arise within 12 months of the accident, except for benefit *4* which is normally only payable after 104 weeks benefit has been paid under benefit *5*.

Only one capital benefit may be claimed in respect of a single accident so that a claim cannot be made for loss of a limb and then a further amount claimed for death, if it occurs within twelve months as a result of the same accident. Some insurers warrant that once a capital benefit is paid the policy is automatically cancelled.

It was the practice, in the past, for benefit *2* to be half of benefit *3* but most insurers now provide the same benefit for each, unless requested otherwise and, as a result, one frequently finds that benefits *2* and *3* are combined to cover 'loss of one or more limbs or eyes'.

Any or all of the benefits can be insured to suit individual requirements—with the exception of benefit *6* which cannot be insured without benefit *5*. Thus, one can insure any one or more of the capital benefits with or without the weekly benefits and similarly the weekly benefits can be insured on their own.

It is also possible to show benefit *4* (permanent total disablement) as an annuity, for example, instead of a £1,000 capital sum, insurers will pay £100 per year for 10 years.

Most insurers offer standard units of benefit quoting a single premium for, say, £1,000 capital sums with £10 per week temporary total disablement and £4 per week temporary partial disablement, as well as offering the selection of benefits. In fact, insurers can meet most requirements and will provide benefits in various forms, particularly under group schemes. For example, some companies offer what is generally known as the 'Continental scale of benefits' instead of benefits *2, 3* and *4* described above. This scale usually provides 100 per cent of the sum insured in respect of permanent total disablement or loss of sight in both eyes but provides lower percentages of the sum insured as compensation for lesser degrees of disablement (for example, 50 per cent for loss of one leg at or above the knee, 60 per cent for the loss of the right arm or hand and 50 per cent for the left—or vice versa if the insured is left-handed—down to 10 per cent for loss of a big toe and 3 per cent for any other toe). Different insurers have different scales. Although all the lists are fairly exhaustive they usually contain a statement to the effect that if any permanent disablement is not specified then the degree of disablement will be assessed by comparison with the scale and benefit paid accordingly.

Special coverage can be arranged for professional people who need great dexterity, such as doctors, musicians and dentists, and for whom an injury that an ordinary person would consider relatively minor, such as damage to a finger, could mean total inability to continue their work.

Medical expenses can also be covered under an accident policy either as a fixed maximum sum or as a percentage of the benefit payable for temporary total disablement. However, if an insured feels he wants medical expenses cover to pay for private treatment, far better cover can be obtained than provided by an accident policy (but naturally at higher cost) and this is described later in this chapter.

Rating

The premium charged will be based in the first place on the level of benefits chosen for each of the various categories of permanent and partial disablement referred to earlier in this chapter.

In respect of individual risks, insurers will also calculate the premium required on the basis of their occupational classification schedule. As the hazard of occupation increases, so does the classification, the following example being typical:

> *Class I*—Administrative, clerical and similar work, for example, accountants, commercial artists, and civil engineers.
> *Class II*—Superintending personnel only, for example, builders merchant, clerk of works, or commercial traveller.
> *Class III*—Manual work (self-employed) not generally involving undue hazards, for example, garage mechanics, engineers, farmers, veterinary surgeons, etc.

Class IV—The more hazardous occupations, for example, steel erectors, window cleaners, and the like.

It is normal to find that the rates for *Class II* are about 20 per cent high than *Class I* and *Class III*, about 35 per cent higher than *Class I* (1982 rates).

For group schemes, various alternatives exist. Cover may be on a 24-hour basis or for occupational risks only, but with the additional benefit of discounts for both numbers of members in the plan and for the size of premium to be paid.

The rating of group policies will vary according to the basis on which the benefits are arranged. Where these are earnings-related the rate will be applied to total payroll, the rate itself depending on the relationship between annual salary and the level of benefits chosen. If, on the other hand, employees are, for benefit purposes, graded into various categories, it may be sufficient merely to declare numbers in each category for the purpose of premium calculation. These approaches have many advantages in that frequent updating of benefits is not required, as with a fixed sum insured, since the policies are normally adjusted at the end of each year.

Territorial limits

Generally speaking, there is no restriction in an accident policy and cover will apply anywhere in the world, although if an insured person is normally resident outside of Europe, insurers may impose some restriction or ask for an extra premium.

Exclusions

The exclusion list in most policies is extensive and only a few of the more important exclusions, suitably abbreviated, are shown below:

1 Pre-existing infirmity.
2 The taking of drugs.
3 Suicide or attempts thereat.
4 Hazardous sports and pastimes—these may well involve popular activities such as football, motorcycling, winter sports, hunting

in which directors or employees may well indulge. Cover may usually be provided for most of the excluded sports and pastimes but, notice must be given to insurers and any required additional premium paid.

5 Flying except as a commercial airline passenger.
6 Pregnancy or childbirth.
7 War risks.
8 Persons below or above certain specified ages (usually 16 and 65).

SICKNESS COVER

The standard personal accident policy may be extended to include sickness but, only for weekly benefits and subject to important age limitations and after provision of detailed additional personal information. This latter requirement may be modified for group schemes. It is to be recommended, however, for such benefits to be covered under a permanent health insurance (disability) policy (see p. 355) in view of the limited cover available under the personal accident policy, which has to be renewed annually with the premium rates thus liable to increase and the policy cover subject to review.

GROUP PERSONAL ACCIDENT COVERAGE

It has been reported that during 1980, in the UK, accidents killed more people in the 20–44 age group than any other cause and were the fourth leading cause of death amongst people of all ages. At least 50 per cent of the population will be killed or suffer a serious injury, as a result of an accident, during their lifetime. Accidents strike without warning. Few families are prepared financially for the sudden hardship caused by the accidental death of the breadwinner. Neither are preparations made, in many cases, for the high cost of preparing for a new way of life following permanent injury or even the sudden loss of income as a result of a temporary disability.

Personal accident insurance is one way to provide the means to offset financial problems, either by means of individual or group policies. One important point which the employer should always bear in mind is, when arranging either personal accident or permanent health insurance, to ensure that the temporary benefits to be received will not be over-generous when considered with local social security benefits, leaving little if any incentive for an employee to return to work. For the individual, personal accident cover is relatively expensive to purchase and requires an effort which the average person is not willing to make. After all, 'it will never happen to me.'

One solution is for the company to help employees meet this need by making personal accident insurance available to them. An overall employee benefit evaluation will show whether this benefit is to be included in the company package and the cost therefore will be borne by the company; or for the company's bulk purchase facilities to be used to obtain competitive premiums for employees to pay themelves, perhaps by means of payroll deduction but, with the possibility of savings up to 50 per cent over those they would have to pay individually.

Any staff scheme involves extra effort on the part of the employer. Any such effort generally will result in increased overheads, but with today's computerised payroll systems, most are able to include the deduction facility without much problem.

Apart from more reasonable rates, the employee will benefit from the lack of need for completion of a health questionnaire, as all employees will be accepted regardless of past medical history. Facilities to insure husbands, wives, and children, may also be made available. The group policy pays in addition to any policies held by the employee personally but may be subject to disclosure to and possible limitation by his own insurers if the benefit is other than discretionary on the part of his employers. An important feature is that the policy may be more broadly worded to eliminate minor exclusions and conditions such as, the exclusion of certain sports accidents.

The advantages for the employer will be:

1 No premium cost (unless included in the company's employee benefit plan).
2 Enhancement of the employee benefit programme.
3 Ease of installation and administration.

4   Creation of goodwill among the employees.
5   It will also help the employees to provide for their families' future financial stability.

Situations in which group personal accident covers may apply

Examples may be summarised as follows:

1   Full 24-hour coverage, including leisure activities.
2   Occupational activities only.
3   Limited to certain defined portions of an employee's work.
4   Overseas travel only.
5   Travel whilst on business only.
6   Whilst the employee is at work, including travel time to and from home.
7   During participation in sports activities (company-sponsored or otherwise).

PERMANENT HEALTH INSURANCE (PHI)/LONG TERM DISABILITY (LTD)

The personal accident policies described above, with or without sickness cover, are annual contracts which means that both insured and insurer have the right at each renewal either to vary the terms as explained earlier, or to discontinue cover altogether.

Many insurers now offer a permanent health or long-term disability form of policy which overcomes these drawbacks. The aforementioned advantages to employer and employee, in respect of personal accident coverage including bulk purchase facilities, are relevant to PHI as well. This form of cover provides benefit, on a weekly or monthly basis, for as long as the insured person is prevented from attending to his usual occupation by reason of accident or illness until the age limit specified, normally 65 (60 for females). Once having accepted the insurance, the insurers cannot vary the terms or cancel the policy, provided the insured pays the premium each year, and has not been guilty of any misrepresentation or nondisclosure on his proposal form.

If anything, a PHI policy is more important than a personal accident policy because it provides a regular amount each month during long-term disability, as a result of accident or sickness, until the employee is no longer disabled, dies, or retires. Employees also tend to understand the PHI policy cover more readily. Many people believe they will not die early in life, but more readily accept that they might suffer serious illness or injury. This form of policy is particularly useful as a mortgage protection cover. Life cover is always considered essential when a mortgage is effected, but cover against prolonged disablement is just as essential. It can also provide a very valuable fringe benefit to senior staff.

Particular features of the PHI are as follows.

Medical examination

(a) Group. It very much depends upon the size of the group. The larger the group, the less likely medical examinations will be required. In most cases, if the size of the insured group is in excess of 50 persons, it is normal practice for insurers to quote without medical evidence, subject to a proviso that no one employee or small number of employees have substantially higher incomes than the others.

(b) Individual. It is normal for insurers to request a medical examination if the insured benefit exceeds a certain amount and/or if the person insured is over a given age provided the proposal form is otherwise satisfactory.

In all cases, the medical examination fee is paid by the insurers.

Benefit

As with personal accident cover, close attention must be paid to the level of benefit made available so that there is always an incentive for the employee to return to work. The usual benefit (including social security payments) is 50 to 75 per cent of the employee's salary. There is now also a tendency to provide a reduced rate of benefit if the insured person is able and willing to undertake work other than his normal occupation. The permanent health policy will pay proportionately to the difference between the reduced income and normal benefit, if a shortfall should occur. If the person is then fully incapacitated, insurers will pay the whole amount of the insured benefit, as before.

Waiting period

The object of this form of policy is to cover prolonged disablement and it is aimed at the executive or professional man, although this is not to say that other occupations do not effect permanent policies. Many such people will be paid by their firm for quite a long period during sickness and will not require cover 'from the first day.' Therefore, as well as 'first day' cover (subject only to a franchise of 7 days in respect of sickness), most insurers offer excesses of up to 52 weeks (and some up to 104 weeks), and this naturally has a distinct effect on the premium. It has been found that the usual excess period chosen, for group policies, is 26 weeks. Where sickness and illness recurs within six months of an employee returning to work, having received benefit, there is generally no waiting period for the insured benefit payment to recommence.

Rating

As with personal accident coverage, PHI policies are rated according to the age of the insured person and classification of occupation, as described earlier under the personal accident section. The following table of rates, although fairly representative of rates applicable in 1982, is given to show the effect age and excess periods can have on the premium required.

Annual rates per £1 of weekly benefit (males)

	Age 30	Age 40	Age 50
First-day cover	1.50	2.10	3.60
4 week excess	1.00	1.40	2.65
13 week excess	.65	.95	1.75
26 week excess	.45	.75	1.40
52 week excess	.30	.60	1.10

Premiums may be paid monthly, quarterly or half-yearly at a small extra charge.

Females

In life assurance, premium rates for females are lower than for males, because females live longer. The opposite is the case in PHI insurance where females present a very much heavier risk. Rates for females can be 10 to 50 per cent higher than for males but some insurers will effect cover without a loading if the proportion of the group to be insured is very low, for example, 10 per cent or less.

Waiver of premium

Most insurers will waive future premiums during periods of disablement. The cost of this feature is normally included within the premiums charged.

Automatic increases in benefits

The group scheme will define the salary level on which the benefit is to be based. It is normally the salary applicable on the renewal date. Some schemes allow for salary increases which may occur during the scheme year, but it must be appreciated that an additional administrative burden may be placed upon the employer. However, it is more usual to find that the salary basis is only changed annually. It is now rare to find group policies written where the benefit is fixed and the level revised only occasionally.

Once the benefit becomes payable, the cover wording will usually allow for benefit increases of 3 to 5 per cent annually, but not to exceed an agreed inflation index.

Exclusions

Exclusions in the permanent policy tend to be fewer than in the annual cover. There is normally no exclusion relating to sporting activities—although questions will be asked about these on the proposal form—but self-inflicted injury, venereal disease, pregnancy, and the effect of drink or drugs are usually excluded, as are war risks or flying except as a passenger.

An additional exclusion is usually made relating to sickness contracted in tropical climates, although this sometimes relates only to the first three or six months of resulting disablement and thus may not apply to cover subject to longer excess periods.

PRIVATE MEDICAL EXPENSES COVER

With growing pressure on the National Health Service resulting in longer waiting lists for surgical operations, together with the trend in the late 1970s to improve fringe benefits rather than pay additional salaries, the private health area has expanded. This expansion has mainly been due to the large number of company-sponsored schemes introduced with BUPA (British United Provident Association), PPP (Private Patients Plan), WPA (Western Provident Association), and other specialist insurers. The basic objective of the schemes available is to cover major expenses of surgical operations or hospital treatment. The insured person can choose the level of benefit he desires and may also extend coverage to include his wife and children. Thus he can cover hospital and nursing-home charges, including home nursing, for a specified maximum amount, including fees for surgeons, anaesthetists, physiotherapists, radiotherapists, etc. Obviously, the premium depends on the amount of cover selected. This would of course need to rise with inflation, which becomes a major factor affecting the scheme cost. Additional premiums are payable if it is desired to include wife and children— although the cost of cover for a family of four is normally only in the region of double the cost of individual cover. Rates also vary with the age of the oldest person covered, and although this means the premiums can change during the currency of a policy, the cover is often 'permanent' in the sense that insurers continue cover without restriction, regardless of health, for as long as the annual premiums are paid.

Group schemes generally offer discounted premiums depending upon the number of members insured and may generally include medical expenses incurred abroad.

TAXATION

This is an area in which professional advice should always be obtained as Finance Acts may vary the taxation treatment of either premiums or benefits from year to year. Particular reference should be made to the impact of taxation in relation to policies providing capital sums when there may be advantages in having the policy issued to the benefit of a person other than the insured person, such as a spouse in connection with an individual policy, or an employer in connection with a group policy.

CONCLUSION

The foregoing has touched briefly the area of insurance of personnel including Employee Benefit Plans (other than life and pensions assurance). New plans are being produced continually by both insurers and brokers whose advice is always readily available to assist the company, when required.

FURTHER READING

E. R. Hardy Ivamy, *Personal Accident, Life and Other Insurances,* Butterworth Insurance Library.
David Bacon and L. J. New, *Principles and Practice of Life Assurance and Other Insurances of the Person,* Buckley Press Ltd, 1971.

16

Kidnap, Ransom and Political Risks Insurance

An AIRMIC member

INTRODUCTION

Insurance cover for the financial loss involved in a kidnap and a demand for ransom has been available for many years. More recent developments in the field of politically motivated kidnappings have considerably increased the demand for the cover from multi-national businesses.

Political risks affecting international business may not in themselves have increased to the same extent. There is however a growing awareness of the financial risks and exposure to various types of losses from political situations. These risks may affect export orders, contract works and capital investments when contemplated or those already in existence. Political conditions in overseas territories can become unstable without much prior warning. In the event of nationalisation for example compensation paid by foreign governments is seldom thought to be adequate and reasonable by the recipients.

This chapter is in two parts. The first outlines the situation regarding the risks and insurance cover involving personnel and the second part examines the risks to the company arising out of potential losses of fixed assets or merchandise and losses arising from the cancellation of capital projects and schemes, together with the various forms of insurance.

KIDNAP AND RANSOM

The developing need for cover

There is something totally repugnant about the kidnap situation where there is a deliberate plan to bargain human life or the potential injury or disfigurement of a person for money or reward or pecuniary or political advantage in some other form. A natural aversion to contemplation of the possibility applying to one's own situation could be part of the reason why demand for insurance was not significant until the weapon of kidnap came into regular use throughout the world particularly by political groups and organisations. This development has had two main effects. In the first instance employees with possibly no significant personal wealth have on account of their position in a business become prime targets. Secondly, there has been a dramatic escalation in the level of ransom demand. For these and other reasons, many multinational businesses now consider an examination of the exposure of their executives and their families to this risk as a logical part of their 'risk management' programme. There is in addition still a large number of private individuals of great personal wealth or influence who remain exposed as individual targets and it is recognised that these persons and the members of their families remain at risk and require help in threat assessment and in considering the purchase of insurance.

Confidentiality

It hardly needs to be stated that the need for discretion and confidentiality in all matters relating to this serious problem is paramount. This is particularly relevant in consideration of insurance cover as the purchase of such cover has been declared illegal in some countries.

Moreover in the recent past it has been alleged that knowledge of the existence of insurance cover was in itself encouraging potential kidnappers to select their victims from among those protected by insurance.

All parties involved in the London market where most kidnap

and ransom cover is effected take realistic precautions to preserve security and the conduct of business is for this reason somewhat different to the procedures adopted in other classes.

Evaluating the risk

Threat assessment is the term commonly used to describe the initial process of considering the need for cover and the characteristics of the company proposing for insurance. There is naturally enough an initial questionnaire which would correspond to the traditional proposal form. In this questionnaire the information sought relates in the main to the company profile.

Important questions included seek information on the spread of the company's activities in the UK and abroad and considerable attention will be paid to the overseas locations in which the company operates. Experience has clearly identified countries where there is a high risk factor to the evaluation. This may arise from political instability, weak law enforcement or the local presence of a cell of an international terrorist group. A serious additional factor has been the tendency of the common criminal element to identify kidnap and a ransom demand as a significant potential source of substantial gain.

The second range of questions relates to the potential numbers of company personnel and their families exposed on account of their residence abroad or their business travel pattern taking them from statistically low risk areas of residence to high risk areas on short business trips.

Finally, information is naturally sought on any prior incidents or threats received by personnel.

Managing the risk

Kidnap and ransom risks placed in the London market, or when there is a serious intention to place the business, may carry a prior condition to the granting of cover or the setting of a premium that the threat assessment be carried out by professional experts. A specialist security consultancy exists in London whose services are used freely by underwriters and brokers. This organisation exists in part to provide the threat assessment service and in part to handle on behalf of underwriters, the negotiations in the resolution of any kidnap and ransom threats or incidents. The resources and expertise of this organisation are impressive and their record in handling many cases has earned them a sound international reputation.

Advice received from this consultancy during or following a threat assessment survey, will include a risk analysis relating to property and personnel and the inter-relationship of property security to security of personnel. The risks to personnel will include risks at the private residence, travelling to and from the main place of business, and while engaged in business travel anywhere in the world. Such a survey may include a visit by a consultant to an overseas location identified to be a high risk exposure.

Persons to be insured

A company may be selective about the persons whom they wish to protect under a kidnap and ransom insurance. Selection may be based on seniority and importance but in addition a main consideration is location and the amount of travel or period of residence in high risk areas.

Where an executive is assessed as being a target, it is relevant to consider including his immediate family in the scope of the cover. This should be standard practice where the risk arises on account of residence in a high risk area. It should also be considered worthwhile for all persons insured where there is a considerable amount of business travel whether or not the wives accompany the husbands on journeys.

Blanket cover can be obtained for example covering all expatriate staff and their families, or all staff while travelling on company business. Any form of blanket cover will be more expensive in total than a selective cover on specified individuals or individuals in specified high risk locations. Blanket cover can be justified on the lower cost per capita which it represents and the absence of the unexpected when an uninsured employee may be the subject of a kidnap.

Purchasing insurance cover

The monetary limits of the cover generally purchased now require to be in excess of £1 million. Ransom demands have regularly been for several millions. Bearing in mind that the cover of the policy will include costs and expenses incurred in the handling of an incident and these will inevitably be high, there is a need to consider carefully the amount of cover purchased to ensure that it is, as far as can be judged, adequate.

Principal perils insured

The cover granted under a typical policy is broadly under two main headings:

1 Loss following an actual or alleged kidnapping of any person insured by the policy in respect of ransom money or the monetary value of any other consideration given as ransom to secure the release of the insured person or persons.
2 Loss following a threat to kill, injure or abduct any person insured by the policy in respect of extortion money or the monetary value of any other consideration surrendered to secure the release of an insured person or persons from such a threat.

Extensions to the cover provided by the policy are:

1 Payment of a loss in transit of any sum being ransom or extortion money being conveyed by an employee of the insured to the persons making the demand.
2 Payment in respect of reward money paid by the insured to an informant for information leading to the arrest and conviction of parties responsible for a kidnapping or threat made against any person covered by the policy.
3 Payment of expenses incurred where any insured person is kidnapped or where there is an extortion demand. These expenses may include payment by the insurers for the services of a specialised firm engaged to carry out negotiations on behalf of the insured to secure the release of any person kidnapped or to handle and negotiate any extortion demand. The use of such

specialists will be offered by underwriters and if accepted by the insured, such specialists will be instructed to render every reasonable assistance in an advisory capacity to secure the safe release of the insured person.

4   Additional payment of expenses incurred in circumstances where action is required by the insured on account of a threat to kidnap, kill or injure any insured person. Provided such demand would, if paid, be a valid claim under the policy, then expenses such as fees for medical or legal advice, travel and accommodation or any cost of an independent negotiator engaged by the insured will be payable in addition to the limit of liability under the policy but such payment shall not exceed 10 per cent of the policy limit.

Policy conditions

Conditions attaching to the policy include requirements as follows:

1   Establishment of a written procedure to be followed in event of an incident.
2   Immediate notification to the insurers of an incident or threat.
3   Exclusion of collusion or fraud on the part of employees of the insured or victims or possible victims of a kidnap attempt.

There are conditions covering contribution, cancellation, limitation of liability, and notification of alteration in risk. Finally, there is a condition requiring non-disclosure of the existence of insurance and a general condition precedent to liability dealing with the fundamental need to establish that:

1   Any ransom or extortion money paid was surrendered under duress.
2   A kidnapping or threat had in fact occurred.
3   Local law enforcement officials have been notified.
4   At least two executives of the insured company have agreed to the payment of the ransom or extortion.

Claims

The policy provides for payment of fees for independent medical and legal advice and with the agreement of the insured for the offer of the services of an independent consultancy to render every reasonable assistance to the insured company to secure the safe release of the insured persons.

It is a condition of the policy that the insured and their representatives shall at all times cooperate with underwriters or their representatives in the carrying out of investigations following any kidnapping or extortion demand.

POLITICAL RISKS COVER

Insurance cover is available to provide compensation in respect of loss sustained under a wide range of exposures relating in general to investment or business transactions undertaken in overseas territories. In some cases insurance is available from government export credit insurance arrangements in the country of origin of the goods or the domicile of the proposer. In the UK the government insurance covers are available through Export Credit Guarantee Department (ECGD). This UK scheme or the National Export Credit arrangements in other countries may not provide full cover or may not provide any cover at all for some reason, and insurance companies and Lloyd's may be available as an alternative market or to provide additional or supplementary cover.

Need for cover

In this less well known area of insurance, it may be logical to argue that it could be necessary to insure against theft in the form of expropriation, confiscation or requisition by foreign government just as much as it makes sense to insure against theft by lawless individuals or against loss or damage by fire and other perils. It must be recognised that foreign legal interpretation of contract conditions entered into in good faith by an exporter or contractor may fall well short of expectations resulting in a serious financial loss. In some cases of expropriation or confiscation, the loss could be total.

Extent of cover available

Property

Insurance is available for protection of property such as buildings, machinery, plant and equipment against the risks of:

1 Confiscation.
2 Expropriation.
3 Requisition or destruction by order of government.
4 Possibility of inadequate compensation in event of nationalisation.
5 Deprivation of use.
6 The inability to repatriate money earned or local compensation paid.
7 Prohibition of re-export of moveable items.
8 Inability to regain title to a ship or aircraft for political reasons.

Financial loss

Cover is available in respect of sums due to a contractor or exporter in respect of a) work in progress, or b) earlier deliveries where a contract or part of a contract is terminated on account of:

1 Force Majeure as defined in the contract.
2 Repudiation.
3 Export or import embargo.
4 Exchange transfer risks from prohibition or delay in permission to remit.
5 Rejection of goods for political reasons.
6 Inability to recover money or outlays in a contract on account of war, civil war or legal disputes beyond the scope of local laws to resolve.

Bonds and guarantees

Bid or tender bonds are requested as evidence of good faith and honest intention to do business. As the bond is payable on demand of the buyer, it may be called even when the contractor or bidder is not at fault.

Insurance cover can provide protection in these circumstances provided the bidder has not contravened the terms of the contract. The cover for the guarantee also applies where the bidder has been unable to fulfil the contract on account of war embargo or political event.

Similarly performance bonds or guarantees may be demanded on an unconditional 'on demand' basis in support of advance payments and/or the performance of the contract.

Insurance can cover the calling of the guarantee unfairly and without reference to the terms of the contract or where a guarantee is not being reduced as provided for in a contract or where there is a threat to call the guarantee in the course of negotiations.

Such insurance cover can assist an exporter or a contractor in obtaining the necessary guarantees and bonds in the first place. This can be important as such guarantees or bonds unprotected by insurance could be tantamount to an increase in the borrowing of a company while the risk of the bond or guarantee being called remains.

Insurance market

Where cover is available from a National Export Credit Insurance arrangement, it will normally be cheaper than that available in the company market and Lloyd's. There are however limitations to government sponsored export insurance schemes and these include:

1   Where goods manufactured in a foreign country are involved.
2   Where cover is required for part only of the contract price.
3   Where cover is required for only part of the range of risks which are generally insured on overseas business.
4   Where the national scheme is already over committed to a particular country.

Information required to underwrite a risk

The information required to arrange cover under the headings described in 'Extent of cover available' is similar whether the cover is to be sought from company insurers or Lloyd's, or under a government scheme such as provided by ECGD.

Property

In addition to basic details of the company and its operations, the following details will be required:

1   Country where the investment exists or is to take place.
2   Details of the local operation or subsidiary including:
   (a)   Local name or title.
   (b)   Date established (if already in existence).
   (c)   Activities.
   (d)   Local shareholding.
   (e)   Net asset value.
   (f)   Amount to be insured.
3   If plant and equipment is being insured as part of the cover, additional details will be required as follows:
   (a)   Type of plant or machinery and manufacturing process.
   (b)   Location.
   (c)   Management i.e. expatriates and locals.
   (d)   Present day value and basis of valuation.
   (e)   Is there the possibility of re-export, and is there a re-export licence in force?
   (f)   Value to be insured.
4   Is cover required against:
   (a)   Nationalisation.
   (b)   Deprivation.
5   If exchange transfer risks are required:
   (a)   Details of official arrangements made for the transfer of funds.
   (b)   Amounts transferred in previous two years.
   (c)   Amount of cover required.

Financial loss on contracts

1   Basic details of company.
2   Buyers details including location and whether or not buyer is wholly or partly a foreign government organisation.
3   Contract details.

4   Law which applies to the contract e.g. English or local law.
5   Previous experience with buyer or other buyers in the same
    country.
6   Whether at time of enquiry contract is firm or in negotiation, or
    whether bid or tender was invited or open to any contractor.
7   Periods of time covering:
    (a)   Manufacture.
    (b)   Shipment.
    (c)   Erection or commissioning.
    (d)   Warranty.
    (e)   Services.
8   Cover required:
    (a)   Import or export embargo.
    (b)   Force Majeure termination.
9   Contract conditions relating to:
    (a)   Termination.
    (b)   Repudiation.
    (c)   Arbitration.

Bonds and guarantees

1   Type of guarantee.
2   Name of bankers:
    (a)   In local market.
    (b)   In country of domicile.
3   Amount of guarantee and whether it reduces in proportion to
    deliveries or work completed.
4   Expiry date of bond or guarantee.
5   Period of cover required.
6   Amount of cover required.

Policy details

The policy can be prepared on a first-loss basis. It is not necessary
when arranging cover to insure the full value of the overseas
investment or the total value of the contract or the amount of the
guarantee.
    The risks insured can be selected individually according to

exposure and the period of insurance agreed as required subject to a normal maximum of three years.

The premium will vary in accordance with the risk and this will be assessed by underwriters relative to the country or countries involved, the type of investment or contract, the experience of the proposer and whether by the nature of the investment or contract, there is a capability of the investor or exporter or contractor to influence the local government. This can apply for example where the project may be of considerable national importance in the foreign country or may be a prestige project sponsored and totaliy supported by the foreign government.

Claims

Whether a particular situation develops into a claim is more often than not a function of time. The very risks insured against and the nature of the cover granted make it logical to state that a valid claim may result from a gradually developing situation perhaps over years.

There is no requirement to inform insurers of matters of public knowledge regarding for example political events in an overseas territory. When events begin directly to affect a company in matters which could result in a claim under a policy, or the calling of a bond or guarantee, these matters should be brought to the notice of underwriters.

Thereafter by regular contact and the reporting of developments, action will be discussed and where possible agreed in advance. In some cases this will involve contact with bankers, auditors and possibly the Foreign Office where there is danger of expropriation or nationalisation. As these risks may well be affecting other companies domiciled in other countries consultation at government level may well take the control of the situation out of the hands of insured and insurers.

DEVELOPMENT OF POLITICAL RISKS INSURANCE

With the dramatic improvement in communications and air travel, subsidiaries or branch factories of multinational companies can be established quickly to take advantage of specially attractive conditions in a particular country. The ease with which such units may be established and a management and production team trained and installed has to be balanced against an assessment of the risk factors. Included in these risk factors is the political risk.

An ambivalent attitude to multinational companies persists at government level in many countries. The identified need to find employment for the citizens of the country is often eclipsed in periods of political instability by a distrust and suspicion of big business and in particular multinational enterprises. Stability in the long term is the factor which is more often than not absent in the evaluation of investment prospects in some overseas territories.

The market for political risks insurance is likely to be with us for a long time.

Glossary

A. S. D. Cross (editor) and H. R. Loader,*
Group Insurance Manager, Tetra Pak

Accidental insurance embraces those forms of insurance not falling within the scope of life, marine or fire insurance. The main types of policy cover personal accident, loss of or damage to property, legal liabilities. In recent years the former strong differentiation between life, marine, fire and accident insurance has been breaking down owing to legislation and developments within insurers.

Adjuster, loss. An independent official employed by an insurer to investigate the circumstances of a claim, and make recommendations upon the extent to which the claim falls for payment under the policy (term used in non-marine insurance).

Adjuster, average. A similar official who calculates and apportions claims in marine insurance (particularly general average claims).

Adjustment. (1) of a claim is the whole process of investigation and reporting made by a loss adjuster.

(2) of a premium is the calculation of additional or return premium under any policy in which, after payment of an initial deposit, the final premium is levied as a rate upon a chosen variable (such as total salaries or turnover).

Agent. The person or firm that introduces the prospective client to the potential insurer, and negotiates the form of insurance required.

*The authors are indebted to Mr. R. W. Rooke for material retained from the previous edition.

Various levels of expertise are available, ranging from fully qualified professional advice to mere introduction. Remuneration is normally by commission paid by the insurer as a percentage of the premium applicable, but may also be by negotiated fee paid by the insured.

Aggregate limit of liability. The total liability of insurers under a policy for all incidents occurring within a stated period, usually one year.

Agreed value policies allow for payment of a fixed sum in the event of total loss of the insured property, and can be obtained for articles subject to much fluctuation in value (such as paintings and motor cars).

'All risks'. The fullest insurance obtainable upon property, covering all physical loss or damage of an accidental nature. Despite the name, various forms of damage are excluded (such as gradual deterioration and attack by vermin).

Assessor, loss. An official employed by the insured to negotiate settlement of an insurance claim on his behalf.

Assurance. A synonym for insurance, but general usage tends to reserve this to life assurance as opposed to other classes of business.

Average. (1) A method of scaling down payment of a claim in proportion where property has been insured for less than its full value. The full claim is reduced in the ratio which the insured value bears to the true value. Policies so written are said to be 'subject to average'.
(2) A term applied in marine cargo insurance to partial loss, as opposed to total loss.

Average, general. An ancient practice in marine insurance whereby certain losses or expenses at sea are shared amongst the interested parties in the venture.

Average, particular. A term used in marine insurance to denote partial loss or damage which is not a general average.

Aviation insurance embraces all those forms of insurance relating to use of aircraft. The main types of policy cover loss of or damage to aircraft, and legal liabilities arising from flying activities.

Baggage. As regards personal baggage, insurance consists of clothing, personal effects, items of personal adornment and the like, whether worn, carried or sent in advance, including the suitcases containing them. Items of particular value should be specially listed and valued. Insurance is usually arranged on 'all risks' terms.

Blanket policy. See Floater policies.

Boiler insurance consists of (1) periodic inspection of the plant, (2) compensation for damage to the plant and surrounding property, (3) liability for damage caused to a third party's property, and injury to persons, caused by such explosion or collapse of the plant. 'Inspection-only' contracts as in (1) above are available if (2) and (3) are not required.

Bonds or sureties are issued as a guarantee of the correct performance of certain court duties, or of the accountability for certain customs dues. Other bonds relate to performance of duties by a tenderer or contractor towards his principle.

Book debts insurance. An insurance covering against loss by reason of non-collection of book debts due to the destruction of accounts records caused by an insured peril, e.g. fire.

Broker. A person whose business consists of arranging insurance on commission or by payment of negotiated fee, with freedom to choose between different insurers. A degree of skilled knowledge in interpreting the needs of the client and placing insurance is offered. Business with Lloyd's underwriters can be effected directly only through specially appointed Lloyd's brokers. Recent legislation under the Insurance Brokers (Registration) Act 1977 is designed to restrict the use of the title 'Insurance Broker' to persons or companies who meet certain minimum criteria as to competence and solvency.

Business interruption. The term preferred by many insurers to the older style 'consequential loss'.

Cancellation notice. The right commonly written into an insurance policy whereby the insurer may give notice within the period of insurance that the policy is to be terminated on a certain date, in return for a pro rata rebate of premium. Similar cancellation by an insured may or may not give entitlement to a premium rebate (pro rata or less).

Capacity denotes the extent to which an insurer is able to offer insurance of various kinds to an insured, and is ultimately based upon the largest amount that an insurer is prepared to afford from his resources upon any particular claim. Market capacity represents the extent of insurance which the entire insurance market together is able to offer to an insured.

Captive insurer. An insurance company which is a subsidiary of the parent company for which it acts as insurer or reinsurer either accepting the risk entirely or spreading it by reinsurance.

Cargo insurance. The insurance of goods transported by sea or air, with or without incidental transit before and/or after shipment.

Certificate of insurance. Document issued by insurers as evidence of: (1) Insurance of a shipment under a marine cargo insurance open cover or policy. This document may be required as part of the documents of title. (2) Third party cover on a motor vehicle as required by the Road Traffic Act 1972. (3) Employers' liability cover under the Employers' Liability (Compulsory Insurance) Act 1969. (4) Cover in respect of some other form of insurance where the policy itself cannot be handed to an interested party, e.g. a person covered under a blanket policy.

Claim. The request by an insured for compensation for a particular misfortune, or protection against a legal liability, according to the terms of a policy. Evidence of the misfortune and the attendant financial loss must be given, together with proof that the claim falls within the scope of the policy wording.

Claims experience denotes the comparison between the cost of claims met and/or estimated as outstanding and premium paid during a certain period, frequently expressed as a percentage ratio.

Claims payable abroad. An arrangement on a marine cargo policy whereby claims may be payable (if required by the insured) by some named person or firm abroad (usually at or near the place of destination), on behalf of the insurers.

Coinsurance. (1) The situation arising from the sharing among insurers referred to in the next definition (*coinsurers*). (2) A requirement in a policy that the insured shares a loss with the insurers in an agreed proportion, usually expressed as a percentage, e.g. the insurers agree to pay 80 per cent of any loss leaving the insured to bear the remaining 20 per cent. Thus, unlike an excess or deductible, the uninsured amount of the loss varies according to its size.

Coinsurers comprise those insurers accepting responsibility for a percentage of an insurance on terms and conditions set out by a first or 'leading' insurer, accepting the agreed percentage of the premium and paying the same percentage of each settled claim. The various coinsurers (including the leading insurer) stand parallel to each other and are only responsible for their particular share of the total insurance.

Collective policy. (1) A policy covering a number of persons each for a separate amount. (2) One policy issued by several insurers sharing a risk. Each is liable only for his own share as stated in the policy.

Commission. The percentage of the premium allowed by an insurer to an agent or broker as remuneration for services rendered. The percentage may vary according to different types of insurance and other factors. In certain cases, mostly marine, a percentage of a settled claim may be allowed by an insured as commission to an agent or broker for services rendered in obtaining the settlement.

When earned by a broker commission is often known as brokerage particularly in marine insurance.

Composite offices. The insurance companies that are prepared to underwrite many of the major forms of insurance that have evolved, and do not limit their business to a certain class of insurance, such as marine or life.

Comprehensive policy. One that covers a collection of named perils. It is less extensive than an all risks policy.

Conditions in a policy comprise the printed terms which apply to various aspects of the policy, and the action to be taken in certain contingencies, such as giving notice of a claim. In addition, various conditions are implied and binding although unwritten (for example, there must be a financial interest by an insured in the subject-matter of the policy).

Consequential loss insurance (or business interruption) gives protection against loss of profits or increased cost of working incurred by a business following certain forms of physical damage (such as destruction of property by fire, or breakdown of machinery).

Contingency insurance, (or risk). A term applied to policies: (1) Covering a specific liability outside the more common types of cover, usually one foreseeable event or type of event, e.g. liability arising out of defect in title to property. (2) Issued by engineering insurers embracing those insurances which are not included in the group of insurances known as 'inspected classes'.

Contractors' all risks insurance (or contract works insurance) is the comprehensive insurance effected by a contractor or sometimes the principal upon a construction project, until handed over to the principal (purchaser). Insurance is provided against all risks of loss of or damage to the contract works (apart from certain stated perils). Third party insurance can also be provided within the policy.

Contractual liability. Liability imposed by contract as opposed to liability at common law.

Contribution. Where double-insurance exists, each insurer will only make contribution of a rateable proportion of the loss so that over-compensation is avoided.

Cover. A commonly used synonym meaning (1) to insure, or (2) the insurance obtained.

Cover note. A document issued by insurers or brokers setting out broad details of the insurance pending the issue of the policy itself.

Credit insurance protects a seller against failure on certain grounds of a purchaser to make payment for goods or services supplied. Insurance may apply to all sales, or only those with specified customers or countries. The insured is commonly expected to bear a proportion of any claim.

Cut through clause. A clause inserted into an insurance or reinsurance contract allowing the policyholder to have direct access to the reinsurer or reinsurers in the event of a loss.

Days of grace constitute the stated period after renewal date of a policy during which the insured must pay the premium for renewing the policy, although insurance may continue by agreement thereafter pending eventual payment. Insurance continues during the days of grace unless it can be shown that there was no intention of renewing the policy. For motor policies, cover is provisionally granted for a period after renewal date but limited to the minimum obligatory insurance under the Road Traffic Acts (that is against injury to certain third parties).

Declaration. (1) The periodic statement of certain variable statistics to an insurer, which show the fluctuation in risk and provide the basis for averaging a premium over the period of insurance.

(2) A detailed statement under open covers or floater policies, for example in goods-in-transit or marine cargo insurance.

Declinature, occurs when the insurer declines to accept a proposed insurance contract.

Deductible. A synonym for 'excess', whereby before payment of a claim by an insurer, a certain amount is deducted and the insured is obliged to accept this cost.

Difference in conditions policy. Individual policies effected by an insured group covering a particular type of insurance in a number of different countries are likely to vary in interpretation and conditions. In order to obtain one standard form of cover the insured group may effect a supplementary master policy on conditions which are understood and are considered acceptable to embrace risks in all countries. This policy will pay only those claims which are not recoverable under the terms of the individual local policies issued in each country. It is known as a 'difference in conditions' policy.

Disclosure. The duty of an insured to reveal all information relating to a desired insurance which will enable an insurer to decide whether to offer cover and on what terms. A similar duty applies at renewal.

Double indemnity. A provision in a life or personal accident policy whereby the insurers pay twice the amount stated in the policy for a particular injury or for death, if such injury or death occurs through certain named events, e.g. death whilst travelling by railway.

Endorsement. An alteration to the normal printed terms of a policy document whether at inception or during the currency of the insurance, making the cover more specific to the particular circumstances. In any apparent contradiction, the endorsement will override the printed terms.

Engineering insurance. The branch of insurance affecting boilers and other pressure vessels, cranes and other lifting equipment, lifts and the like. Inspection services provided satisfy the requirements of the Factories Acts where periodic inspection is obligatory.

Excess. The amount deducted by the insurer (and met by the insured) before payment of a claim under the policy.

Excess of loss. A form of reinsurance whereby the reinsurer in return for a stated premium, meets all that part of any claim on the original insurer which exceeds an agreed amount. There may be a financial limit to the reinsurer's liability.

Ex gratia payment. A payment made by an insurer which he asserts he is not liable to meet under the terms of the insurance.

Expense ratio. The proportion of an insurers total premiums represented by his expenses, usually expressed as a percentage.

Explosion. The sudden, violent expansion of a gaseous substance held under pressure in a confined space, with shattering effect.

Export Credits Guarantee Department. The government department that provides insurance to a seller against failure of an overseas buyer, on political or commercial grounds, to make payment for goods or services supplied.

Extra perils comprise the additional, specific risks which can be insured against by extension of a basic fire policy.

Fee. The payment of an agreed figure by an insured to an insurance broker for the services rendered over the period involved. In return, all commission on insurance placed is passed to the insured.

Fidelity guarantee insurance protects an employer against theft of stock or money by an employee. In a claim, it is normal for insurers to insist upon legal proceedings being taken against the offending employee.

First-loss insurance applies to those areas where the risk of a total loss is extremely small. A maximum loss is estimated (the 'first loss') and insurance for that amount arranged, but the premium takes into account the value of the whole.

Floater policies provide for an agreed total sum insured to apply over a number of locations or persons, that sum being applicable to any one or more of them.

Franchise in a policy exempts an insurer from paying claims below a declared figure, but claims exceeding that figure are paid in full.

Full value. The basis on which many sums insured should be calculated, normally being the full market value of all the property to be insured.

Funding, self. The process by which an insured can make financial provision against possible losses as an alternative to effecting insurance.

Goods-in-transit insurance covers the inland transit of goods by road, rail, post or other conveyance, and may, where required, cover the risks of loading at point of departure and unloading on arrival at destination. Single journeys may be insured or all transits during a certain period, with or without definition of the carrying vehicles.

Gross profit. A term used in consequential loss insurance being specified standing charges plus the net profit (or less the net loss) of the insured business, or alternatively can be calculated by deducting specified variable charges from the turnover of the insured business.

Hazard denotes both the physical and more personal features of an insurance which are noteworthy to an insurer in assessing the form and cost of protection to be given. The 'physical hazard' comprises the actual tangible features which make up the subject-matter of the insurance. The 'moral hazard' concerns the more intangible, personal aspects.

Hull insurance. The form of marine or aviation insurance covering loss of or damage to the actual ships, marine structures, or aircraft.

Impact. The damage caused to property by vehicles, horses or cattle (normally only when owned by another person) colliding with it. Impact constitutes a 'special peril' which can be insured by extension of a fire policy upon the property.

Indemnity. A basic principle of insurance that, in the event of a claim being made under a policy, compensation paid will place the insured in no better financial position that he was before the incident causing the claim. This does not apply to life and personal accident insurance, where the insured is held to have an unlimited interest in his personal well-being, although there may be some limit to the amount claimable in the case of assurances covering the life of a person other than the insured, e.g. in the case of insurance by a creditor on the life of a debtor.

Inspection. The service provided in engineering insurance whereby trained surveyors periodically examine the machinery insured, and submit recommendations regarding repairs and safety precautions applying to it.

Institute of London Underwriters. The trade association of insurers (other than Lloyd's underwriters) transacting marine insurance in London.

Insurable interest. A basic principle of insurance whereby the insured must stand to benefit by preservation of the object insured, and suffer loss by its damage or destruction.

Insurance. The pooling of financial resources by those exposed to the possibility of a particular loss, to produce a pool from which those members suffering such a loss can be recompensed. Contributions (premiums) are assessed by the guardian of the pool (the insurer) according to the likelihood and possible extent of such damage occurring.

Knock-for-knock agreements. Mutual agreements between insurers aimed at simplifying and reducing the administrative costs involved in settling motor insurance claims. Each insurer meets the cost of damage to the car he insures (according to the terms of the policy), without counter-claiming on the other insurer. If a cost is not covered by the policy, the policyholder is free to attempt recovery from the third party.

Layer. The amount between agreed financial limits for which an insurer accepts responsibility in any claim falling within the terms of the insurance. By successive layers with appropriate financial limits, insurance may be obtained up to a high limit of liability.

Leading office. The insurer who negotiates the terms of an insurance but accepts responsibility for only a percentage of the cover, leaving coinsurers free to accept other percentages.

Liability (directors and officers). The type of insurance effected for or by directors or officers of a company to indemnify them against claims arising from negligence, wrong advice, breach of trust and other wrongful acts in the exercising of their duties with the company.

Liability, employers'. The branch of insurance which protects an employer against his legal liability to an employee suffering injury (including death) caused by the employer's negligence or a breach of statutory duty. The policy meets the cost of damages awarded against the employer, and the expense of negotiating settlement of the claim (including legal costs if need be).

Liability, products. This form of insurance gives protection against legal liability for accidental death of or injury to third parties, or damage to their property, arising from goods manufactured, sold, or processed in any way by the insured. The policy meets the cost of damages awarded and the expense of negotiating settlement of the claim (including legal costs if need be) up to stated limits per claim and in all per year.

Liability, professional. Such insurance gives protection to persons offering professional skills and abilities against legal liability arising from failure to show reasonable care in exercising these skills and abilities. The policy meets the cost of damages awarded and the expense of negotiating settlement of the claim (including legal costs if need be) up to stated limits per claim and in all per year.

Liability, public. This type of insurance (also known as third party insurance) gives protection to the insured against legal liability for accidental death of or injury to third parties or damage to their property, arising from activities defined in the policy. The policy meets the cost of damages awarded and the expense of negotiating settlement of the claim (including legal costs if need be) up to stated limits per claim and in all per year.

Liability, umbrella. An insurance for limits in excess of those provided by more specific liability policies also including some risks not specifically included in those policies. An Umbrella Liability policy is normally subject to a deductible when covering risks not specifically insured under primary policies.

Limit of liability. The maximum amount which an insurer will pay in settlement of a claim or claims arising under a policy. For claims expected to exceed the limit of liability, the insurer normally reserves the right to pay this maximum amount to an insured and leave him to negotiate settlement of the claim (applicable to liability insurance claims).

Lloyd's. The insurance market in London formed of syndicates of underwriting members, open to transact insurance offered to them on behalf of clients by specially appointed brokers (Lloyd's brokers). Each underwriting member offers his capital as surety, each for his own share of the insurance provided. The Corporation of Lloyd's supervises the market but accepts no financial obligation for business transacted by the syndicates.

Long-term agreement. A mutual agreement whereby in return for agreeing to continue the insurance for a fixed number of years, the insured is allowed a discount on each annual premium. The insurer normally retains the right to vary the terms of the insurance during the period but, if exercised, the insured may cancel the agreement without forfeiture of earlier discounts.

Loss adjuster defined under 'adjuster, loss'.

Loss assessor defined under 'assessor, loss'.

Loss ratio. The proportion of claims (paid and outstanding) to total premiums, usually over a period of one or more years, expressed as a percentage. (See also Claims experience.)

Material fact. Any information concerning a proposed insurance which influences an insurer upon whether to offer insurance and, if so, upon what terms. The prospective insured is under a strict duty to disclose all material facts.

Money insurance gives protection against loss of money in all negotiable forms while in transit or contained in premises, whether in safes or not. Loss through theft by employees may be covered in limited form, as well as damage to safes. Premium is payable by fixed charges and by percentage of the total value carried in any year. Money insurance is often linked with personal accident insurance for those engaged in carrying money, as well as protection against damage to their clothing occasioned in a hold-up.

Motor fleet insurance concerns the terms and conditions on which insurance is offered to the owner of a number of cars or commercial vehicles.

Motor insurance. The form of policy providing compulsory insurance to comply with legislation, but also offered with provision for damage to the property of third parties, loss of or damage to the insured vehicle, and personal accident to the driver. The policy normally extends to cover other persons driving the insured vehicle, and the insured driver while driving other cars (third party cover only).

Motor Insurers' Bureau. The working arrangement between motor insurers to provide a fund from which claims from injured third parties may be met where these arise from a cause for which motor insurance is compulsory but the policy of the offending driver is ineffective or absent. Claims may also be considered from injured third parties where the guilty driver is unknown.

Mutual company. An insurance company in which those insuring share, by way of dividend, in any profits which may be earned.

Names. The individual Lloyd's underwriting members, grouping together in syndicates to transact insurance business.

Net profit as used in consequential loss insurance denotes the figure obtained by deducting from the turnover of an insured business both the standing charges and the variable charges.

No-claim discount. The reduction allowed in a renewal premium in recognition of no claims having been paid by the insurer during the previous period of insurance.

Non-tariff insurers. Insurance companies that decide their own terms of cover and premium rates without consultation with the companies (tariff companies) that cooperate together on such aspects. With the abandonment of tariffs in many fields of insurance, the terms 'tariff' and 'non-tariff' are tending to lose relevance.

Open cover. A policy under which the defined insurance is automatically provided upon each separate operation of a particular kind, subject to full details being provided later to the insurers and appropriate premium paid. An open cover is particularly suitable for insuring transit of goods.

Operative clause in a policy defines the insurance protection given and any general exceptions.

Permanent health insurance provides a weekly benefit in the event of disability from following either normal or any occupation, caused by accident or sickness. Payment of benefits may be deferred for an agreed period if required, but must continue to be paid to a certain age limit provided the policy is maintained by the insured until that time.

Personal accident group insurance provides insurance on similar terms to those for an individual person, but applicable to all members of a certain group (who may or may not be named in the policy). The scale of benefits may be fixed sums or multiples of annual salary, and the total premium may be calculated according to the number of persons insured or the total annual salary payments.

Personal accident insurance provides for payment according to a schedule of fixed sums in the event of death of or bodily injury to the insured caused by violent accidental external and visible means.

Policy. The printed document embodying the terms and conditions of the contract made between the insurer and the insured, defining the scope of the cover and the premium to be paid. The policy consists of (1) recital clause, making reference to the two parties involved, (2) operative clause defining the insurance and any general exceptions, (3) attestation clause confirming the authenticity of the document, (4) conditions on which the insurance is granted and procedure to be followed in certain circumstances, (5) schedule giving details special to the particular policy, (6) endorsements making cover more specific to the particular circumstances.

Premium. The sum to be paid by the insured for the protection given by the insurer.

Primary insurance. The insurance of the first layer of cover as opposed to the excess insurance.

Probable maximum loss. The maximum loss which it is estimated is likely to occur arising out of one event, not taking account of remote possibilities or unlikely catastrophes.

Proposer. The person or organisation seeking insurance, who submits relevant details (usually by completing a proposal form) to the insurer for consideration.

Quotation. The summary of important terms and conditions upon which the insurer would be prepared to provide insurance, in response to an enquiry from a proposer. The quotation is otherwise subject to the standard policy wording which the insurer would use for that class of insurance.

Rate. The percentage which, when applied to the sum insured or other chosen figure, produces the premium payable to the insurers.

Recital clause (or preamble). The opening section of the policy, which makes reference to the parties involved.

Reinstatement basis certifies that in the event of loss, the insurers will meet the cost of a new replacement of the same kind but not superior to or more extensive than the original, to the limit of the sum insured. If reinstatement is not carried out, the basis of settlement is the value of the property at the time of the loss (indemnity basis). Reinstatement basis is mostly found in fire insurance upon buildings or machinery, but may also apply to new cars or household effects.

Reinsurance. A method of spreading more widely the cost of possible claims under a policy, in return for a proportion of the original premium. The original insurer (known as the direct insurer) agrees to cede all or part of the business to the secondary insurer (known as the reinsurer), and the reinsurer agrees to reimburse the whole or predetermined part of any claim under the terms of the policy. The latter may themselves further reinsure with other reinsurers (i.e. retrocede) a part or the whole of the liability they have accepted from the original insurer or previous reinsurer in the chain. There is no contact or relationship between the insured and the reinsurer.

Rejection risk insurance. A cover to insure certain types of export goods, e.g. frozen foods, against the possibility that they will be rejected by the health or other authorities of the importing country as unacceptable by their standards resulting in loss to the exporter.

Renewal. Continuation of an insurance for a further period from a chosen date (the renewal date). Apart from most forms of life assurance and permanent health insurance, an insurer can refuse to renew a policy, or may vary the terms upon which insurance may continue. Similarly, an insured is entitled to cancel the policy at renewal or seek an alteration in the terms and conditions.

Riot is held to occur when three or more persons assist each other to execute a common purpose, with sufficient display of force to alarm other persons. Insurance against this risk, usually linked with strikes and malicious damage, may inter alia be obtained by extension of a fire policy. Compensation may be claimed in certain defined circumstances from the police or local government authority.

Risk. (1) In general terms, objective doubt as to the outcome of an expected event.

(2) The sum total of all those features against which insurance protection is required.

(3) The particular peril which may cause loss or damage.

Risk control is the practice by a company of safeguarding against losses and of minimising the risks to which it is exposed.

Room. The open section of the Lloyd's Building in London which constitutes the market-place housing the desks (or boxes) of the underwriting agents transacting insurance business for the syndicates of underwriting members they represent.

Salvage. (1) Property damaged by an insured peril which still retains some potential value and usefulness. In payment of a claim, an insurer is entitled to retain any salvage and sell it to reduce the outlay. If the salvage is valueless, the insured will bear the cost of its removal and destruction unless provision against such costs had been made in the policy. (2) Money payable to a third party for services rendered in saving life and property in distress at sea.

Schedule in a policy comprises those details grouped together which are the special features of the particular contract.

Selection against an insurer is the deliberate separation and insurance of only the more hazardous aspects of a particular situation. Withholding the less hazardous increases either the possibility or the extent of a claim arising.

Self-insurance. The retention of losses from a cause against which protection could be obtained from an insurer. Provision can be made for bearing such losses by creation of a special fund in readiness, but frequently losses are met from revenue if and when they occur.

Short-period insurance comprises insurance effected for less than the normal yearly period. The nature of the cover may lend itself to short-period insurance. Where an annual policy would be more normal, the premium for short-period insurance is likely to be greater than pro rata, to allow for disproportionate administrative costs and the possibility of selection against the insurers.

Slip. The summary of relevant information upon a required insurance which a broker presents to prospective insurers.

Special perils comprise the additional, specific risks which can be insured against by extension of a fire policy, such as (1) explosion, (2) riots, strikes and civil commotion, (3) malicious damage, (4) aircraft and articles dropped therefrom, (5) storm, tempest and flood, (6) water damage, (7) impact, (8) spontaneous combustion.

Spread of risk represents the attempt by insurers to distribute their potential liabilities as widely as possible so that exposure to disproportionate claims is reduced.

Sprinklers. Automatic safety devices which help to prevent outbreak of fire in enclosed areas. A sprinkler system consists of a network of water pipes beneath ceilings in a building, with 'sprinkler heads' at regular intervals which detect any increase in temperature above a permissible level and automatically release water from the system. Such dousing is designed to extinguish any incipient fire before it can gain a firm hold. Installation of a sprinkler system finds favour with insurers and normally attracts a substantial reduction in fire insurance premiums. Sprinkler leakage insurance covers the cost of water damage caused by wrongly acting sprinklers or following damage to the sprinkler installation.

Standing charges as used in consequential loss insurance denote the charges normally met out of income which would continue after dislocation of production from an insured peril. The actual nature of the standing charges may depend upon the type of business.

Storm, usually linked with tempest, is a possible source of damage against which insurance may be obtained by extension of a fire policy.

Subrogation. The right of an insurer, by virtue of handling a claim under a policy, to pursue any rights of recovery which the insured may have against another party, in order to reduce or counterbalance the amount of the settled claim.

Subsidence. Collapse or damage to buildings caused by their sinking or settlement.

Sum insured represents the maximum payment the insurer will make in settlement of a claim, and the basis upon which premium is calculated. The sum insured should normally represent at least the value of the property as it stands at the time of any loss or damage.

Surveyors. (1) Fire, burglary or liability surveyors. Employees of an insurer or broker trained to inspect risks, assess the possibility of an insured loss occurring and its potential extent, and recommend precautions to prevent such an event.

(2) Loss prevention surveyors. Title applying to persons employed by the insured themselves, or consultants they engage, who carry out similar duties with the object of minimising loss or damage caused by various types of accident or misfortune.

(3) Marine surveyors. Persons who inspect and report on the probable cause(s) of damage, and the extent, to a ship or cargo resulting from an accident.

Syndicate the group of underwriting members at Lloyd's open to transact insurance business. Many such groups or syndicates are operating in the market.

Tariff companies constitute the group of insurance companies that cooperate in devising minimum premium rates and standard policy wordings for certain types of insurance, discussing terms for more unusual forms of cover within those fields, and collating statistics of various kinds. Most tariff arrangements were abandoned in the United Kingdom some years ago and at present the only tariff agreements still in force there are those covering fire and consequential loss (business interruption) insurance.

Tempest, usually linked with storm, is a possible source of damage against which insurance may be obtained by extension of a fire policy.

Term assurance. A simple form of life assurance whereby in return for a premium, an insurer agrees to pay a fixed sum if the proposer should die within a stated period. No benefit is payable if the proposer survives the period. Under a decreasing term assurance, the benefit payable decreases from year to year.

Third party. Any person or body other than the parties to an agreement, relationship or dispute.

Total loss is (1) actual if the subject matter of the insurance is totally lost or destroyed, or damaged beyond repair, or (2) constructive if its total loss appears unavoidable or the cost of repair would exceed its value thereafter.

Treaty. The agreement whereby a direct insurer will cede to a reinsurer an agreed part of every insurance falling within the terms of the treaty with appropriate share of premium, in return for the reinsurer agreeing to meet part of each qualifying claim paid under the policy. The apportionment between direct insurer and reinsurer is defined by the terms of the treaty. Treaties may be identified by type such as quota share and surplus or by class of business such as non-marine or aviation.

Underlying insurance. An insurance which is required to meet its liability before the next (excess) policy comes into effect.

Underwriter may be used as a synonym for 'insurer', or a title given to the person within an insurer's organisation who determines the terms and conditions upon which insurance is offered.

Utmost good faith. A basic principle of insurance signifying that the proposer is in duty bound to disclose all material facts when first seeking insurance and throughout the currency of the policy. The insurer is likewise duty bound to disclose all relevant features of the cover when offered and continued thereafter.

Valuation may be (1) a professional estimate of the value of property to be insured or (2) an investigation of the assets of a life assurance company to check that these exceed the insurer's potential liabilities.

War risks insurance. Obtainable for hulls and cargo in marine and aviation policies, but cover is not obtainable in the normal insurance markets for property inland. Life and personal accident insurance can also include this cover.

Warranty. A guarantee made by the insured and written into the policy that a certain situation continues to exist, or that certain actions continue to be done (or not done, as the case may be). Breach of a warranty allows an insurer to make the policy voidable if so desired, but by current practice most insurers will not avoid liability if the breach of a warranty is not material to the loss occurring or to its severity.

Index

Brokers—*contd*
  specialist services, 48
  with worldwide operations, 51
  see also British Insurance Brokers Association; Insurance Brokers Registration Council
Broker's slip, 62
Buildings
  collapse following fire, 87
  fire insurance, 88
  foundations, 98
  householders' cover, 105, 105-6
  in course of erection, 107
  rebuilding costs, 75
  reinstatement, 97
  temporary, 317, 336
  valuation for fire insurance, 96
  see also Premises; Property
Bulldozers, commercial vehicle insurance, 274, 275
BUPA *see* British United Provident Association (BUPA)
Burglary, definition, 145
Buses *see* Coaches and buses
Business hours, definition, 166
Business interruption, 111-43, 159, 377
  all risks cover, 107, 141-3
  applying average, 120-1
  auditors' fees, 129
  basis of contract, 112-15
  characteristics, 111
  claims settlement procedure, 130-1
  duty to reduce loss, 124-5
  effect of drop in income, 112
  effect of trends and variations, 117-18
  effects of tax on insurance, 119-20
  effects on business, 125
  employees retained, 125-6
  estimates of future earnings, 117
  factors influencing period, 116
  insurance of wages and salaries, 123-8
    dual basis, 127-8
    payroll basis, 128
  material damage proviso, 113-15
  need for cover, 112
  period of indemnity, 115-17, 143
  policy wording, 113
  premises, 128-9
  provisions related to increased cost of working, 122-3
  return of premiums, 121-2
  risks
    computer, 139-40

Business interruption—*contd*
  cover for advance profits, 137-8
  damage to factory chimneys, 135-6
  denial of access, 135
  deterioration of goods in cold store, 133-4
  epidemics, diseases, murder and suicide, 131
  exhibitions and displays, 136-7
  failure of public utilities or steam supplies, 134-5
  loss of rent, 138-9
  plant and machinery breakdowns, 132-3
  standard risks, 131
  theft, 132
  transit by land, sea and air, 132
  sum insured, 115, 117-22
    methods of calculating, 118-19
    related to indemnity period, 121
  tariff offices, 35
  traders' policies, 106
  see also Consequential loss
Buyers in insurance market, 28-30
  business potential of, 30
  management efficiency of, 28-9
  'own case' agencies, 40
  relationship with broker, 40
  size of account, 29
  spread of risk, 30

Cancellation notice, 377
Capacity, definition, 377
Captive insurance companies, 14, 282, 377
Car sharing, 280
Caravan insurance, 277-80
  baggage and personal effects, 278
  territorial limits, 278
  third party liability, 278
Cargo insurance, 377
  see also Marine insurance
Carriage by Air Act (1961), 220
Carriage of Goods by Road Act (1965), 217
Carriage of Goods by Sea Act (1971), 213
Carriers, 205-6
  by air, liability, 220-1
  by rail, liability, 215-16
  by river, liability, 223
  by road, international, 217-19
    liability, 216-20
  by sea, liability, 213-15
  combined transport and through transport contracts, 221-2